ArtScroll® Series

Rabbi Nosson Scherman / Rabbi Gedaliah Zlotowitz
General Editors
Rabbi Meir Zlotowitz ז״ל, *Founder and President*

JAFFA FAMILY EDITION

RABBI MEIR ZLOTOWITZ

HIS VISION, WISDOM, AND WARMTH
LIT UP THE WORLD

YISROEL BESSER

Published by

ARTSCROLL®
Mesorah Publications, ltd

FIRST EDITION
First Impression ... June 2018

Published and Distributed by
MESORAH PUBLICATIONS, LTD.
4401 Second Avenue / Brooklyn, N.Y 11232

Distributed in Europe by
LEHMANNS
Unit E, Viking Business Park
Rolling Mill Road
Jarow, Tyne & Wear, NE32 3DP
England

Distributed in Australia and New Zealand
by **GOLDS WORLDS OF JUDAICA**
3-13 William Street
Balaclava, Melbourne 3183
Victoria, Australia

Distributed in Israel by
SIFRIATI / A. GITLER — BOOKS
POB 2351
Bnei Brak 51122

Distributed in South Africa by
KOLLEL BOOKSHOP
Northfield Centre, 17 Northfield Avenue
Glenhazel 2192, Johannesburg, South Africa

ARTSCROLL® SERIES
RABBI MEIR ZLOTOWITZ
© *Copyright 2018, by* MESORAH PUBLICATIONS, Ltd.
4401 Second Avenue / Brooklyn, N.Y. 11232 / (718) 921-9000 / www.artscroll.com

ISBN 10: 1-4226-2071-9 / ISBN 13: 978-1-4226-2071-7

Typography by CompuScribe at ArtScroll Studios, Ltd.
Printed in the United States of America
Bound by Sefercraft, Quality Bookbinders, Ltd., Brooklyn N.Y. 11232

Humbly but proudly, we dedicate this biography of
our incomparable, irreplaceable friend and mentor,

Rabbi Meir Zlotowitz ז״ל

He devoted his enormous talent and indefatigable energy
to spreading the light of Torah —
and he succeeded in illuminating the world.
He was the greatest *marbitz Torah* of our era,
the rebbi of hundreds of thousands, the dynamo
who inspired and led the "ArtScroll Revolution"
that is changing the Jewish world.

The world knows the public Meir Zlotowitz.
The private Meir Zlotowitz was just as great.
He combined charisma, incisive judgment,
creative intelligence, and warm sensitivity, and used it
to help, counsel, guide, and encourage everyone
who knew him, and even strangers.
To us and to many others,
he was our beloved "Uncle Meir."

To read the story of his blessed life is to be inspired to
become a better person and servant of Hashem
and Klal Yisrael — and that will be the greatest tribute
to his living legacy.

The Jaffa Family

RABBI MEIR ZLOTOWITZ
SCROLL OF ETERNITY

We honor the bearers of Meir's legacy for their commitment to spread his life story and continue his meaningful work.

SHAYA AND ALIZA ACKERMAN
STEVE AND RENEE ADELSBERG
RAANAN AND NICOLE AGUS
SIMCHA AND SHANIE APPLEGRAD
ARBOR REALTY TRUST —
IVAN KAUFMAN AND STEPHEN YORK
EPHRAIM AND MALYA ARNSTEIN
ERIC AND JOYCE AUSTEIN
DAVID AND TIKVAH AZMAN
BANK LEUMI
HENRI AND BELLA BEER
MOSHE AND ESTHER BEINHORN
MARC AND SHANI BELSKY
BERGMAN FAMILY
BINYOMIN AND CHANIE BERKOWITZ
YOCHONON BERMAN
SHIMMY AND LAYLA BERTRAM
EZRA AND DEBBIE BEYMAN
SHLOMIE AND MIRIAM BIDERMAN
EZRA AND GITTY BIRNBAUM
JJ AND RIVKIE BISTRICER
SHOLOM AND SURI BLATT
ZVI AND GOLDIE BLOOM
BINYOMIN AND ESTY BLUMENKRANZ
DUVIE AND NAOMI BODNER
BOOK AUTOMATION INC
GERSHON AND LEA BRAFMAN
STEVEN BREITMAN AND FAMILY
AARON AND RAQUEL BRODY
YOSEF CHAIM AND CHANI BROOK
HARRY M. AND PERL BROWN
RABBI AND MRS. DOVID COHEN
CROSS RIVER BANK
RICHARD A. EHST, CUSTOMERS BANK
CHANANIAH AND GITTY DANZIGER
RABBI AND MRS. YECHEZKEL DANZIGER

YOSEF AND EDIE DAVIS
LEVI AND LEEBA DESSLER
ARI AND ARIELLA DEUTSCH
DAVID AND CHANEE DEUTSCH
DAVID AND TZIPI DIAMOND
ASHER AND ESTIE DICKER
URI AND DEVORAH DREIFUS
EASTERN UNION
SHIMON AND CHAYA ECKSTEIN
EDMOND J. SAFRA FOUNDATION
MEYER AND LEAH EICHLER
DAVID AND CHUMI EISEN
YECHIEL AND NECHI EISENSTADT
MICHAEL AND LINDA ELMAN
EFROIM FASTEN, FASTEN HALBERSTAM LLP
MENDY AND DEBBIE FEIGENBAUM
GREINER-MALTZ COMPANY OF NY, INC.
AVI FEINBERG, GUY SOLOMOV, JACOB BEER
ARYEH AND MALKY FELLER
MOSHE AND MIRIAM FEUER
YANKY AND CHAYA FEUEREISEN
LIPPY AND MATI FISCHMAN
DOV AND JUDY FISHOFF
JOEL L. FLEISHMAN
AVROHOM AND BOBBY FLUK
HESHY AND SUSAN FREUNDLICH
MICHAEL FRIED
SAM AND LAURIE FRIEDLAND
MATIS AND DEVORAH FRIEDMAN
MOTTI AND RIKI FRIEDMAN
RABBI AND MRS.
AVROHOM FRUCHTHANDLER
MOSHE AND ROCHEL FUCHS
YITZCHOK AND DEVORIE FUCHS
SONNY AND SHANI GANGER
MENACHEM AND RACHEL GASTWIRTH
YERUCHEM AND YEHUDIS GELB

LAIBEL GERSON

GITLER FAMILY

EFREM AND YOCHEVED GOLDBERG

JOSH AND SHARI GOLDBERG

LEON AND AGI GOLDENBERG

JACOB AND PNINA GRAFF AND FAMILY

CHAIM AND HENCHY GREENFELD

SHULKY AND FAIGY GREENWALD

TZVI AND CHANA GREENWALD

STEPHEN ROSENBERG — GREYSTONE

ETHAN AND YAEL GROSS

HAB BANK: SALEEM IQBAL,
ZILAY WAHIDY, NASIR U.KHAN.

MORDECHAI AND LOIS HAGER

YITZY HALON

ASHER AND JUDITH HANDLER

DAVID AND DENISE HARARI, PANAMA

HERTZ AND LIBBY HASENFELD

YITZCHOK AND GITTY HAAS

HASHI AND MIRIAM HERZKA

MOTTY AND MINDY HERZOG
HERZOG WINE CELLARS

YAAKOV AND BEATRICE HERZOG

MOSHE AND SUE HESCHEL

NATE AND SHIRA HYMAN

INVESTORS BANK

THE JEWISH PRESS

MR. AND MRS. ALBERT (NOSSON) KAHN

YEHIEL KALISH AND YACOV FEILER

LAIBISH AND TANYA KAMENATSKY

LLOYD AND BETH KEILSON

MEIR AND FRUMI KESSLER

MEIR AND IDY KESSNER

CHAIM AND BAYLA KIFFEL

LESTER KLAUS

BORUCH BER AND RIVKY KLEIMAN

GEORGE KLEIN

MOTTI AND MALKA KLEIN

YAAKOV REUVEN AND RIVKY KLUGMANN

BARRY AND TOBY KOHN

PHILIP KRISPIN AND NACHUM SOROKA

RABBI AND MRS. PAYSACH KROHN

SHAUL KUPERWASSER AND YITZY KLOR

SHIMSHON AND BATSHEVA KLUGMAN

LAKELAND BANK

IRVING AND MIRIAM LANGER

YERUCHUM AND SIMI LAX

MOTTI AND CHANIE LAZAR

SHOSHANA LEFKOWITZ

CHAIM AND ILDI LEIBEL

DANNY AND BLIMY LEMBERG

YEHUDA AND RASIE LEVI

RAFI AND DEBBIE LICHTSCHEIN

YISROEL AND MENUCHA LIPPEL

RABBI AND MRS. PINCHOS LIPSCHUTZ

LOEB AND TROPER LLP

BEN AND MIRIAM LOWINGER

JUDITH LOWINGER

ROBERT LOWINGER

L'ZECHER NISHMAS SHALOM BEN YOSSEF

MADISON COMMERCIAL
REAL ESTATE SERVICES

MOSHE AND MARGA MARX

MEYER & SHULAMITH MAY

MR. AND MRS. YAAKOV MELOHN
AND FAMILY

DOVID AND ROCHIE METZGER

ASHER DAVID AND MICHAL MILSTEIN

STEPHEN AND EVE MILSTEIN

SHLOMIE AND SURI MILWORM

ADAM AND CHAVIE MIRZOEFF

MISHPACHA MAGAZINE

RABBI AND MRS. DOVID MORGAN

DOVID AND DVORAH MORGENSTERN

JEAN-CLAUDE AND DEBBIE MULLER

MOSHE AND MICHAL MULLER

YEHUDA AND TZIVI MUNK

MIKE NAJARIAN

ANDY AND NANCY NEFF

MOSHE AND BROCHIE NEIMAN

NEXUS CAPITAL INVESTMENTS

ALLAN AND CHAIKIE NOVETSKY

AARON AND AHUVA ORLOFSKY

ARI AND RUTHY PARNES

RABBI AND MRS. MAYER PASTERNAK

DAVID AND MICHELINE PELLER

EFRAIM AND FAIGIE PERLOWITZ

YISROEL AND BETH RABINOWITZ

BARRY AND HARRIET RAY

CREDIFI CORP. AND ELY RAZIN

SHLOMO YEHUDA AND TAMAR RECHNITZ

CHANINA AND TAMMY REISCHER

IRA AND INGEBORG RENNERT

REONOMY

DANIEL AND MARGIE RETTER

ELIE AND RACHEL RIEDER

SHMUEL YOSEF AND LEA RIEDER

SHMULIE AND CHANALE RIEDER

RIDGEWOOD SAVINGS BANK

GEOFFREY AND MIMI ROCHWARGER

PHIL AND MALKI ROSEN

MECHI AND CHANIE ROSENBERG

AARON AND ADINA ROSENFELD

DANIEL AND CHAVA ROSS

DAVID AND GAIL RUBIN

ZVI AND BETTY RYZMAN

YITZCHOK AND ESTHER SHAINDEL SAFTLAS

GEORGE AND STEPHANIE SAKS

JUDAH AND BAYLA SAMTER

BENJAMIN AND GABI SAMUELS

DOVID AND CHANI SCHARF

YITZCHOK AND ZISI SCHICK

AVI AND MEIRA SCHNUR

JAY AND JEANIE SCHOTTENSTEIN

JOEY AND LINDSAY SCHOTTENSTEIN

JEFFREY SCHOTTENSTEIN

JONATHAN AND NICOLE SCHOTTENSTEIN

SCHRON FAMILY

RIVIE AND LEBA SCHWEBEL

NEW SPRINGVILLE JEWISH CENTER,
CHAIM NATE SEGAL — RABBI

HESHE AND HARRIET SEIF

BERYL AND SABINA SEPTIMUS

JUDAH AND BAILE SEPTIMUS

SHARESTATES

YOSEF CHAIM AND NINA SHENKER

RABBI AND MRS. SHIMSHON SHERER

JOSEPH DEPAOLO, JOSEPH FINGERMAN
AND JOHN ZIERAN — SIGNATURE BANK

MARK AND BARBARA SILBER

NACHUM AND MALKIE SILBERMAN

JEFFERY AND DANIELLA SILVER

MR. AND MRS. YERACHMIEL SIMINS

TZVI AND DEVORAH SINGER

JORDAN AND LAURIE SLONE

MORRIS AND DEVORAH SMITH

PINKY AND ANN SOHN

ADAM AND SURI SOKOL

AHRON AND RACHEL SOLOMON

YECHIEL AND CHUMIE SPERO

GERSHON AND LEAH SPIEGEL

ZEV SPIRA

DAVID AND RACHEL STEINBERG

ARI KLEIN, STERLING NATIONAL BANK

BRENDA WIENER,
STERLING NATIONAL BANK

A. JOSEPH AND RUCHI STERN

YITZCHOK AND MIRIAM STERNHELL

ELLIOT AND DEBBIE TANNENBAUM

YANKY AND ESTHER TAUBER

SOL AND RUTH TEICHMAN

JAY AND SARI TEPPER

THE BATTERY GROUP

THE REAL DEAL

JAMES AND MERRYL TISCH

GARY AND MALKA TORGOW

MARC AND SHULI TROPP

SHMUEL UMLAS

SHALOM AND REENA VEGH

ZECHARIA AND ESTEE WALLERSTEIN

STANLEY AND ELLEN WASSERMAN

CHAIM AND AVIVA WEALCATCH

MORTY AND CHAYA MALKIE WEBER

NAFTALI AND NAOMI WEINBERGER

AVRUM AND D'VORAH WEINFELD

JOE AND MIRIAM WEISS

CHANOCH AND HADASSAH WEISZ

MICHAEL (ZVI) AND KATIE WEISZ

SHLOMIE AND ESTHER WERDIGER

ADAM AND DAYNA WESTREICH

BENZION (BENNY) AND JOYCE WESTREICH

LESLIE WESTREICH

STEVEN ROMER & ABE ROMER, WESTROCK
APPRAISAL SERVICES

RONNIE AND DINA WILHEIM

YAAKOV AND CHAYA WILLINGER

ROBERT D. MERCURIO, MITCHELL A. GILBERT
AND ALAN WINTERS,
WINDELS MARX LANE & MITTENDORF, LLP

JERRY AND SORA WOLASKY

MRS. HIRSCH WOLF

MOSHE AND ARIELLE WOLFSON

CHAIM AND SHIRA ZLOTOWITZ

BARUCH AND CHANI ZLOTOWITZ

YISROEL (IRA) AND ROCHI ZLOTOWITZ

TABLE OF CONTENTS

FOREWORD

by Rabbi Gedaliah Zlotowitz

F OR ELEVEN MONTHS, THREE TIMES A DAY, I SAID THE
words, again and again: in crowded *shtieblach* and spacious *batei medrash*, a *minyan* at the airport, along the
New York Thruway, and at ArtScroll headquarters. In Brooklyn,
the Catskills, or Yerushalayim, I expressed the timeless Jewish
reaction to profound loss: *Yisgadal v'yiskadash Shemei rabba.*

The vacuum left by the passing of a Jew is somehow filled by
these words, the prayer for increased *kevod Shamayim*, a hope
that the glory of Heaven be increased.

And on the very day that those eleven months end, I sit down
to write these words.

This book is sort of a Kaddish as well, an enduring call of
Yisgadal v'yiskadash Shemei rabba.

It's a guidebook, an in-depth look at how my father *z"l* managed to do it, how he elevated every interaction and lived with a clear sense of his own mission. He saw each moment as a gift and an obligation, ever-attuned to the mandate of *Yisgadal V'yiskadash Shemei rabba.*

Each person he met — each colleague or relative or employee or neighbor — was worthy of respect and sincere attention. Each challenge was an opportunity to call forth resources of fortitude and courage, each juncture of his life a moment of reckoning at which the eternal call to bring glory to the Name of Hashem prodded him to action.

This is a story about being close to *talmidei chachamim,* about reveling in the role of husband and father and grandfather, of radiating warmth and *chizuk* to those who need it so badly, about building and building and building and still remaining humble. It's a book about a man who, early on, absorbed the lesson that life is the ultimate Kaddish and determined to live that way.

Ima, my siblings, and I all mourned bitterly over our loss. As we sat *shivah* we knew that so many people felt that they lost their best friend, their favorite "uncle," their place to turn for advice. But I can hear him encouraging us every day to move on, as every person has a special mission to accomplish with his or her precious days on this world.

Of course you will read about the man who created a Torah revolution through ArtScroll. However, what he would want you to take away from the book is how to be a better parent, a better child, a better boss, a better employee, a better friend: to open your heart to each and every person and just show them that you care.

I will never forget the Monday evening of the *shivah.* An acquaintance from the neighborhood came by. I saw that he was very emotional and wanted to tell me something. The room was crowded, and when I looked up a few minutes later he was gone. Several minutes later I received a text from him asking that I contact him when the last person leaves the house. That turned out to be very late, so I texted him asking if he would please pass by the next morning.

After Shacharis I was told that someone was at the door to see me. I went to the door and there he was with tears streaming down his face. I hugged him and asked him to please share what was on his mind. What he told me next was a lesson I will never forget.

Fifteen years earlier his grandfather had passed away. He was very close to that grandfather and for reasons we will never understand, he decided to stop wearing tefillin to show his anger. No one knew this. He looked like a regular guy in the neighborhood with a beautiful family. Whenever my father would see him walking in the street, my father would go over to him, give him a hug, and ask how he was doing. The man went through many challenges — *parnassah*, *shidduchim*, and more — and my father always just showed that he cared and was willing to lend a helping hand.

When this person heard on Motza'ei Shabbos that my father had passed away that day, he decided that the next morning he would start putting on tefillin again as a merit for my father. He was there to tell me that he put on tefillin for the third day in a row…all because my father showed him love and genuinely cared about him.

The same Reb Meir Zlotowitz who created a Torah revolution throughout the world, who will be remembered generations from now as one of the greatest *marbitzei Torah*, who inspired so many Jews to daven better, was able to stop and care about the countless people who turned to him throughout his life, as well as many people who, he sensed, needed a good word and a smile. As we internalize the lessons from his life and we become better people, this will be the ultimate *zechus* for his *neshamah*.

I thank Hashem for granting me the privilege of carrying on my father's forty-two-year mission of *harbatzas Torah*. It's an obligation I do not take lightly. My father *z"l* allowed me to work with him side-by-side for twenty-four years. That unique opportunity allowed me to observe and absorb his approach to people and projects, and that experience *baruch Hashem* prepared me for the moment I prayed would never come.

My father always taught me that the most important thing in life is to have a rebbi. He attributed the success of ArtScroll to his relationship with Hagaon Harav Dovid Feinstein *shlita*, Hagaon Harav Dovid Cohen *shlita*, and Hagaon Harav Reuven Feinstein *shlita*. These Torah giants have shown me the same love they showed him and I am grateful for their guidance. I am thankful for my rebbi of thirty-three years, Hagaon Harav Avrohom Ausband *shlita*, who constantly showers me with love and guidance.

———

When Jerome Schottenstein passed away twenty-six years ago, my father was at Jay and Jeanie's side as an older friend and mentor. Hours after my father's passing, on that difficult Motza'ei Shabbos, Jay and Jeanie returned the favor, and they have been there for me every day since. Their wisdom, concern, and commitment have carried me through this long, hard winter. I am truly blessed by their friendship, and am gratified to feel a similar eternal bond with their exceptional children.

I remember what my brother-in-law, Rabbi Duvie Morgenstern, said in his *hesped* — that my father's steady, inevitable approach to any request could be contained in a single word: *Hineni, I am here for you.* My father stood ready to serve, to help, to get involved — whatever the need was, whoever was asking. I am deeply grateful to all his friends and supporters who sounded that same call of *Hineni* — echoing my father's call to them. To them I say, "Your loyalty to my father in life, and your warm encouragement and assurance that you will always be with me, has given me strength during the most difficult moments." I am blessed that so many new friends as well have rallied around me, reassuring me that they are here to help me in any way. I look forward to reciprocating your kindness.

To my partners in our *avodas hakodesh*, Rabbi Nosson Scherman, Rabbi Sheah Brander, and Shmuel Blitz, it's a pleasure working with you *every* day. My father always spoke about the "genius cluster" he assembled. I am humbled to be a part of it. I am thankful to our special staff at ArtScroll. You have all persevered through the collective and individual loss of my father whom you loved and you knew cared so much about you. Keeping his mission alive is how you are showing your appreciation. You let me know *every* day in so many ways that we are all in this together.

To our special team of *talmidei chachamim*, it's a *zechus* to have the opportunity to be here for you. You keep raising the bar as you produce masterpiece after masterpiece. Let us all pray that Hashem will continue to grant us all *siyata d'Shmaya* to continue spreading Torah and to continue the ArtScroll Revolution that my father began forty-two years ago.

Ima, you have been the rock of the family. Your *emunah* is legendary. A special thank you to all my siblings — Asher and Estie, Efraim and Faigie, Duvie and Dvorah, Yehuda and Tzivi, Yisroel and Rochi , Boruch and Chani, Chaim and Shira — and all my nieces and nephews, for their constant support throughout this difficult period. Knowing that you are rooting for my success is very comforting.

A special thank you to Mommy for always believing in me and cheering me on.

To my wife, Daniella, you are the real hero. No matter how hard it gets, you are always there to encourage me to stay focused and to keep Dad's Torah mission alive. In your quiet way, you are the strength that keeps me going. It's because of you that our children, Ahron and Etty, Eli and Chana, Yechiel and Shoshana, Shmuli, Hadassah, Tzvi, and Yosef, share the

Torah values that we hold dear. I thank Hashem for having the most supportive family. You all understand the special *zechus* that was given to us. I am proud of each and *every* one of you. I am grateful and I love you all.

As I put the final touches on this book, I am sad that this particular *avodas hakodesh* is coming to an end. I created an eternal friendship with Rabbi Sruli Besser, whom I can now call my mentor and guide as I steer ArtScroll into the future. Your insights into the needs of the *klal* are always on target. My father appreciated your talents and I am grateful to have had the opportunity to work with you over the past eleven months. A special thank you to my sister Estie and brother Yisroel, who put in countless hours with me on the phone.

I daven to Hashem that all of us involved in this work did justice to the lessons of my father's life.

I sit in his chair, in his office, in the building he conceived and loved, working so hard to carry on his holy mission; it is so fitting that this book is our first offering as the year of mourning concludes.

Because now we stop *saying* Kaddish and start *living* Kaddish.

AN APPRECIATION

by Harav Dovid Feinstein
Rosh HaYeshivah, Mesivtha Tifereth Jerusalem

THIS IS THE ACCOUNT OF THE DESCENDANTS OF ADAM (*Bereishis* 5:1).

This is the biography of a religious Jew. Chazal say (*Shekalim* 7a): אֵין עוֹשִׂין נְפָשׁוֹת לַצַּדִּיקִים, דִּבְרֵיהֶם הֵן הֵן זִכְרוֹנָן, *We do not make monuments for the righteous — their words are their memorial.* One might think that a biography, like a monument, is necessary to ensure that its subject not be forgotten; but Reb Meir will be remembered whenever someone opens an ArtScroll *sefer* and sees his name. Why this biography? Because it tells the story of why and how he grew up to become the one who made Talmud Bavli and Yerushalmi, and many other *sefarim*, accessible to the masses of our people.

The Gemara (*Niddah* 16b) says that it is decreed for every

person, before he is even born, whether he will be גִּבּוֹר אוֹ חַלָּשׁ, חָכָם אוֹ טִיפֵּשׁ, עָנִי אוֹ עָשִׁיר, *strong or weak, smart or foolish, poor or rich.* For our benefit, Reb Meir was blessed with all three positive traits.

When Reb Meir entered the yeshivah, he was already geared for such greatness. His love of Torah was instilled in him when he awoke every morning hearing the sweet sound of his father's voice as he sat engrossed in his learning. As a *talmid*, Reb Meir compiled copious notes on *Mishnah Berurah*, in addition to learning the regular *seder*. Therefore, Hashem granted him the חָכְמָה, *wisdom*, to pursue his mission to spread Torah.

He suffered physical pain virtually his entire life. Therefore, Hashem granted him גְּבוּרָה, *strength*, to persevere in the face of obstacles.

He took on the responsibility to engage and fund scores of *talmidei chachamim* to work on projects. He accepted the burden of constant fund-raising to support the Torah scholars by having new projects ready for them, so that Klal Yisrael would continue to benefit from them, and they would continue to have a livelihood. This was חֶסֶד, *generosity*, of a very high order.

There is another aspect of Reb Meir's generosity. His creation of the ArtScroll enterprise was motivated by his desire to perpetuate the memory of a dear friend — a huge act of *chessed*. He was therefore granted עֲשִׁירוּת, by raising vast sums of money to cover the creation, production, and publication of dozens of projects benefiting Jews from all walks of life.

Because he had these three vital attributes — wisdom, strength, and generosity — it is understandable why Providence chose him to bring תּוֹרַת חֶסֶד, *the Torah of Generosity*, to the Jewish people.

Additionally, Chazal (*Tanchuma, Ha'azinu* 7), teach that a person's destiny can be seen in his name: מֵאִיר [he illuminated] יַעֲקֹב [the nation of Yaakov] בֶּן אַהֲרֹן [Aharon was the one who loved peace and benefited the Jewish people]. This epitomized Reb Meir.

The Mishnah (*Avos* 4:2) teaches: שְׂכַר מִצְוָה, מִצְוָה, *the perfor-mance of a mitzvah is rewarded with the ability to perform more mitzvos*. It is fitting, therefore, that Reb Meir's contributions to Klal Yisrael have been rewarded by an outpouring of recognition and support by so many people who are dedicating new works as a memorial and monument to Rabbi Meir Zlotowitz. Surely they will be generously rewarded for all that they do and will continue to do.

Reb Meir followed in the footsteps of R' Chiya, and emulated his manner of spreading Torah to Klal Yisrael. Just as Rabbeinu HaKadosh said (*Bava Metzia* 85b) גְּדוֹלִים מַעֲשֵׂי חִיָּיא, so can we say about Reb Meir: גְּדוֹלִים מַעֲשֵׂי חִיָּיא, *great are [Reb Meir's] life's work*, which resulted in unprecendented *harbatzas Torah*.

We take leave of Reb Meir with the words (*Daniel* 12:13): וְאַתָּה לֵךְ [לשלום] לַקֵּץ וְתָנוּחַ וְתַעֲמֹד לְגֹרָלְךָ לְקֵץ הַיָּמִין, *As for you, go to [your] end; you will rest-then arise for your portion at the End of Days*. Gedaliah is taking your place and continuing your work. The harmony among Gedaliah, Reb Nosson, and Reb Sheah will continue and your mission will endure.

AUTHOR'S PREFACE

R ABBI MEIR ZLOTOWITZ WAS A RADIANT MAN. HE HAD this glow about him, and when he spoke with you, you felt it too.

I considered myself his friend.

But now I know that I "only saw Reb Meir from behind" (*Eruvin* 13b).

I had grasped the externals, the charisma and humor and power of his personality. I had marveled at his accomplishments, the way he had illuminated the Jewish world, the significance of the gift he had given his brothers and sisters, but I had missed the real story.

Early in the summer, when I conducted the first of hundreds of interviews with the people who made up his world, I started to notice it. The way they spoke about him, this collection of employees and neighbors and donors and old camp friends: he didn't have a relationship, it seemed, that wasn't impactful.

In Reb Meir's absence people began to realize that his casual conversation, his smile, and his advice and encouragement had been carrying them. Over that summer, I sat at their tables and in their studies as they struggled with the fact that he was gone, that the role he filled would remain vacant.

They spoke of "Uncle Meir" not just with fondness and warmth, but with evident pain and longing.

His generosity of spirit — and actual generosity — made him the one they looked to for a good joke, level-headed counsel, perhaps a loan, help finding a job or getting a child into school. His innate respect elevated them as well: he brushed them with his own dignity. His steadfast loyalty to them and their families was a firm wall they could lean against during stormy times.

This was the story that started to come together.

It was unique in another way, as well. I write about accomplished people for a living. Over the years, I've observed, being great outside the home and being great inside the home don't always go hand in hand. At times, people who are gifted, determined, and focused get lost in their personal crusade or campaign, and there isn't much room for anything else.

Not Reb Meir.

Like a digital picture frame, in which the images keep shifting even as the frame remains unchanged, Reb Meir was himself in every situation, filling that frame with whatever was needed in order to fulfill his mission.

He danced effortlessly between different *middos*, capable of meeting each situation with the appropriate tool. A serious man with a remarkable sense of humor, a punctual person with an ability to drop everything in the middle of a workday to sit and listen to the problems of another, precise with money yet extraordinarily generous, a man with hundreds of close friends and a dizzying array of business relationships, who picked up the phone whenever a child or grandchild called, a frequent traveler who showed up for baby namings and Chumash parties, an independent thinker with strong opinions who would shift — no, completely negate — his view to adapt to the approach of his rebbeim.

I wondered what it was, the inner force that drove him and enabled him to be so many things to so many people. What was the defining characteristic of this man, of Rabbi Zlotowitz?

Then, I heard my rebbi quote an explanation of the Rambam in *Maseches Demai* (2:3). Why are *talmidei chachamim* called "*chaveirim,*" which literally means friends? Because, says the Rambam, *chaveirasam ne'emana*, one can depend on their friendship. They are loyal. They are steadfast.

To become a *talmid chacham*, one must take words seriously, take information seriously, be capable of serious reasoning. To become a *talmid chacham*, one must take other people seriously, for Torah is acquired only through give-and-take, shared toil.

Talmidei chachamim are steadfast and loyal to what they believe because their own opinions are developed. They are steadfast and loyal to others because they have learned to appreciate the contributions of other people.

Reb Meir was a "*chaver,*" the friend whose loyalty to others was merely a reflection of his spirit, the lifelong *talmid* to his great rebbeim, rooted, until his final day, in the *beis medrash* of Rav Moshe Feinstein. That *middah* — his being a *chaver* — made him the faithful *talmid*, the loyal friend, the devoted husband, father, and grandfather — and it was this *middah* that would make ArtScroll so successful.

People often ask me which story in the book is my favorite. The answer, of course, is that they all are, but there is one line that moved me deeply, which gave me real insight into the depth of Reb Meir's vision.

*An industry colleague once pointed out that some publishers preferred to create books that would eventually rip, so that customers would be forced to buy new ones. "That makes sense if you're running a business," Reb Meir said, **"not if your*** *mission is to give someone a Siddur that can become their best friend."*

Reb Meir wasn't only a *chaver,* a *talmid chacham,* and a loyal friend to other people. He was determined to create products that were themselves *chaveirim*: dependable, faithful companions. The Siddurim made the shul a welcoming place, and the Gemaros made the *beis medrash* feel like home.

Only someone who appreciates the poetry, the depth, and nuance of the word *"chaver"* can express the hope that a Siddur would "become a best friend."

Talmidei chachamim marbim shalom ba'olam. This boy from the Lower East Side, who — in a way — never really left its bustling streets, succeeded in reaching the farthest corners of the Jewish world, walked a path that took him well beyond the confines in which he had been raised, and exposed him to Jews of all sorts — and all along the journey, he gathered friends. He pulled them close, shared the vision and the inspiration, filled them with his enthusiasm — and together, he and his many friends gave a nation new sorts of friends: *sefarim* and Siddurim and books they could connect with, cherish, hold close.

———

The interviews were one thing; the conversations with Reb Meir's immediate family led me into another dimension. They mourned and laughed and cried and reminisced and exulted in the great gift they had been given, the father and father-in-law, the grandfather and grandfather-in-law who had carried their worries and fears in his own heart, who had rejoiced in their successes and never, ever, stopped rooting for them.

His pride in each of them, his joy in their accomplishments — and, he always said, his wife Rachel's fervent *tefillos* — paid off, *bli ayin hara.* He was happiest when he was with his family, ever mindful and expressive of his gratitude to the Creator, the One Who had blessed him with so much *nachas.*

To his mind, they were the greatest accomplishment of all.

In interviewing them, their spouses, and their children, I observed something interesting. There was none of the guilt one often finds in children who have lost a parent, *lo aleinu*, none of the regrets about "we should have said" or "we should have been." They miss him terribly, but they know that they were privileged: they knew how much he loved them and that he knew how much they loved him.

It is customary for an author to pen not just an introduction to the book, but also an acknowledgments section. It's true for every book, but in a book about Reb Meir, it's part of the story. Reb Meir was a man of gratitude. Perhaps it was because he experienced health issues, or maybe it was because he had tasted challenge and hardship in his early years, but he was grateful for each and every day. As you'll read in the pages ahead, *be'ezras Hashem*, he didn't see himself as having accomplished, but rather as having seized the opportunities given to him. The Ribbono Shel Olam had something He wanted done, and Reb Meir had been fortunate enough to have been selected as a *shaliach*. He was effusive in his thanks to those who helped him realize it: in ArtScroll works, the thank-you section was never an afterthought.

And so, we turn to the acknowledgments: there is no introduction more appropriate for a work about Reb Meir and his legacy.

The Ribbono Shel Olam allowed me the *zechus* of writing this book. It elevated my life, and that of my family, and I'm overwhelmed by thanks to Him for all His kindness. I daven that we always be able to sense the *siyata d'Shmaya* we felt while working on this project.

Among the many gifts He has given me is the friendship of Rabbi Gedaliah Zlotowitz. I looked on in awe as a man mourning his father, who had the burden of a massive company and its considerable payroll thrust onto his shoulders almost over-night, was somehow able to honor his father's legacy beyond ArtScroll as well — the responsibility to family and friends, the bright smile and warm, encouraging words.

And I made a true friend — a *chaver*, like his father before him.

Reb Gedaliah, this isn't the first time you've done it for me. At a different time, a simpler time, when I was an uncertain teenager and you were a dynamic head counselor, you took me for a walk in Camp Munk and said, "You can do it." You touched my life once, and now you've done it again. I think I know whom you inherited it from, this *ayin tovah* and desire to see others succeed.

Thank you for late nights and long rambling conversations, for shared laughter and tears, for being my partner in discover-ing your father's true story. Thank you for letting me do this.

The Zlotowitz family is special. Mrs. Rachel Zlotowitz is a queen. She exudes the *temimus, ehrlichkeit,* and sincerity of Jewish women of generations past. Along with the stories, she took me to a time before ArtScroll, when her husband was just a dreamer, a man whose secret ambitions had not yet been realized. It was her support that allowed those secret dreams to burst forth and, as he often said, "*Sheli veshelachem shelah hi.*" She was the pillar holding up one of the great *marbitzei Torah* of the modern era.

Each one of the Zlotowitz children has clearly inherited Reb Meir's giving nature; were it not for their generosity and warmth, this book would never have happened. They allowed me in, opening up the storehouses of treasured memories and sharing deeply moving personal conversations. They trusted me and encouraged me and did all the things he would have done.

To Gedaliah and Daniella Zlotowitz, Asher and Estie Dicker,

Efraim and Faigie Perlowitz, Yehuda and Tzivi Munk, Duvie and Dvorah Morgenstern, Yisroel and Rochi Zlotowitz, Baruch and Chani Zlotowitz, and Chaim and Shira Zlotowitz, thank you. I'm eternally grateful for the trust you showed me and blessed by the friendship formed with each of you.

To the Zlotowitz grandchildren and grandchildren-in-law: Thanks for the conversations, phone calls, texts, pictures, and continuous stream of precious memories. Clearly, you know how fortunate you are to carry his legacy forward; may you never forget, even for a moment, who your zaidy was and how he viewed each one of you.

Reb Nosson. You were a mentor long before this project began, a wise, experienced, patient, gracious voice of reason and depth. Your gifted pen inspired so many of us to try writing, showing us just how elevated a craft it can be.

Reb Sheah. The world knows your genius from printed letters, designs, and layouts; in this book, the "white space" too is filled with your *seichel*, clarity, and insight.

Reb Shmuel. I landed in Yerushalayim hours after committing to this book and you were the first interview; as soon as I sat down in your office and listened to you speak, I knew it would be okay.

I've worked with the ArtScroll staff before, but in this book we were partners. Reb Avrohom: you just get it. Whatever it is, you understand in a way that makes words redundant.

To the talented production staff: Mrs. Judi Dick made many valuable editorial contributions; Mrs. Mindy Stern and Mrs. Esther Feierstein proofread with great diligence. Mrs. Estie Dicker handled the complicated pagination with exemplary skill. This book was not just another project — it was the story of her father's life and legacy — and she treated it as a labor of love.

This book is graced with the reminiscences and insights of *gedolei Torah*. I am grateful for the time given to me by Rav Dovid and Rebbetzin Malka Feinstein and Rav Dovid and

Rebbetzin Leah Cohen. It was a *zechus* to sit with them, as well as with Rav Avrohom Ausband, Rav Yaakov Bender, Rav Elya Brudny, Rav Yosef Efrati, and Rav Aryeh Elyashiv, Rav and Rebbetzin Avrohom Chaim Feuer, Rav Moshe Mendel Glustein.

The conversation with Mr. Jay and Mrs. Jeanie Schottenstein pulled back a curtain on one of the great Torah partnerships in Jewish history. That afternoon in Florida was far more than a trip down memory lane: it was an ode to what can be accomplished when there is shared commitment, shared vision, and true friendship.

To Mr. Shimmy Bertram, Rabbi Yaakov Biderman, Rabbi Heshy Billet, Rabbi Shmuel Bloom, Rabbi Zvi Bloom, Rabbi Reuvain Borchardt, Mr. Yitzchok Brezel, Mr. Harry Brown, Rabbi Raphael Butler, Mr. Menachem Butler, Rabbi Ami Cohen, Rabbi Eli Cohen, Rabbi Simcha Bunim Cohen, Rabbi Eric Coopersmith, Rabbi Yechezkel Danziger, Mr. Reuven Dessler, Rabbi Shimon Finkelman, Mrs. Susie Fishbein, Mr. Benny Fishoff, Rabbi Yissocher Frand, Mr. Howard Zvi Friedman, Mr. Adrian Garbacz, Rabbi Aryeh Zev Ginzberg, Rabbi and Mrs. Zvi Gluck, Rabbi Avrohom Glustein, Rabbi Avie Gold, Rabbi Shalom Gold, Rabbi Hillel Goldberg, Rabbi and Rebbetzin Yisroel Gornisch, Mr. Charlie Grandovsky, Mr. Yitzchak Meir Greenwald, Rabbi Mordechai Yehuda Groner, Mr. Yitzy Gruen, Rabbi Sholom Hecht, Rabbi and Mrs. Yehuda Heimowitz, Mr. and Mrs. Moshe Hellman, Rabbi Eli Herzka, Mr. Yaakov Herzog, Rabbi Avraham Heschel, Mr. Malcolm Hoenlein, Mr. Amir Jaffa, Rabbi Burton Jaffa, Mr. Ilan Jaffa, Mr. Jack Jaffa, Mr. Chaim Kahn, Rabbi Yechiel Kalish, Rabbi and Mrs. Hillel Kapenstein, Rabbi Yosef Chaim Karmel, Rabbi Ahron Kaufman, Mr. and Mrs. Chaim Kiffel, Mr. Mendy Klein *a"h*, Mr. Elly Kleinman, Rabbi Eliyahu Meir Klugman, Rabbi Aaron Kotler, Mr. Chananya Kramer, Rabbi Paysach Krohn, Rabbi Meir Levi, Rabbi Michoel Levi, Rabbi Yehuda Levi, Mr. Tobias Levkovich, Rabbi and Mrs. Pinchos Lipschutz, Rabbi Chaim Malinowitz, Rabbi Shmuel

Mayer, Mr. Yoni Mayer, Mr. and Mrs. Yaakov Melohn, Mr. Yosef Melohn, Mr. and Mrs. Asher David Milstein, Mr. Adam Mirzoeff, Rabbi Ezriel Munk, Rabbi Ezzy Munk, Rabbi Pinny Munk, Mrs. Raye Munk, Rabbi Shragi Neuberger, Mr. Aaron Orlofsky, Mr. Mayer Pasternak, Rabbi and Mrs. Shlomo Dovid Pfeiffer, Mr. Mark Platnick, Rabbi Meir Platnick, Mr. Geoffrey Rochwarger, Mr. Phil Rosen, Rabbi Itche Rosenbaum, Rabbi Yonoson Rosenblum, Mr. and Mrs. Zvi Ryzman, Mr. Yitzchak Saftlas, Mr. Dovid Scharf, Mr. Aubrey Scharfman, Mr. Avrohom Scherman, Rabbi Yitzchak Zev Scherman, Mr. and Mrs. Joey Schottenstein, Mr. Barry Schwartz, Mr. Elliot Schwartz, Mr. Ronnie Schwartz, Mr. and Mrs. Rivie Schwebel, Mr. Charles Selengut, Rabbi Shimshon Sherer, Mr. Avi Shulman, Mr. and Mrs. Nochum Silberman, Rabbi Chaim Smutni, Mr. Adam Sokol, Rabbi Yechiel Spero, Mr. Jacques Stern, Mr. Woli Stern, Rabbi David Sutton, Mr. Sol Teichman, Mr. Gary Torgow, Rabbi Yosef Wartelsky, Mr. Chaim Wealcatch, Rabbi Berel Wein, Rabbi Naftali Weinberger, Mr. Avrum Weinfeld, Rabbi Yonah Weinrib, Mr. Chanoch Weisz, Mr. Shlomo Werdiger, Mr. and Mrs. Mendy Yarmish, Mr. Pinchas Zagelbaum, Rabbi Yosef Zoimen, and Rabbi Chaim Dovid Zwiebel, thank you for your memories.

The conversations with the various members of the ArtScroll staff were enlightening: they spoke with the passion and heart of family. Thank you to Mrs. Lea Brafman, Mrs. Judi Dick, Mrs. Shaindy Friedman, Mr. Mendy Herzberg, Rabbi Eli Kroen, Mrs. Chana Rothstein, Mr. Benjy Seror, Mrs. Mindy Stern, and Mrs. Faigie Weinbaum. It was evident that working with Reb Meir day in and day out didn't minimize their respect for him, but just the opposite.

I very much appreciated the insights in the various articles that appeared following Reb Meir's passing, and I drew on the material contained in written appreciations by Rabbi Avrohom Birnbaum, Rabbi Shimon Finkelman, Rabbi Hillel Goldberg, Rabbi Yehuda Heimowitz, Rabbi Yaakov Horowitz, Rabbi

Yitzchok Hisiger, Rabbi Pinchos Lipschutz, Mr. Yitzchak Saftlas, Rabbi Yechiel Spero, Rabbi Berel Wein, and Mrs. Mimi Zakon.

And finally, to those near and dear to me who were very much part of this project.

It's an honor to work for and learn from Rabbi Pinchos Lipschutz of *Yated Ne'eman* and Mr. Eli Paley of *Mishpacha* magazine. I have gained immeasurably from being exposed to the talented editorial staff at *Mishpacha*, and I'm grateful for the opportunities they have given me.

A central theme of this book is the benefit of having a rebbi; my own rebbi, Rav Aron Tabak, is a continuous source of Torah, guidance, and encouragement.

Another thread that runs through the chapters is the importance of family; in this regard, we too have been blessed.

Having grandparents such as Rebbetzin Ahuva Besser, Rabbi and Mrs. Hertzel Schechter, and Rabbi and Mrs. Gershon Morgenstern is a *zechus*; we are grateful for the shining example they set for us.

My parents, Rabbi and Mrs. Shlomo Besser, raised us to appreciate the greatness of all Jews. This book is a tribute to their vision and *ayin tovah*. My father, my greatest role model, also conveyed the unique flavor of the world of RJJ and Rav Moshe's MTJ, helping me with the background to this work.

With their steady unwavering love and support, my parents-in-law, Rabbi and Mrs. Avrohom Schechter, are partners in all we do. They are with us at every juncture, always finding ways to give and be helpful.

My wife, Riki, makes it all possible. A great man once told me that, in this generation of *chinuch* challenges, a man can travel for work only if he is truly confident in his wife's abilities. "If you cannot completely depend on her wisdom, kindness, and warmth," he told me, "then you cannot travel."

I travel.

Simi, Yitzchak, Miri, Yechiel, Eliyahu, and Esti make every

moment of life joyous and fulfilling; thanks for listening to the stories, and then listening again. You're *everything* to us. May we continue to have *nachas* from each of you.

"Changed my life" is a very dramatic expression. Speeches, songs, and encounters that are impactful often change that moment, or maybe the day: It takes a special kind of person to make change last longer than that.

I daven that I manage to hold onto these emotions, to allow them to continue to influence me.

Reb Meir taught us so much. He taught the joy of service, of being charged with a Divine mission. He taught that conversations with children, with parents, with friends — each one is life itself. He taught that no person is insignificant, and no task is too small to be done with precision.

This isn't an ordinary biography, not just a collection of dates and places. The magic of Reb Meir's story lies in the many threads that run through it, how the experiences of his youth shaped who he would become, how the lessons seared onto his soul by his parents and rebbeim would become his legacy. It's one long short-story of a life well-lived.

Someone once commented that politicians promise to effect certain changes if elected, but then, when they're in office, they don't follow through. The person remarked that clearly, politicians are liars.

Reb Meir took issue with the statement. "No," he said, "it isn't that they're liars. When they make the promise, they are sincere, and intend to carry it out. But the reality is that when they sit on the other side of the desk, in a position of power, things appear different and then they forget."

"But," Reb Meir concluded, "a sign of greatness is when a person reaches a place of power, and is still able to remember how things looked from a position of weakness."

Reb Meir never forgot. He never forgot the difficult times, never forgot the challenges, never forgot what it was like to have a dream buried in his heart and wonder if it would ever be set free.

He sat on one side of the desk — builder, architect, innovator — but remembered the view from the other side.

He understood adversity and despair because he had survived adversity and despair.

He understood loneliness because he had survived loneliness.

But he did more than remember: along his journey, he learned to cherish the gifts of life, family, rebbeim, friends, happy occasions. He learned to seize opportunities, to share whatever was given to him with others.

And he managed to convey that appreciation, elevating all those fortunate enough to know him.

Perhaps, *be'ezras Hashem*, this book will give them — give all of us — a taste of what was, a sense of being around him.

Perhaps we too will be counted among those who knew Reb Meir.

1

FIRST RAYS OF LIGHT

IT WAS A DECISION NO HUSBAND SHOULD EVER HAVE TO make.

The doctor spoke quietly and quickly, conveying the urgency of the situation. "It's either the life of your wife, or your unborn child," he said. "We can't save both."

Harav Ahron Zlotowitz had no questions: halachah was clear, and there was no other reality.

"The mother," he said, and resumed saying *Tehillim*.

The doctor nodded grimly and went back into the operating room.

The medical team tried once more, breaking the fragile bones of the unborn infant in an attempt to bring him safely into the world; this time, they were successful.

The child — born on the 10th of Tammuz/July 13th, 1943 — would live. He would spend the first few months of his life confined to a cast and endure pain throughout his life, but he would live.

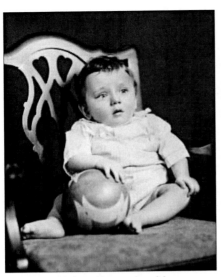
Meir at 10 months old

His *bris* was celebrated in his parents' Brooklyn apartment, two months after his birth. The event was marked by the presence of a unique guest, Rav Yechiel Mordechai Gordon, rosh yeshivah of the Lomza Yeshivah in Poland, who had been prevented from returning to Europe because of the war.

The connection between the rosh yeshivah and the *avi haben*, the father of the infant, was deep-seated.

As a young man in Poland, Reb Ahron Zlotowitz had spent many years as a *talmid* in the Lomza Yeshivah. He had left home before his bar mitzvah and returned to visit his parents just three times over a twelve-year period. He was looked up to as one of the *masmidim* of the yeshivah, the *chavrusa* of Rav Yaakov Kamenetsky.

During the First World War, the yeshivah *bachurim* were being harassed by local authorities. The rosh yeshivah, Rav Yechiel Mordechai, understood that he had to act to save his *talmidim* from imprisonment or worse. He therefore decided to task one of the *bachurim* with the mission of acquiring an illegal skill: learning how to forge passports. He conducted a *goral haGra*[1] to identify which *bachur* would be suited to the job; the results pointed to "Ahron," and the quiet, studious *masmid* turned his diligence to this new pursuit, saving the lives of his fellow *talmidim*.[2]

---

1. A lottery conducted according to a mystical tradition, passed down from rebbi to *talmid* and father to son, dating back to the Vilna Gaon.

2. The *pasuk* referred to Moshe and Ahron working together to save Jews, and Ahron Zlotowitz worked with the yeshivah's *mashgiach*, Rav Moshe Rosenstein,

When the local baker, Chaim Tzvi Pasternak, came to yeshivah seeking a *talmid chacham* as a match for his daughter Fruma, the roshei yeshivah directed him to Ahron Zlotowitz.

They got married and Ahron earned *semichah*. The future, Fruma felt, was in America; in 1923, the newly certified rav and his wife set sail for the United States, where they hoped he would find a position teaching Torah in safety and peace.

But things did not go as smoothly as they had hoped.

Rav Ahron and Fruma started off in Albany, New York, where relatives welcomed them — but that welcome came along with expectations: that the newcom-

Rav Ahron Zlotowitz as a *bachur*

ers adapt to the new reality, the American way. Shabbos, the hosts gently told them, was a relic of the past and the new arrivals would be wise to adapt. They argued persistently that Rav Ahron and his family would starve if he wouldn't work on Shabbos, but the young couple had no intention of agreeing with their argument. Rav Ahron and Fruma left Albany and traveled to New York City, where they had very few acquaintances. They settled in the Lower East Side, among people who

on this mission. Among those *talmidim* they saved was a respected *talmid chacham* named Rav Yosef Feldman, who would become a prominent rav in Baltimore. His sons are Rav Emanuel Feldman, the beloved and impactful rav of Atlanta, presently of Yerushalayim; Rav Ahron Feldman, the rosh yeshivah of Ner Israel in Baltimore and a member of the *Moetzes Gedolei HaTorah*; and Rav Chaim Yoel Feldman, a respected, veteran *mechanech*.

Rav Ahron Zlotowitz

cherished the Shabbos, so they felt at home. Rav Ahron found work as a *mohel*, and once his reputation as a *talmid chacham* spread, he found a position teaching Torah too. In 1927, he was appointed rav of Congregation Etz Chaim, Anshei Luban.

The family would experience grinding poverty, and endure the agony of losing a child to illness. When Rav Ahron went to summon a doctor and beg him to come treat the ailing child, the doctor refused because the desperate parents did not have money to pay him. Through the hardship and pain, Rav Ahron sat and learned Torah. The sound of his learning would welcome each new day, and long after the children had gone to bed, the singsong of their father's learning still filled the apartment.

He had never really left Lomza.

Unfortunately, so many others had come to America and erased the past; Rav Ahron Zlotowitz, however, lived with the vision of those years in the great yeshivah before his eyes.

And now, as he and Fruma prepared a *bris* for their youngest child, Rav Ahron saw the opportunity to give his newborn son a precious gift, a merit that would stand in good stead for the child. Rav Yechiel Mordechai Gordon, the Lomza rosh yeshivah and Reb Ahron's rebbi, was trapped in New York during that summer of 1943. The boy's father would be *mohel*, but the visiting rosh yeshivah would be *sandak* at the *bris*.

Meir Yaakov Zlotowitz, named for Reb Ahron's father, was welcomed to the covenant

Rav Yechiel Mordechai Gordon, the Lomza rosh yeshivah

of Avraham Avinu on the lap of the Lomza rosh yeshivah; the child would spend his entire life pursuing relationships and becoming close with *talmidei chachamim*.

Meir Yaakov — or Martin as he was known at the time — was the youngest of four children: Bernie, Shirley, and Diana were the siblings who preceded him.

RABBI & MRS. ARON ZLOTOWITZ	ב"ה
cordially invite you to attend the	הרב אהרן והרבנית פרומא זלאטאוויץ
	לאדען אייך העפליכסט איין צום
CIRCUMCISION	**ב ר י ת מ י ל ה**
(ברית מילה)	פון זייער ניי-געבארענעם זוהן
of their son	וואס עם וועט שטאטפינדען בעז"ה
Wednesday Morning, Sept. 8th, 1943	מיטוואך, ח, אלול, התש"ג
at 11 A. M. sharp,	(סעפטעמבער דעם 8-טען 1943)
at RABBI'S RESIDENCE	11 אוהר אין דער פריה שארף
763 Greene Avenue	אין רב'ס וואוינונג 763 גרין עוו.
near Sumner Ave. Brooklyn, N. Y.	ניער סאמנער עוו. ברוקלין, נ. י.

Bris Announcement

The dominant story of those early years was that of his father's Torah. Rav Ahron worked hard to feed his family; along with performing *brissim*, he was a *shochet* as well, but his passion was learning Torah. Meir grew up on an island of Torah, absorbing its splendor and beauty even before he could speak.

There were days when Meir woke and his father was gone, having left in the middle of the night for a series of bus trips that would take him to one of the New Jersey slaughter-houses, or to the Sands Hotel in Long Beach, where he served as *mashgiach*. Reb Ahron would return late at night, but would soon be seated by the table, the Gemara open in front of him.

Rav Ahron was fluent in the entire *Shas*. If someone would quote a Gemara or halachah, he would react with a unique motion, rubbing a finger across his forehead before quoting the precise source. The margins of his own *sefarim* were filled with

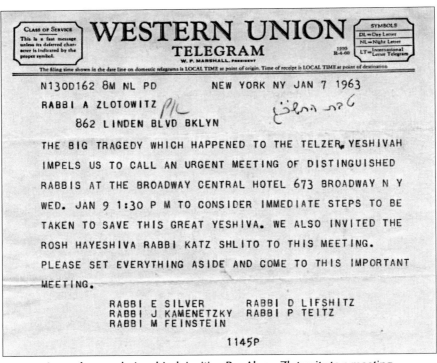

Letter from roshei yeshivah inviting Rav Ahron Zlotowitz to a meeting

chiddushim, and, a gifted writer, he would pen scholarly Torah articles for the periodicals popular at the time.[3]

Students at the Rabbi Jacob Joseph Yeshivah (RJJ) on the Lower East Side recall that Meir inherited his father's gifted pen. Unlike the other boys, he wouldn't just write standard notes in class; Meir preferred to use intricate calligraphy and pictures instead. He was a normal child, by all accounts — mischievous,

Rav Ahron and Fruma Zlotowitz

popular, and funny — with an artist's eye for detail.

He had no younger siblings, and was thirteen years younger than the sister immediately above him. It might have been a lonely childhood, but Meir had a close friend within the family: his mother, Mrs. Fruma Zlotowitz, who would have a profound impact on him. In later years, he would credit her elegance and refinement with shaping his own career choices.

Once his sisters built their own families, Meir became very close with his nephews. Both Shirley Kiffel and Diana Platnick had young sons, and they loved their Uncle Meir, with his accordion, easy smile, and endless supply of jokes.

Meir with his mother and nephew

3. See *Igros Moshe, Choshen Mishpat* I, 108, where Rav Moshe Feinstein refers to a question posed by Reb Ahron as a "*kushya gedolah*, a powerful question."

Meir as a young boy at the wedding of his brother Bernie

Along with music and art, Meir had another hobby: he loved to talk about the greatness of *gedolei Torah*, to discuss *talmidei chachamim*. A friend remembers a teenage Meir urging him to accompany him to a wedding taking place near the yeshivah, on the Lower East Side. "If we go, we'll get to see Rav Henkin," Meir exclaimed, excited about the opportunity to observe one of the great *poskim* of the generation.

He showed originality in learning as well. He had a *chavrusa* session with a friend during the lunch break; they learned Midrash Rabbah,[4] a *limud* that Meir enjoyed greatly. Rather

---

4. More than five decades later, Reb Meir would send an enthusiastic email to Elly Kleinman as the ArtScroll Midrash Rabbah went to print: There is no *peirush* on *Sheishes Yemei Bereishis* that equals the Midrash Rabbah — the primary source of Chazal — and there is no *sefer* in any language that does as much justice to it as this Kleinman Edition. It is an unparalleled elucidation, and you have the timeless *zechus* for making it possible! That is why we waited to work on this volume until the staff was more immersed in the *derech* of the Midrash — so we can do it historic justice.

With siblings: (L to R) Diana Scholar, Bernie Zlotowitz, and Shirley Kiffel

than learn in the *beis medrash* of their own yeshivah, RJJ, where people might notice and comment, the two boys slipped out and learned in Mesivtha Tifereth Jerusalem (MTJ), the yeshivah of Rav Moshe Feinstein.

Along with the anonymity, Tifereth Jerusalem afforded Meir the chance to soak up the atmosphere of the yeshivah and revel in the proximity of the rosh yeshivah, Rav Moshe.

During the summer break, Meir — like most of his friends — went to summer camp, but unlike most of his friends, he faced challenges that made it hard to enjoy the experience.

Along with the persistent pain in his legs that had accompanied him since his birth, he was overweight and couldn't really participate in sports activities, the primary pastime in summer camp. Meir faced another obstacle as well: the teenager suffered from a pronounced stutter, making it difficult for him to chat in the presence of unfamiliar people. At home or in school, he managed, but in camp, with new faces all around him, it was painful to speak.

Camp could have been a miserable experience for him — but it wasn't. It was in Camp Munk that seeds of a glorious future were first planted.

2

DARING TO DREAM

HAPPY LAUGHTER ROSE FROM THE FIELDS AND COURTS dotting the sprawling grounds of Camp Munk, in Ferndale, New York. City boys who spent ten months a year in yeshivah luxuriated in the sunshine and relaxed schedule, discovering new talents and hobbies in the tranquil environment.

Meir Zlotowitz was no different. The camp's founder, Rav Yechiel Aryeh HaKohen Munk, was a *talmid* of the Slabodka Yeshivah, an heir to the path of *gadlus ha'adam* transmitted by the Alter of Slabodka, Rav Nosson Tzvi Finkel: every person has a role, a singular mission, a means of becoming great.[1]

Rabbi Munk looked at Meir Zlotowitz, not inclined to athletics, hampered by a severe stutter — and envisioned the glory that would yet come.

---

1. Interestingly, Meir's father, Reb Ahron, was a *talmid* of Rav Yechiel Mordechai Gordon of Lomza. The Lomza rosh yeshivah was a *talmid* of Slabodka as well, and he had been especially close to the Alter, so at home too, Meir had absorbed this approach of seeing the greatness in each individual.

Meir (top right) with a group of friends in Camp Munk

The boy was an artist: creative, innovative, and thorough.

And so Rabbi Munk gave him a job. In an alcove near the small head office in the main building, Meir Zlotowitz stood, pen in hand, and worked. With papers fanned out all around him, he took on one project after another: a beautiful *bentching* chart, then an attractive Eishes Chayil poster. Each week, the boys who had been awarded best in learning saw their names, written in calligraphy, mounted on the wall. There was scenery for the various plays and, of course, the banner for color war.

In camp, Meir Zlotowitz became a star.

Along with artistic flair, these jobs called for an appreciation for the messages he was meant to convey. He developed a depth in *hashkafah*, an ability to use images to express the eternity of Klal Yisrael, the centrality of Torah, the spiritual valor of a Jew. Rabbi Munk taught him how to use art, the significance of each letter and picture.

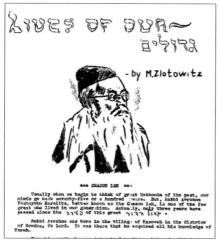

A sampling of Meir's Camp Munk artwork

Rabbi Michel Chill, a friend from those camp days, remembers that it went beyond talent. Meir Zlotowitz exuded a special *ruach*, an elevated spirit. Even though he was young, he was looking for ways to contribute to Klal Yisrael.

In camp, Meir forged enduring friendships, broadening his own horizons — and he would also find a lifelong mentor.

Rav Dovid Cohen was a brilliant young *talmid chacham*, a *talmid* of Rav Yitzchok Hutner in Yeshivas Rabbeinu Chaim Berlin — and, as such, yet another heir to the *chinuch* approach of Slabodka. Rav Dovid knew Rav Ahron Zlotowitz, and he drew the rav's personable teenage son close.

Rav Dovid appreciated Meir's refreshing sense of humor and Meir, in turn, was taken by Rav Dovid's sweeping knowledge of Torah, Jewish history, and Torah personalities. In their conversations, Meir discovered that everything had relevance; every idea, every *ma'amar Chazal*, each word used by a *Rishon*, was suffused with meaning.

An unofficial custom evolved over the summer of 1959: Meir Zlotowitz would join the newly married Rav Dovid and Rebbetzin Leah Cohen each day for lunch, sitting at their table in the camp dining room.

They seemed to enjoy his company, and he looked forward to these daily interactions.

Fifty-seven years later, Rabbi Zlotowitz — founder of ArtScroll/Mesorah Publications and architect of one of the greatest *harbatzas Torah* initiatives in recent history — called Rebbetzin Leah Cohen, wife of one of the most respected *poskim* in the world.

"I used to come eat lunch with you every day in Camp Munk," he said, taking her back to a simpler, quieter time, "when you were in *shanah rishonah*, newly married. I didn't realize it then, because you were so warm and welcoming, but it was wrong of

With Rav Dovid Cohen in Camp Munk

me to intrude upon that private time. I just want to apologize."

Rebbetzin Cohen laughed and assured Reb Meir that it was perfectly fine. She told him that they had enjoyed his company over that summer and were grateful for the beautiful relationship that had evolved. There was no reason to apologize, she said.

Six weeks later, Rabbi Zlotowitz passed away.

Many years earlier, Reb Meir had experienced a seminal *chinuch* moment with Rav Dovid. Reb Meir was visiting Camp Munk and Rav Dovid noticed that his young friend was wearing a stylish pair of burgundy pants.

Rav Dovid called him aside and put an arm around Meir's shoulders. "Those are very nice pants," he said, "but a 'Meir Zlotowitz' doesn't wear burgundy pants!"

Reb Meir would repeat the story often. Well before the *chinuch* establishment preached the message, Rav Dovid had made him big, rather than small, had conveyed a message without a word of censure, had let him know who he was. Meir Zlotowitz had been touched by the glory of Slabodka.

Those summers in camp gave him exposure to the world of *chinuch* as well. In creating posters and materials for younger children, he learned how the right image or graphic could capture the imagination and communicate an idea.

Rabbi Yehoshua (Josh) Silbermintz was head counselor, and the perfect partner for Rabbi Munk. They understood that most of their campers were children of Holocaust survivors: these two *mechanchim*, Rabbi Munk and Rabbi Silbermintz, invested the campers with a sense that *they* were the answer, the ones who would rebuild that which lay in ruins.

While Rabbi Munk tended to the spiritual needs of his campers, his wife, Mrs. Miriam (Martha) Munk, a trained psychologist, ensured that each and every camper was receiving physical

(L to R) Rabbi Eli Munk, Rabbi Yechiel Aryeh Munk, and Rabbi Joshua Silbermintz

and emotional nourishment as well.[2] Her ability to correctly diagnose the root of a problem gave the counselors tools of insight and understanding not readily available. It's no surprise that many of the young men who summered in Camp Munk, influenced by Rabbi and Mrs. Munk, would become effective *mechanchim* and leaders.

In Camp Munk, there were children of roshei yeshivah and day-school boys — they were all cherished. On that summer day in 1957 when Rav Ahron Rokeach of Belz was *niftar*, Rabbi Munk addressed the campers. Too overcome with pain to speak, he wept instead, conveying the magnitude of the loss with his tears. There was one central message in that camp and it wasn't about any party or affiliation: it was about *Yiddishkeit*, and the role of each individual Jew.

---

2. Camp Munk was established in 1949. When the buses pulled out of camp on the last day of that first season, Mrs. Munk sat down on a bench and began to cry, tears of relief that each and every boy had made it through the summer, healthy in body and soul.

Tishah B'Av in Camp Munk was a special day. Rather than reason that there was little point in trying to make *Kinnos* meaningful, Rabbi Munk invested the few hours on Tishah B'Av morning with extraordinary significance. He would share memories of the Nazi atrocities he had witnessed, sharing painful personal recollections. He would then apportion the *Kinnos* between the various rabbanim and staff members, so that each *Kinnah* was given an introduction and context, presented in a way that was relevant and interesting to the boys.

Just a few years after the Holocaust, the boys of Camp Munk were being given the tools to understand the *churban* — and the task of rebuilding.

(More than a quarter-century later, ArtScroll would release its ground-breaking translation and commentary on the *Kinnos*. Camp Munk would be among the first to purchase the volume, ordering several cases and encouraging each and every staff member and camper to own a copy.)

Rabbi Munk had an original approach to color war. Rather than give the teams the standard names, like red and blue, he termed the activity "*Hashkafah* war" and gave each team

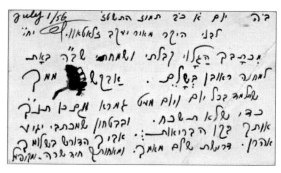

Corresponding with his parents
during the summer months

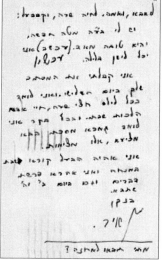

With Rabbi Eli Munk,
son of Rav Yechiel Aryeh

a name to reflect an ideological path, like *Beis Hillel* and *Beis Shammai*, or *Mekarvei Harechokim* and *Mechazkei Hama'aminim*. It fell to the artist to transmit the potency and power of a position through the banner — and Meir Zlotowitz was made for the role.

Rabbi Munk had another remarkable idea. He harnessed the talents of his staff, and charged them to work together to construct a model of the Mishkan. It would call for exhaustive learning of the sources along with dexterity, patience, and artistic skill. As construction progressed, the campers became fluent in the halachos and the counselors learned to consult with leading *talmidei chachamim* — including Rav Yaakov Kamenetsky — regarding details of the Mishkan. When the Camp Munk Mishkan was completed, it was celebrated, taken to be shown at numerous yeshivos throughout the year.

In Camp Munk, Meir learned a new skill — art not just as a hobby, but as a means of *chinuch*.

Over the course of the following year, he would become active in writing and drawing for the Pirchei and Bnos leader guides, a handbook of ideas and inspiration for the teenage boys and girls who devoted their Shabbos afternoons to leading groups for children.

As his confidence grew, Meir began to articulate some of his dreams. He had a sheaf of papers that he guarded zealously, and spent hours working on. He showed it to his nephew and a few friends: it was an English translation of the *Mishnah Berurah*, a project he had undertaken in his spare time. In this private mission he had assigned himself, Meir Zlotowitz revealed some

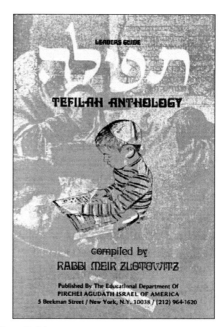

Pirchei Leaders Guide

of what lay within his soul: not just a desperate drive to spread Torah, but a keen sense of where the future lay, an awareness that a new generation that spoke English was arising and could achieve clarity in Torah if it was presented in their language.

And it was there, in the peace and serenity of Camp Munk, that Meir Zlotowitz shared a secret dream, one he harbored deep in his heart. "One day," he confided to a close friend, "I will translate all of *Shas* into English!"

Fittingly, in 1983 — before the ArtScroll *Shas* was published, but after the company had established itself as a leading disseminator of Torah — they released a book titled, *The Wisdom of the Hebrew Alphabet;* it was written by Rav Yechiel Aryeh HaKohen Munk:[3] things had come full circle.

Years earlier, Rabbi Munk had seen Meir's *Mishnah Berurah*

---

3. Rabbi Nosson Scherman recalls that ArtScroll published the book as an expression of gratitude to the author, not anticipating that it would be a commercial success. In time, the book would become one of their most requested titles, reprinted several times.

notes and said, "You are very talented. You should continue writing." Now, with that vision realized, Rabbi Meir Zlotowitz was honored to publish the *sefer* of the man who had believed in him early on. The book proved extremely popular, and after Rabbi Munk's passing, Mrs. Martha Munk worked with Reb Meir to have it translated into Hebrew and published.

In a journal ad written a few years before his passing, Rabbi Meir paid tribute to the camp of his youth: *Camp Munk instills a ruchniyus in each camper that carries him throughout the year and throughout his life. I am one of those campers. The feeling never leaves you.*

The inspiration I absorbed spending summers in the makom Torah called Camp Munk, among gedolei Torah and chinuch, who honed my sensitivities and have remained close to me as guides all these years, is the impetus that motivates me daily.

When it came to writing skits and comedy routines in camp, Meir's sense of humor was on full display. He embarked on an early publishing venture, a camp newspaper he titled *Kol Meshugaim*, a compendium of camp jokes and news.

A friend remembers a typical Meir joke — creative, teasing and original.

Meir was singing *grammen* in color war and, in the presence of Rabbi Munk, he poked gentle fun at the good-natured competition between two of the leading summer camps of the time, Camp Munk and Camp Agudah.

The color-war team names were *Shamayim* and *Eretz*, and Meir sang, "*Eretz means earth, while heaven is shamayim,*" then paused. He took a deep breath and sang, "*L'shanah haba'ah...,*" and as the audience anticipated the obvious ending, the word to rhyme with *shamayim*, Meir concluded, "*L'shanah haba'ah b'Camp Agudah,*" to delighted laughter from the crowd.

In fact, it would go beyond the joke. The next summer, Meir would join some of his yeshivah friends in Camp Agudah, where he was given the job of arts and crafts director.

With Rabbi Boruch Borchardt

If Rabbi Munk was the first great summertime influence in his life and Rav Dovid Cohen the second, then Rabbi Boruch Borchardt would be the third. The director of Camp Agudah would become a role model in *achrayus*, complete dedication to a cause.

Rabbi Borchardt, who had been born and raised in Germany, was a punctilious person. Working under him, Meir's mischievous nature rose to the fore — and the camp director appreciated it.

Meir was shown his lodgings on the first day of summer, a decrepit room with peeling paint. He complained to the director that the room was ugly, and Rabbi Borchardt shrugged. "Feel free to paint it," he said.

It was exactly the response Meir had been hoping for. Along with his two friends and roommates, Avie Gold and Mair Fogel, he headed to the hardware store in nearby Liberty to buy paint.

Rabbi Borchardt had expected them to purchase the standard

(L to R) Mair Fogel and Reb Meir

brown paint, as in all the other rooms, but Meir came back to camp with cans of purple, yellow, and black paint, painting the doorframe one color, the walls another, and the windowsills a third.

Rabbi Borchardt smiled.

Before the following summer, Rabbi Borchardt asked the maintenance workers to paint the camp's main building. They started the job, but quickly grew tired of the tedious task.

Meir, with his keen understanding of the artistic temperament, had the solution. He drove to Liberty and bought several gallons of paint in different colors. "Please do the moldings in a darker color and the doorways in a bright color," he instructed the workers. Stimulated by the challenge, they got back to work.

One day, the campers were on a trip and there were no scheduled activities: Meir Zlotowitz had the afternoon off. He sat down at the top of the hill overlooking the camp, the landscape spread out in front of him, and, with a large easel before him, he started to paint. He spent the entire afternoon depicting the magnificent scene, the rolling hills and charming bunkhouses and mountains pressed against the clear blue sky in the distance. A beautiful picture emerged; onlookers marveled at the painting, but Meir Frischman recalls that the artist himself wasn't impressed. Meir Zlotowitz took a marker and drew a large X across the painting. "It's not perfect," he shrugged in explanation.

Meir, along with his two roommates, grew very close to Rabbi Boruch and Mrs. Miriam Borchardt. In later years, Meir would

Rabbi Boruch Borchardt speaking at the bar mitzvah of his son, Naftoli,
in the Camp Agudah dining room, August 1964;
Meir is seated at far left.

often remember overhearing how Mrs. Borchardt complained
to the camp cook when there was no coleslaw one Shabbos.
"The boys need to enjoy Shabbos," she protested.

"I would love to make coleslaw for them," the cook countered, "but I don't have time to check the cabbage for insects."

"I'll do it," Mrs. Borchardt replied.

The camp director's wife spent her summer Wednesdays
standing by the window of her small bungalow checking cabbage — so that the boys should fully enjoy the Shabbos meals.

Meir would also recall how he and his friends had gone fish-
ing in the lake near camp. The boys filled a bucket with fish, and
then brought them to Rebbetzin Teitelbaum, wife of the camp's
rav, Rav Yaakov Teitelbaum. They asked her to cook the fish
for them and the rebbetzin accommodated them, showing the
boys how kosher fish are cleaned and prepared. Meir would
often recall the dedication he had seen in camp, how no one
was confined by the formal parameters of their job. These illustrious people all shared a common mission of giving the boys

a happy, productive summer, and so they saw everything as a personal responsibility. The images — Mrs. Borchardt checking cabbage and Rebbetzin Teitelbaum cleaning fish — would remain with him, underscoring the lesson.

If, in yeshivah, Meir showed his serious, focused side, and camp revealed his fun-loving nature, it was at home that Meir developed the approach that would shape his own path to *chinuch*.

"It was a time when many parents, having endured so much pain and difficulty, had no idea how to express love for a child; Meir's home was different. You felt his parents' love for him as soon as you walked into the apartment; they would light up when they saw him. Even though money was tight, you had the sense that they would do whatever they could to make him happy," recalls a childhood friend. "That wasn't the norm then."

(L to R) Rav Shlomo Zalman Sonnenfeld, Rav Ahron Zlotowitz, Reb Meir

A generation later, friends would notice that Reb Meir followed that approach with his own family; he never kept his love for his family under wraps.

Meir — who considered himself a lifelong *talmid* of his father — had a lot in common with Reb Ahron.

"They had the same *eyes*, the same ability to look right through you," remarks a friend. "They were both able to gauge a person just by looking at him."

There was the love of *sefarim*: teenage Meir had a large number of eclectic *sefarim*, and enjoyed helping his bar mitzvah-age nephews assemble their own collections. He was particularly proud that he owned every single *sefer* mentioned or quoted in the *Mishnah Berurah*.

Meir's nephew, Meir Platnick, received a gift from his grandfather, a set of *Aruch HaShulchan*. Reb Ahron found a beautiful way to express his love for his grandson: He wrote a separate inscription inside the flyleaf of each volume, penning the *berachos* and words of encouragement again and again. This way, whichever volume of the *sefer* his grandson might use, the young man would remember his grandfather's love.

In 1990, Reb Ahron Zlotowitz was *niftar*. Reb Meir sat *shivah* and, throughout the week, friends and family filed by and offered words of comfort, but Reb Meir didn't cry. He sat stoically as he shared stories and memories, completely in control of his emotions. At one point, an old friend came in and sat there, listening quietly.

He looked at the *avel* and said five words.

"He loved you so much."

Reb Meir listened and then burst into tears, crying for several minutes without speaking.

"Yes," he finally said, "my father loved me so much."

3

TO BECOME A TALMID

I N THE 1961 RJJ HIGH SCHOOL YEARBOOK, EVERY GRADUATE has a *pasuk* or *ma'amar Chazal* listed near his name. Next to Martin J. Zlotowitz (Journal art editor, Tablet art editor, Designer of the senior button and graduation flag), the *pasuk* from *sefer Yechezkel* (31:9) appears: "*Yafeh asisiv b'rov dali'yosav* — I made it beautiful with its many branches."

After graduating RJJ high school, Meir Zlotowitz became a *talmid* in Mesivtha Tifereth Jerusalem; to a certain extent, he would never leave.

He was a respected *talmid*, learning seriously and eventually earning *semichah* at

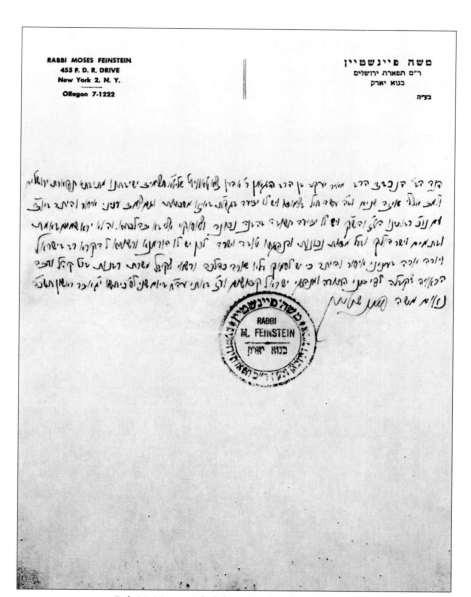

RABBI MOSES FEINSTEIN
455 F. D. R. DRIVE
New York 2, N. Y.

ORegon 7-1222

משה פיינשטיין
ר"מ תפארת ירושלים
בנוא יארק

בע"ה

Reb Meir's *semichah* from Rav Moshe Feinstein

the yeshivah. Though he had put formal artistic study on hold, the young man made it a personal mission to ensure that each of the yeshivah's *sefarim* had a beautiful binding and an attractive label on the inside.

RJJ elementary graduating class; Meir is on far right (circled)

But what would characterize those years at MTJ was the way he became a *talmid*.

Well beyond the actual *sedarim* and *shiurim* in yeshivah, he found reasons to be in the rosh yeshivah's presence, listening and learning. Those experiences and encounters would shape him and guide him.

Many years later, Rabbi Nosson Muller — a *mechanech* and notable speaker who had grown close to Reb Meir — was preparing a speech for a *Zayin Adar Seudah*, the traditional gathering for members of the *chevrah kaddisha* held on the *yahrzeit* of Moshe Rabbeinu. His address was meant to focus on *kevod habriyos*, respect for all of Hashem's creations, and the mandate to perform *chessed*; he happened to be speaking with Reb Meir and mentioned that he was working on the *derashah*.

Greeting Rav Moshe Feinstein at a wedding

Reb Meir asked Rabbi Muller if he wanted to hear a story about Rav Moshe. When Rabbi Muller eagerly said that he would, Reb Meir shared a memory from his years as a *bachur* in Mesivtha Tifereth Jerusalem. One day, he noticed a group of unfamiliar men waiting to speak to the rosh yeshivah after Minchah in yeshivah was over. Intrigued, he approached and asked what brought them to the yeshivah. They explained that Rav Moshe was to preside over a *chalitzah* ceremony,[1] and they had come to escort him. Meir asked if he could join, and they acquiesced.

They drove to a decrepit apartment building and led Rav Moshe up several flights of stairs to where an old, disheveled man lived in squalor. Rav Moshe spoke with him, patiently explaining the halachos of the process, and then asked the

---

1. A mandated halachic procedure that would permit the widow of a childless man to marry someone other than the brother of her deceased husband.

elderly man to remove his shoes and socks, since the rosh yeshivah had to check his foot.[2]

Moments later, the small apartment was filled with the most revolting odor; the man's foot was covered with blisters and fungus. The participants struggled to breathe, but Rav Moshe calmly asked for a brush, a cloth, and a bucket of water with soap. He cradled the man's foot in his hands and started to scrub. No one else could handle the oppressive smell, but Rav Moshe worked slowly and tenderly, ensuring that the foot was perfectly clean.

Some of the people present had to step outside, Reb Meir recalled, but Rav Moshe didn't stop until all the fungus was removed. "Now we're ready for *chalitzah*," he said softly.

This was the story — this account of sensitivity and selflessness — which Rabbi Muller repeated to the *chevrah kaddisha* members in Chicago, who were deeply moved.

The next day, Rabbi Muller sent a message to Rabbi Zlotowitz, thanking him for the impactful story.

Reb Meir replied by text message: *That scene will never leave my mind. It was a mitzvah and Rav Moshe handled that person's feet as if they were tashmishei kedushah.*

At the *shivah* for Reb Meir, Rabbi Muller flew in from Chicago to be *menachem avel* the Zlotowitz family. He wanted to share that story, since it reflected Reb Meir's own approach to life. He had learned the lesson well.

Rabbi Muller retold the story and then read Reb Meir's text message aloud; as he reached the conclusion, he heard soft weeping — not from one of the *aveilim*, but from one of the rabbanim seated next to him.

He turned to see Rav Moshe's son, Rav Reuven Feinstein, crying at the story, the lesson, the memory of the great rebbi

---

2. Before performing the *chalitzah* ceremony, the *beis din* must ascertain that the right foot is clean, so there is no *chatzitzah*, barrier, between the foot and the shoe used for the ceremony.

With Rav Reuven Feinstein

— and the *talmid* who had lived with the scene before his eyes.

In his preface to the ArtScroll biography of Rav Moshe, Reb Meir shared some of his own impressions, written *"as a talmid who felt a personal closeness to him as to no other."*

Reb Meir wrote of the rosh yeshivah's schedule, of the *shiurim* and halachic rulings — but also of the atmosphere in the *beis medrash.*

The rosh yeshivah, Reb Meir wrote, would walk through the *beis medrash* and notice groups of *talmidim* speaking in learning; he would pause and look on with obvious pleasure. *"He would not come over to us, because he knew that would make us self-conscious and interfere with our learning, but we knew he was there and the thought that the rosh yeshivah was pleased with our efforts made us extend ourselves further in the fray of Torah..."*

In this sentence, Reb Meir revealed the depth of his connection to his rebbi: it wasn't just learning Rav Moshe's Torah, but

With Rav Dovid Feinstein and Rabbi Burton Jaffa

being a *talmid* of Rav Moshe. It wasn't just the *shiur*, but the connection.

For the rest of his life, Meir Zlotowitz would define himself by that relationship: he was a *talmid* of Rav Moshe Feinstein.

During those years in MTJ, Meir also formed a close relationship with his rebbi's son, Rav Dovid Feinstein. Years later, Rav Dovid would tell Rabbi Burton Jaffa that Rabbi Meir Zlotowitz's impact on the world came as no surprise to him. One who had observed Meir carefully in yeshivah would have been able to foresee a bright future.

Along with his growth in learning, Meir decided to formally study toward a career in art. In 1964, he registered at Brooklyn's prestigious Pratt Institute, where he broadened the scope of his artistic and graphic abilities. He eventually dropped out after being assigned a project that he felt compromised the Torah values of *tzniyus* and decency, but he was confident that he had found his career path.

Talented, bright, well-regarded in yeshivah, and the scion of a respected family, Meir Zlotowitz was very much in demand when he reached the age of *shidduchim*: he was soon a *chassan*, engaged to Miriam Mayer. Her parents, Reb Yosef and Chana Mayer, were among the esteemed members of the Washington Heights community.

As in the Zlotowitz home, Torah learning was at its core. Long before it was commonplace, Reb Yosef started each workday with an intense learning *seder,* and he and his family attached themselves to *talmidei chachamim.* Reb

Reb Yosef and Chana Mayer

Yosef and Chana Mayer would raise an exemplary family of *bnei Torah* and *askanim.*

Meir and Miriam married in 1965 and settled in Boro Park. While learning in *kollel*, Meir was able to earn some side-money through writing and illuminating *kesubos*, so when he felt the time was ripe to open a business, he already had a glowing reputation.

Leon Goldenberg worked at the Washington Heights butcher-shop owned by his father, and he remembers delivering meat to the Zlotowitz apartment. Reb Meir was working from home — his desk a board of wood he had affixed to the wall near the entrance, space so tight that whenever the door to the apartment opened, he was in the way.

On that bare piece of wood, though, he was creating art — and dreams.

Charlie Grandovsky, a close friend and early partner, remembers sitting on the porch of Meir's apartment on Boro Park's 53rd Street, between 13th and 14th Avenues, discussing

Early ads

different names for the printing and graphics business they hoped to open in partnership.

Scrollart seemed to be the favorite, since Reb Meir's handwritten calligraphy scrolls had become very popular, but then someone asked, "What about ArtScroll? Doesn't that have a better ring to it?"

ArtScroll Studios opened in Manhattan, a higher-end graphics studio servicing organizations, businesses, and private clients.

With a flourishing business and growing family, Reb Meir needed a spiritual base as well: the Kopyzcynitzer *shtiebel* in Boro Park would become that place.

The Kopyzcynitzer Rebbe, Rav Avrohom Yehoshua Heschel, lived on the Lower East Side, but as more and more young families were choosing to settle in Boro Park, the Rebbe's son, Rav Moshe Mordechai, had opened a *shtiebel* there as well, on 55th Street between 14th Avenue and 15th Avenue. At his son

Rav Moishe'le's urging, the Rebbe would come to Boro Park for Shabbos and lead the *shtiebel*.

The Rebbe had only one condition as to who could daven in the *shtiebel*: he wouldn't accept any member who was already a steady *mispallel* in another shul. That rule resulted in the shul attracting a young crowd, newcomers to the neighborhood — Reb Meir among them.

Kopyzcynitz took some getting used to for him. Reb Meir had grown up in his

Kopyzcynitzer Rebbe

father's shul, which reflected the glory of Lita and its yeshivos; a chassidishe *shtiebel* was a new experience for him — but at the same time, he felt an instant bond with the Rebbe.

The fact that the Rebbe had a close relationship with Rav Moshe Feinstein made Reb Meir feel at home. He recalled hearing that one year, it had been raining on Succos and Rav Moshe's succah had no *shlock*;[3] when the rain stopped, the rosh yeshivah wanted to eat in the succah, but it was still too wet. Rav Moshe and his family joined the Kopyzcynitzer Rebbe in his succah, which had been covered by a *shlock*.

The Rebbe — whom Rav Aharon Kotler would refer to as a "*gaon* in *chessed*" — imbued these young "chassidim" with a sense of their own abilities and responsibilities. He taught, by example, that life is meant to be viewed as a means to help others. The Rebbe was a master of how to give. One of the young

---

3. A makeshift succah cover that can be spread out in case of rain.

couples in the shul received the traditional *"drosha geshank,"* a wedding present from the Rebbe, the customary *becher.* Inside the silver Kiddush cup, the new husband found a thick, rolled-up wad of bills.

He hurried to the Rebbe's home to thank him for the gift — and return the money he assumed the Rebbe had mistakenly left there.

"No," the Rebbe smiled, "it's part of the gift. A newly married couple always needs some extra money while they get settled. Use it well."

The Kopyzcynitzer Rebbe didn't often speak formally, but there was a *vort* he shared on Rosh Hashanah that the young *mispallelim* saw as a mission statement.

The Rebbe discussed the day's Torah reading — the *parashah* of *Akeidas Yitzchak* — and the merits accrued by Avraham Avinu for this act of supreme self-sacrifice.

"Wouldn't any intelligent human being heed a command that they hear directly from the Master of the Universe?" the Rebbe wondered. "How come the *zechus* of the *Akeidah* gives us such merit that we still rely on it, after all these years?"

The Rebbe shared a memory. He recalled being led to Gestapo headquarters to be tortured by the Nazis, *yimach shemam.* The Rebbe accepted the will of Heaven, and painful as it was, he was serene and at peace, since this was the Ribbono Shel Olam's decree. But then, the Rebbe continued, he heard the cries of other Jews who were being beaten, and that was too much to bear — so much harder than having endured a beating of his own.

"When the decree was on Avraham Avinu, of course he rose up to the situation and accepted the will of Heaven. By the *Akeidah*, however, he was asked to give over his son Yitzchak for slaughter, and then the pain was much more intense — because it was the pain of another!"

Reb Meir's fellow *mispallelim* at the table in Kopyzcynitz

would become lifelong friends, most notably Ronnie Greenwald. A friendship formed in an atmosphere of pure *chessed* would lead to a lifetime of shared *chessed* projects. Even after both men moved away — Reb Meir to Flatbush and Ronnie to Monsey — they would speak frequently, each one encouraging the other in his quest to change the Jewish world.

With Ronnie Greenwald

Ronnie's activities were behind the scenes while much of Reb Meir's work was public — but they shared a deep insight into people and a fierce commitment to helping others.

There were many memorable moments in the presence of the Kopyzcynitzer Rebbe, but one remark made by the Rebbe would illuminate Reb Meir's own path and life's work.

The Rebbe introduced this group of young American yeshivah graduates to the joy in the performance of mitzvos, the experience of shaking *daled minim* or blowing the shofar. They would join him each year as he went to bake matzos, each of them assuming a specific task as part of the Rebbe's *chaburah* and observing his sublime delight in the mitzvah.

One year, after they finished baking matzos, the Rebbe circulated among the workers at the matzah bakery, thanking each one for their devoted work. The Rebbe noticed that a chassidic young man who worked as a kneader appeared quite destitute: the Rebbe handed him several bills, a tip in honor of the approaching Yom Tov. The worker gratefully accepted the money.

A few days later, the Rebbe announced that he was going back to the matzah bakery to bake "Erev Pesach matzos," in accordance with his custom, and they joined him once again. After they finished baking, the Rebbe again sought out the young kneader and approached him with a wad of bills. "Here, *l'kavod Yom Tov*," the Rebbe said.

This time, the gentleman protested. "*Der Rebbe huht shoin yotzeh gevehn*, the Rebbe has already fulfilled his obligation," he said.

The Kopyzcynitzer Rebbe looked at him. "*Ich bin nisht gekummen oif di velt*, I didn't come down to this world," the Rebbe said, "*yotzeh tzu zein*, just to fulfill my obligations."

Rav Avrohom Yehoshua Heschel, the Kopyzcynitzer Rebbe, was *niftar* in 1967, just a few short years after establishing the little shul, but his words and message would reverberate throughout the years, the families he inspired going forward, each in their own way, to live lives of genuine accomplishment — never just "*yotzeh tzu zein*."

4

TRANSITIONS

P EOPLE LIKED BEING AROUND MEIR ZLOTOWITZ. THE
young graphic artist always seemed to have a kind word,
warm smile, and good joke to share. With healthy,
delightful children and a circle of close friends, a growing list
of satisfied clients and a brilliant professional reputation, he
seemed to be living a charmed life.

Only those closest to him knew how much effort that smile
took.

The business struggled. Impressive as their work was,
ArtScroll Studios always seemed to be operating at a deficit.

In later years, someone once accused Reb Meir of being "too
generous," unable to turn down anyone who appeared to be
in need. Reb Meir conceded that it was true, and commented
that he could never forget how, during the years when he was
struggling for every dollar, he was once seated at a *simchah*
surrounded by a group of acquaintances. They were discussing
what to buy their wives for the upcoming Yom Tov, complaining how hard it was to find the right gift.

He was struck at how "tone-deaf" they sounded, how oblivious they were to the real challenges facing others; while he was wondering how he would purchase food for Yom Tov, they were distressed about which sort of gift to buy. At that moment, he promised himself that if he would ever be in a position to help others, he wouldn't forget what it was like to be worried about buying basic necessities. "It's not that I have a better or more generous nature than others," he explained, "it's just that I have a good memory!"

But those difficulties were small next to the personal challenges his young family was facing.

In 1971, he and his wife divorced.

It was an era when divorce was virtually unheard of in the community, before the support networks that would be available years later existed. He was alone, a young father charged with the care of three young children, faced with a much heavier burden than a floundering business.

It was a difficult time — but later, he would point to that period as a time of blessing, because it was then that he developed the faith, resilience, and optimism that would allow him not just to succeed, but also to encourage others. Throughout his life, he would seek out those facing difficulties and reassure them that better days would come — and, he would say, he was speaking from experience!

At the darkest point, the flicker of light that ushered in brighter days came from the most radiant man in Reb Meir Zlotowitz's world — his rebbi, Rav Moshe Feinstein.

It came at a time when Reb Meir felt he had hit rock bottom. The business was in debt, he was raising three children on his own, and his friends were busy with their own lives while he was alone. He wasn't able to learn properly, since after long, wearying days at work he would come home and take care of his children.

He went to Rav Moshe's Lower East Side apartment, waiting

in the familiar foyer for a chance to share his pain with his beloved rosh yeshivah.

But Rav Moshe was meeting with a group of rabbanim, involved in a complicated halachic issue, and after Reb Meir sat there waiting for a long while, the rebbetzin came out and apologized. The rosh yeshivah wouldn't be able to see him after all. Reb Meir was despondent; even this, it seemed — the opportunity to unburden himself to his rebbi — was being denied to him.

He returned home, the load feeling heavier than ever before.

The next day, New York suffered a major snowstorm, making car travel difficult. Schools were closed, and Reb Meir spent the day at home, watching his young children. That evening, as the harried young father struggled to get the children to bed, the doorbell rang. Reb Meir walked downstairs and opened the door, wondering who would have ventured out on the snowy night.

It was Rav Moshe Feinstein.

The rosh yeshivah, *posek* of his generation and leader of thousands, accompanied his *talmid* up several flights of stairs, coming into the apartment and taking in the scene. Rav Moshe lifted one child, then the next, and finally the third one. He tucked each one into bed, telling them a story and kissing them good night. Then, when the house was settled, Rav Moshe looked at Reb Meir.

"I came to schmooze, to hear what's on your mind," he said.

Reb Meir spoke — really spoke, sharing his doubts and fears about the future, and Rav Moshe listened.

The rosh yeshivah offered *chizuk*. He offered encouragement. He reassured his *talmid* that things would get easier. And then Rav Moshe offered a *berachah*, a single statement that would carry Meir Zlotowitz through that period and accompany him every single day, for the rest of his life, the chorus in the song that played in his mind and heart.

"Your children," Rav Moshe said, "will become *bnei Torah*, and they will marry *bnei Torah*."

Those words would become the raft that would carry Reb Meir through the stormy sea, the goal he would visualize and imagine, the hope that allowed him to rise above loneliness and despair.

And as Rav Moshe foretold, things began to turn.

ArtScroll Studios invested in cutting-edge technology, purchasing a machine capable of printing Hebrew characters, *alef, beis*: a novelty in the *frum* world.

"Meir," recalls Elliot Schwartz, a longtime business associate

(L to R) With Elliot Schwartz, Steve Adelsberg, and Dave Schwartz (seated)

and partner, "understood the business and also saw exactly where things were headed. He was always a step ahead of the game and ready to meet whatever demand would come next. He didn't only have vision, he was confident enough to invest in that vision, and when the market evolved, he was right there, ahead of the game."

Things began to stabilize on the professional front, and in his personal life too, Reb Meir saw blessing.

As an early-childhood teacher, Faigie Schulman was beloved by students for her warmth and good nature and appreciated by parents for her educational capabilities.

It was Mrs. Tobi Handlesman, wife of Rav Moshe Handlesman, executive director of the Mirrer Yeshivah, who thought of the *shidduch*, along with Meir's sister, Shirley Kiffel.

Faigie came with her own illustrious background. Her maternal

Montreal's first *cheder*

grandmother, Miriam Devorah (Weinshenker) Zaltsman, was a sixth-generation descendant, mother to daughter, of Rav Yonasan Eybeschutz. After leaving Russia, Reb Yisroel Yehuda Zaltsman arrived in Montreal, where he was met by a local Jew, Reb Benzion Hershkowitz.[1] Right there, Reb Benzion asked the new arrival to teach Torah to his own sons. That group of young *talmidim* would evolve into the city's first *cheder*, located on Hutchison Street, with Reb Yisroel Yehuda, who was also a gifted *ba'al tefillah* and *ba'al korei*, serving as *melamed*.

After their oldest daughter married Rabbi Dovid Barenholtz of Toronto, Reb Yisroel Yehuda and Miriam Devorah relocated to New York, so that the other Zaltsman girls might find committed Jews to marry.

Chaya (Ida) Zaltsman did. Chaim Chaikel (Irving) Schulman was American born, a public school graduate with a Talmud

---

1. Reb Benzion, a poor man who lived in a basement apartment with his wife and eleven children, would go to the docks each day and welcome new arrivals, offering help and advice. When he saw Reb Yisroel Yehuda, he immediately realized that this was an elevated Jew, and he made the request on the spot.

Reb Chaim Chaikel and Chaya Schulman

Torah education, blessed with exceptional *simchas hachaim* and faith: his motto was, *Ivdu es Hashem b'simchah*,[2] and his life's aspiration was to serve Hashem in joy.

He was a member of Brownsville's famed Rayim Ahuvim shul, a stronghold of authentic *Yiddishkeit* in a new world. Like so many others in that shul, Chaim Chaikel Schulman would be fired from his latest job every Monday, since he refused to work on Shabbos. He realized that there was little hope of making a living as long as he was subject to the schedule imposed by an employer, so he opted to open his own business and hire other *shomrei Shabbos* to work for him. The way he saw it, Shabbos and Yom Tov were not just meant to be kept, but honored.

The company manufactured moderately-priced blouses and succeeded for several years, until a brand-name blouse company dropped its prices. Chaim Chaikel Schulman's business was wiped out, and even as well-meaning friends urged him to declare bankruptcy, he resisted. "What will happen to all the people that I owe money to?" he asked, taking on various jobs and struggling to pay back every last dollar.

Even in his most difficult times, his daughter remembers, there was always money for Shabbos expenses. "There's a special pocket for Shabbos and Yom Tov," he would tell his family, "and whatever you take out from there has no effect on the other pockets."

---

2. *Tehillim* 100:2: "Serve Hashem with joy."

After moving from Brownsville, Reb Chaim Chaikel became a devoted member of Rav Avigdor Miller's shul.[3] He would join the Kings Highway Shabbos Parades, in which the rabbanim and laymen would walk up and down the busy street, trying to gently and respectfully persuade Jewish shopkeepers to close their stores on the holy day.

The very first decision his daughter Faigie made after her 1972 engagement to Meir Zlotowitz was a portent of what was to come: one of the Zlotowitz children was named Faigie, just like she was. It was clear that one of them would have to change her name, and the three-year-old girl seemed the obvious choice.

No, said the new *kallah*, it would be unsettling for the child during what was already a tumultuous period. Faiga Rachel Schulman switched to her second name. She stood under the *chuppah* as Rachel Zlotowitz.

At the *sheva berachos*, the *chassan* got up to speak. He mentioned that his own middle name was Yaakov, and now his *kallah* would be known as Rachel.

"Yaakov had to work long and hard until he finally married Rachel," he said.

Meir and Rachel at their wedding

3. Four generations later, Frumie Morgenstern, a granddaughter of Reb Meir and Rachel Zlotowitz, would marry Zevi Leshinsky, a great-grandson of Rav Avigdor Miller, solidifying a bond fashioned at an earlier time.

(R to L) Rabbi Boruch Borchardt, Rav Ahron Zlotowitz, Rav Moshe Feinstein,
Yankel Kiffel, Meir, Rachel
Rear: Charlie Grandovsky and Josh Grossman

Reb Meir Zlotowitz was able to set his sights on new goals: not too many people saw the dreams in his heart, but there was someone who perceived the latent potential of the young artist.

On Simchas Torah afternoon of 1972, Rabbi Moshe Sherer and his son, Rav Shimshon, were walking down Boro Park's Fourteenth Avenue on the way to shul for Minchah. They passed Reb Meir — who did the printing and graphics for Agudath Israel of America — and Rabbi Sherer embraced the younger man. They spoke for a few minutes, and then walked on.

"That man," Rabbi Sherer remarked to his son, "will yet make a real contribution to Klal Yisrael."

5

REVEALING THE HIDDEN

THE FIRST FEW YEARS AT 156 FIFTH AVENUE IN MANHAT-tan had been slow, but in time, business picked up. Along with invitations and brochures, the company would do *kesubos*, diplomas, scrolls for dinner honorees, and even *kisvei rabbanus*.

Even when the company struggled, Reb Meir had a reputation for being fair and reliable, on time with payments to suppliers and employees.

The small group at ArtScroll Studios saw the spirit and pride back then. Charlie Grandovsky recalls an old-style New York City mafia shakedown, when a burly hoodlum came into the office and demanded money. Reb Meir refused.

"Listen, we clean the garbage here. We work with the sanitation department and you've got to pay us, there is no choice," the thug said menacingly.

Reb Meir stood firm. "We work hard for our money, and we pay our taxes. I can't just give it to you, sorry."

The unwelcome visitor took a step closer and Reb Meir, undaunted, grabbed the garbage pail.

"Really?" Reb Meir asked. "Are you sure you want our garbage?"

Reb Meir, who ran his business with meticulousness and integrity and wouldn't put up with nonsense, lifted the garbage pail and prepared to throw it at the hooligan, who turned on his heels and fled.

Despite his determination not to spend his hard-won earnings unnecessarily, Reb Meir kept his priorities straight.

Reb Meir's employees knew of his insistence on perfection; if there was the slightest error, the invitation or brochure was thrown into the trash and the project started again.

He was constantly looking for ways to streamline the process. He invested in screen-printing machinery so that they would be able to do the work in-house. He bought a state-of-the-art machine capable of printing Hebrew letters, as if sensing that one day his company would be printing its own *sifrei kodesh*.

The stage was being set for a revolution.

Eishes Chayil plaque made by Meir, presented to Rabbi and Mrs. Borchardt

Even though money was tight, Reb Meir decided to upgrade to larger quarters, moving the business to 212 Fifth Avenue.

Along with up-to-date equipment, he was assembling a staff of top-notch people around him. He had an exceptional eye for talent and surrounded himself with the team with whom he would change the world.

(L to R) With Reb Nosson and Reb Sheah

Rabbi Borchardt, Meir's mentor from Camp Agudah, sent his secretary to deliver documents to Meir's office. While there, she mentioned that she was engaged; her *chassan*, she continued, designed monograms.

"Bring him in, I'd love to meet him," Reb Meir said, and the *chassan* — Sheah Brander — was offered a job on the spot.

The day after completing *sheva berachos*, Rabbi Sheah Brander — without formal training or real work experience — joined the staff at ArtScroll. Reb Sheah would ultimately partner with Reb Meir in creating the ArtScroll typeface, layout, and font: not just visually stimulating and aesthetically pleasing, but also user-friendly. In time, he would be the one to develop the ArtScroll design and look — the trademark Hebrew-English translation with running English text alongside the *lashon kodesh*.

During his years working at 156 Fifth Avenue, a building that

With Reb Avi Shulman

was home to several Jewish organizations, Reb Meir made many new friends, among them Mr. Avi Shulman of Torah Umesorah. One day, Reb Meir asked Mr. Shulman if he could recommend a gifted writer to help review some copy ArtScroll had done for a yeshivah.

Mr. Shulman mentioned the name of a close friend, Rabbi Nosson Scherman, the *menahel* at the Karlin-Stolin Yeshivah in Boro Park. The name was not unfamiliar to Reb Meir.

An article in the October 1974 issue of the *Jewish Observer* had caught Reb Meir's eye — and it had been penned by Rabbi Scherman.

Entitled, "The Chofetz Chaim Comes to Vienna," the writer described the magic of the great Knessia Gedolah of 1923 and the significance of the Chofetz Chaim's arrival. Reb Meir was very moved by the depiction, the fusion of historical exactitude with reverence for the subject. It was a new type of literature: detailed, but not detached and academic. Accurate, but also inspiring.

Reb Nosson did some work for ArtScroll, offering editorial input into advertising copy, but something bigger was happening. With Reb Nosson's literary ability and Reb Sheah's graphic genius, Reb Meir was ready to actualize his dreams.

But first he had to reach into his heart and share the vision he had articulated to his close friends.

The conversation had taken place in Nochum Silberman's large Buick somewhere along the Staten Island Expressway, on the way back from Mair Fogel's *levayah*. The *niftar* had been a Camp Agudah roommate of Meir Zlotowitz and Avie Gold, and they had become close friends. The pain at the *levayah* was intense: Mair Fogel, a talented young *mechanech*, had left this world before he and his wife had merited having children. The fact that he had passed away without having built a family compounded the tragedy of his passing.

In the car with his longtime friends, Meir Zlotowitz could still talk with the enthusiasm of a teenager, expressing old dreams.

"We need to do something to allow his name to live on. I want to do something in his memory," he said.

It was the middle of the winter — the third day of Teves 5536/December 7th, 1975 — with less than 2½ months remaining until Purim.

"Maybe we should translate *Megillas Esther*?" he pondered.

Reb Meir asked Rachel for permission to embark on a project that would consume him, to invest his heart and soul into perpetuating the memory of his friend.

In retrospect, says Rav Elya Brudny, that decision was itself indicative of his character. "Many people would have that initial thought, to do something to eternalize the *neshamah* of a friend who died without being blessed with children — it's a sign of kindness," says the Mirrer rosh yeshivah, "but not too many people would instantly grasp that Torah is the greatest source of merit."

The son of Rav Ahron Zlotowitz, the *talmid* of Rav Moshe Feinstein, knew just what to do.

For the next few weeks, there were no invitations and no *kesubos* and no brochures: there was just the Ibn Ezra, the Alshich, the Vilna Gaon, and the Malbim. He wrote and wrote, seated at his desk through most of the day and part of the night, *sefarim* spread out all around him as words flowed from his pen.

At the time, Reb Meir and Rachel lived in Flatbush, where they rented the upper floor in the home of Rabbi Yisroel Gornish, rav of Chizuk Hadas, on East Fourteenth Street. Rabbi

A labor of love: Reb Meir writing at home in the early years, during the midnight hours

Gornish, who has an extensive *sefarim* library, recalls his tenant coming to borrow *sefarim*. "He went through every one of the *meforshim* on *Megillas Esther*, every *sefer* he could find."

Rebbetzin Gornish remembers the steady rhythm of the typewriter keys. "His dining room was above ours, and we heard the sound clearly; the kids would go to sleep and then the typewriter would come to life, deep into the night."

One month later, Reb Meir had the rough draft of *Megillas Esther* ready. He showed it to Rav Dovid Feinstein and Rav Dovid Cohen, both of whom offered encouragement and insights that were incorporated into the text.

Friends and family told him it was ground-breaking, but no one was really sure what to expect.

Reb Meir consulted with his friend Mr. Avi Shulman, who asked several publishers how many copies of the newly translated Megillah they estimated would sell. Most suggested printing between five hundred and one thousand copies, their assessment of the potential demand for such an English-language work.

(L to R) With Rav Dovid Feinstein and Rav Dovid Cohen

The company had no experience with retail — distribution, sales, and collection — so Mr. Shulman and Reb Meir developed a creative sales concept. They would print in soft-cover and offer one institution in each Jewish community the right to purchase copies: the *mosdos* could then use these copies as gifts, the perfect mailing to their donors.

The first indication that the book they were selling had more value than they realized was Rav Simcha Wasserman's order: The rosh yeshivah of Ohr Elchonon in Los Angeles ordered fifteen hundred copies of the *Megillas Esther*!

Reb Zundel Berman, a lifelong friend of Reb Meir, handled the distribution from the back of his station wagon. Reb Shmuel Blitz, who ran the Hebrew Publishing Bookstore at the time, recalls his initial order: eighteen hardcover copies and twelve paperbacks. The next day, he remembers, he called Reb Zundel, pleading for another hundred copies.

The *mosdos* that initially placed orders called a few days

First ad for the new *Megillas Esther*

later with urgent requests to reorder, explaining that they desperately needed more. Those who saw the new Megillah loved it and people were asking for additional copies. ArtScroll printed and printed some more: that first year, twenty thousand copies of *Megillas Esther* were sold!

It was clear that the *sefer* had disclosed a new need. Not just masses of *ba'alei teshuvah*, newly returned to the faith of their fathers, but even yeshivah-educated English speakers, a generation born and raised in America, were looking for sophisticated Torah works in their native language.

During those years, Reb Meir davened at Congregation Sfard, on Coney Island Avenue, where Rav Sholom Hecht served as rav. Rabbi Hecht clearly remembers Reb Meir's pride in the work.

"He came to shul with a box of the new *sefarim*, we were all so full of compliments and excitement. We all knew he was on to something, even though he himself wasn't sure yet."

That Purim night, Reb Meir got an inkling of what was to come as he saw Jews walking home from *Krias HaMegillah* with copies of the newly released *Megillas Esther* under their arms.

"You have to understand just how innovative the work was," Reb Sheah Brander points out, "and not just the inside. There was no concept of a full-color cover in the Orthodox Jewish world, but Meir wanted to bring all the beauty and meticulousness of the secular world to our publishing industry. He invested in an attractive cover, confident that our audience would appreciate it. He felt that the *sefarim* and the people learning them deserved no less."

Another innovation was the overview, conceived by Reb Meir, but penned by Reb Nosson. More than an introduction or foreword, it would offer a sweeping analysis of the Yom Tov, melding the warmth of the chassidic Rebbes with the profundity of the *ba'alei mussar*. A close *talmid* of Rav Gedaliah Schorr, whose Torah synthesized chassidus, halachah, and *mussar*, Reb Nosson's overviews would become part of the brand, an entryway into the true essence of the *chag* for generations of readers.

"Do something well the first time and you won't have to do it again," Reb Meir would often say, pointing to the layout of that initial offering. The design of the ArtScroll *Megillas Esther* would become the standard look for the stream of books that would follow: it was classic, so there was no reason to change.

But there was something else beyond the quality of the work.

In his introduction, Reb Meir offered the usual

PAGE 13   THE JEWISH WEEK-AMERICAN EXAMINER   WEEK OF MARCH 7-1

Esther megilla published in a new translation

A new translation of the Megillas Esther (The Book of Esther) in lucid English and Hebrew has been published by Artscroll Studios Press. Translated and compiled by Rabbi Meir Zlotowitz as a memorial to a friend who died some months ago, the book has a lengthy introduction called an "Overview," which deals with the period and miracle of the Purim story. The introduction is by Rabbi Nosson Scherman.

Although the book only appeared three months ago, the publisher says that he has virtually exhausted a press run of 10,000 hard cover and 6,000 soft cover copies. He explains this kind of sale as being due to the fact that the book has won wide acceptance among a wide spectrum of Jewish religious and educational experts.

A feature of this new translation of the Book of Esther is a commentary authologized from Talmudic, Midrashic and Rabbinic sources. The volume sells for $6 in hard cover and $4 in soft cover. Artscroll Studios Press is 212 Fifth Ave., New York, N.Y. 10010.

An article about the new translation

acknowledgment and appreciation, and then allowed himself a moment to reflect on his goal. It would be the very same goal of every one of the two thousand-plus titles that would follow.

It must be made clear that this is not a so-called "scientific" or "apologetic" commentary on the Megillah. That area has, unfortunately, been too well covered, resulting in violence to the Jewish faith as well as incorrect interpretation. It is in no way the intention of this work to demonstrate the legitimacy or historicity of Esther or Mordechai to non-believers or doubters. Belief in the authenticity of every Book of the Torah is basic to the Jewish faith, and we proceed from there. It comes as no surprise to me — nor should it to any Orthodox Jew — that the palace in Shushan, as unearthed by archaeologists, bears out the description of the palace in the Megillah in every detail: nor do we deem it necessary to prove, by means of the "Persian borrow-words," nor by whatever means, that the Book was indeed written in the contemporary period.

Rather, the aim was a specifically traditional commentary reflecting the Megillah as understood by Chazal. No non-Jewish sources have even been consulted, much less quoted. I consider it offensive that the Torah should need authentication from the secular or so-called "scientific" sources.

That he felt a need to write this makes it clear that Reb Meir was very much aware of the role he was to play. A generation later, he would tell young people that when he had started out, he'd been mocked: he, along with Reb Nosson and Reb Sheah, were disparaged as "yeshivah guys," black-hatters without any major experience with the world of secular printing and literature. It's clear that early on, he was determined not just to produce a work more sophisticated and striking than anything else in the world of Jewish literature, but also to be the unapologetic voice of complete faithfulness to the Mesorah.

He made another fateful decision on the heels of the astounding success of *Megillas Esther* — what was meant to be a

Dancing with Reb Nosson and Reb Sheah at an ArtScroll hosted *sheva berachos*

one-book project — looking at Reb Nosson and Reb Sheah and saying the words they would hear again and again over the years: "What's next?"

Reb Meir had been swept into a new world. In his introduction to *Megillas Esther*, he had written that *the moment of bidding farewell to this book is indeed nostalgic. It marks the conclusion of a delightful quest, of many hours spent in intimate contact with Chazal and their profound insight into every facet of Torah study.*

And he wasn't ready to let go.

He looked at the calendar and got back to work. He embarked on his next project, *Megillas Rus*, but this time, he had a clear-cut sense of his mission. In the introduction, he writes: *I again end with a prayer that this work be received by the Torah world as a tool toward understanding and appreciating yet another one of the Sacred Books of the Bible as our Sages wanted us to understand and appreciate it...so that the hidden depths of Torah will become the possession also of non-Hebrew-reading*

Jews — too many of whom have been condemned to varying degrees of spiritual pauperdom — so that their souls will be drawn close to Hashem and His Torah…

Then he started on *Megillas Eichah*, and, since there was still a business to run, he reached out to literary friends, asking them to review the work and offer suggestions.

Mrs. Faigie Weinbaum had been his teacher in RJJ. Just as she had once corrected his work, she stepped in again to review these manuscripts.

Reb Meir solicited his talented camp friend, Rabbi Avie Gold, for his opinion as well. Reb Avie obliged, sending Reb Meir a marked-up version of the manuscript on *Eichah*. In later years, Reb Meir would tease him. "You were very rough on me. I read your edits on Tishah B'Av and I immediately sat down on the floor and cried!"

At the time, none of them realized that they were joining a team, being called into service. Each one would play a major role as the project became a mission.

Reb Meir encountered his first major hurdle in the road when it came to publishing *Sefer Yonah*, which was slated for a Yom Kippur 1978 release. Preoccupied with other projects, he had commissioned a recognized scholar to work on the translation and commentary.

There wasn't much time until Yom Kippur, and this scholar worked long hours to have the draft ready for the deadline: he succeeded, triumphantly handing it in on schedule. Reb Meir happily accepted the manuscript and sat down to review it.

His excitement grew as he read through the brilliant commentary, the curtains being pulled aside to reveal the true depth of the *sefer* — but then a line caught his eye. The author was examining the meaning of a *pasuk*, and after quoting Rashi's understanding, the author concluded that Rashi had made a mistake, disparaging Rashi's explanation.

Reb Meir stood up and showed the offensive paragraph to

his colleagues. They all agreed that it was disturbing: their disagreement was about how to react.

"The pressure was tremendous," recalls someone who was in the room that day. "We needed to get *Yonah* out. Meir had invested money we didn't have, and he desperately needed the cash flow that sales would have brought in. He was proud of the reputation he was developing, and missing a deadline would have ruined it. We all felt that he should insist that the author remove that paragraph and then move forward. Meir felt differently."

Rabbi Zlotowitz looked at his colleagues and said, "There is no way that this company, ArtScroll, will release a *sefer* written by someone who even *thinks* this way, even if he erases that paragraph. Someone who can consider the possibility that Rashi was wrong cannot be part of what we're doing here."

Reb Meir paid the author for the completed work, and then personally got to work on a new translation and commentary on *Sefer Yonah*, authoring it along with Reb Nosson.

Once the five *Megillos* and *Sefer Yonah* were completed, it was decision time again: Would ArtScroll dedicate itself fully to this new mission, to servicing an audience thirsty for more?

Reb Meir called a meeting, asking a group of trusted friends to weigh in.

Along with Reb Nosson and Reb Sheah, he invited Rabbi Nisson Wolpin and Mr. Avi Shulman; presiding over the meeting was someone Reb Meir considered a mentor.

The relationship between Rabbi Joseph Elias and Reb Meir had been formed at 156 Fifth Avenue, where Torah Umesorah had offices as well. Reb Meir was very taken by the German *talmid chacham* — an educator and gifted writer. Rabbi Elias embodied the intellect and erudition of *yahadus Ashkenaz*. As an educator at the Hirsch Realschule in Frankfurt, he had been trusted to transmit the sacred Mesorah of Rav Samson Raphael Hirsch to the next generation. After leaving Germany, he had studied at England's Cambridge University, where he had learned — and mastered — the English language.

Upon arriving in America, Rabbi Elias wasted no time in addressing the youth, combining his two gifts — education and writing — in a series of pamphlets called Jewish Pocketbooks. Rather than listing halachos, the books aimed to present the *hashkafah*, the Jewish view on contemporary issues, in simple English.

Rabbi Elias carefully studied the *Megillas Esther* and knew that he was witnessing the start of something great: he offered a brief history lesson at that meeting, impressing the significance of the mission on the young American men seated around the table.

When someone floated the idea of doing a translation and commentary on the *Haggadah shel Pesach*, the room grew quiet. It was a daunting task, because the words of the *Haggadah* represent the most fundamental part of our faith, the essence of what has been passed down from father to son ever since that glorious night.

"I would do it," Rabbi Elias said.

Reb Meir's spirits soared. Along with the prestige of being associated with someone of Rabbi Elias's caliber, there was another detail as well.

Rabbi Elias was a very close *talmid* of Rav Yaakov Kamenetsky. Reb Meir knew that Rabbi Elias would never have made an offer like that if he hadn't first consulted with his rebbi — so in his willingness to undertake the project, Reb Meir saw a sign of Rav Yaakov's approval for their work.

ArtScroll had seen its last wedding invitation.[1]

Rav Yaakov hadn't given ArtScroll his automatic approval — it took time to earn the rosh yeshivah's trust. Reb Nosson Scherman had been a *talmid* of his in Torah Vodaath, where

---

1. From that point on, Reb Meir and Reb Nosson turned full-time to working on books. Reb Nosson resigned from his position as *menahel* of Yeshivah Karlin-Stolin and Reb Meir stepped back from day-to-day running of ArtScroll Printing, which is operated until today by Reb Meir's close friend Elliot Schwartz.

With Rav Yaakov Kamenetsky and Reb Nosson

Rav Yaakov served as rosh yeshivah, and Rav Yaakov had been a *chavrusa* with Reb Ahron Zlotowitz back in Lomza — but still, his early support had been tempered with caution.

The rosh yeshivah was watching carefully, eager to see where this new path would lead. In the early days, he wrote a letter in support of ArtScroll; while it was warm, it was not particularly effusive. It underscored how harmful the written word could be if it was not used properly. Reb Meir felt that it would be a mistake to print it, since it fell short of being a real *haskamah*. (The letter wasn't printed, and several years later, Rav Yaakov wrote a glowing letter in support of the Mishnayos series. The rosh yeshivah laughed as he handed it over. "This one you'll be able to print," he quipped.)

Rav Yaakov prized clarity above all. For many years he had been a proponent of teaching American *cheder* children in English, reasoning that if it was the language they were speaking at home and with their friends, then they ought to learn Torah in that language as well.

When Rabbi Joseph Elias became a member of the ArtScroll team and his rebbi began to hear reports from the "inside," Rav Yaakov went from being a friend to being an active supporter. He welcomed Reb Meir and Reb Nosson to his Monsey home for consultations and direction, praising the nascent Torah venture to his colleagues.

Another of the *gedolei Torah* who perceived what ArtScroll might accomplish was Rav Mordechai Gifter. Rav Gifter was unique among the senior roshei yeshivah in that he was American born and raised, and English was his first language. He was that rare synthesis of master of the English language who was also a staunch and unyielding defender of the authenticity of the Mesorah. Torah was pristine and pure and had to be transmitted as such; he well understood the challenge of maintaining the reverence for each letter while translating it into a different language.

And Rav Gifter felt that the staff at ArtScroll was up to the task.

Like Rav Yaakov, Rav Gifter went a step beyond giving his approval, blessing the company with his personal involvement and support.

In the winter of 1977, the newly formed team faced a dilemma. They planned to translate *Shir HaShirim* for Pesach, but they weren't sure what manner of translation to follow — literal or figurative. "We understood that this was above our pay grade, something we couldn't approach without clear direction," recalls Rabbi Scherman.

Rav Yaakov Kamenetsky welcomed Reb Meir and Reb Nosson to his home and listened to their question. He told them

With Rav Mordechai Gifter at the ArtScroll office

that the allegorical references in *Shir HaShirim* are the only true *peshat*, so the translation should follow Rashi's allegorical commentary, which, Rav Yaakov stressed, is the accurate translation.[2] Rav Yaakov offered to lend them a valuable, out-of-print *sefer* called *Divrei Yedidya*, by Rav Yedidya Lipmann Lipkin — a nephew of Rav Yisroel Lipkin of Salant — which he felt would be helpful.

Rav Gifter agreed with Rav Yaakov's ruling, but still, he worried that the project would engender opposition just the same. The Telshe rosh yeshivah pre-empted any possible resistance by reading through the entire manuscript, then writing an actual introduction, in *lashon kodesh*; it was his way of not just agreeing, but enthusiastically endorsing it as a Torah work. (In time, the Telshe rosh yeshivah would offer his literary services to Reb Meir and Reb Nosson, telling them he'd be happy to read and comment on the galleys of other *sefarim* as work on them progressed: Rav Gifter did this for about two years.)

---

2. The literal translation — *peirush hamillos* — appears in the commentary on the bottom of the page.

Incidentally, that translation made its mark throughout the Jewish world. Shortly after the English *Shir HaShirim* was released, Reb Meir received a phone call from Reb Leibel Groner, secretary to the Lubavitcher Rebbe. The Rebbe had apparently read Reb Meir's introduction, in which he thanked Rav Yaakov for loaning them the precious, out-of-print copy of *Divrei Yedidya,* and the Rebbe wanted to know if he could borrow the *sefer* and review it as well. Reb Meir called Rav Yaakov, who immediately agreed, and Reb Meir sent the *sefer* to Crown Heights for the Lubavitcher Rebbe's use. (Reb Meir also sent his own translation and commentary on *Bereishis* to the Lubavitcher Rebbe, who would acknowledge the gift with a letter of thanks, a blessing, and copies of his own *sefarim, Likkutei Sichos.*)

With leading roshei yeshivah behind them, the ArtScroll team planned to turn to *Torah Shebe'al Peh.* Their confidence was further bolstered at a 1977 meeting, a summit on the shores of the Atlantic Ocean.

Rav Gifter was in New York for a private meeting with the *gedolei hador,* and, determined to help the fledgling company, he had an idea. Since he was reading galleys of unpublished ArtScroll works, he invited Reb Meir to bring the materials to the Ocean Breeze Hotel in Seagate, Brooklyn. When Reb Meir arrived, Rav Gifter introduced him to the other roshei yeshivah who were present. Rav Moshe Feinstein and Rav Yaakov Kamenetsky were familiar with Reb Meir's work, but Rav Yaakov Yitzchak Ruderman met him for the first time. Rav Gifter shared his vision of what ArtScroll might become, and the other roshei yeshivah provided words of encouragement and blessing.

Rav Yaakov issued a new challenge: He wanted to see all of Tanach translated into English. He felt that commentary on *sefarim* like *Divrei HaYamim* was a necessity, because there is a scarcity of classic commentaries. In later years, Reb Meir would discuss how difficult this was, because, while works like *Megillas*

Esther turned a profit, he knew that the elucidation of works like *Trei Asar* and *Divrei HaYamim* never would. "The *gedolim* told us what we had to do, but they never told us how to make payroll while doing it," he would joke.

To implement Rav Yaakov's challenge, ArtScroll kept adding *talmidei chachamim* to the senior staff. Reb Meir followed his partner's recommendation and brought Reb Nosson's former Beth Medrash Elyon friend, Reb Hersh Goldwurm, on board. Reb Hersh, a brilliant *talmid chacham*, possessed the erudition and breadth to write the translation and commentary for *Sefer Daniel*, and was soon indispensable.

"Meir perceived the greatness that lay beneath Reb Hershel's humble exterior," Reb Nosson recalls, "and he became very devoted to him."

It was the presence of Reb Hersh Goldwurm, Rabbi Scherman reflects, that gave Reb Meir the dream of having a "*kollel*,"

(L to R) Rabbi Hersh Goldwurm, Rabbi Yechezkel Danziger,
Rabbi Yossi Davis, Rabbi Hillel Danziger

a team of accomplished *talmidei chachamim* on staff not just to write, but to clarify, answer, and illuminate.

Rav Gifter also encouraged Reb Meir to go in that direction. "Imagine," the Telshe rosh yeshivah said, "if you can provide *talmidei chachamim* a means of using their talents to make a *parnassah*. This way, they can remain in the '*beis medrash*' and still earn a living doing what they love to do, learning and teaching Klal Yisrael."

Reb Meir took the charge seriously, and, in time, the high-caliber scholars on ArtScroll's payroll would be as much a source of pride to him as the work they produced.

Once work on the *Nevi'im* was underway, it was time for the next major project. The Yad Avraham Mishnah series, sponsored by Mr. and Mrs. Louis Glick, was launched; the new release was a milestone, because it was ArtScroll's first work of high-level scholarship on *Torah Shebe'al Peh*. "The Mishnayos," reflects a veteran writer, "called for a different level of *talmid chacham* and a different sort of engagement in learning. Once we saw we could do that, we felt that no project was beyond us, with *siyata d'Shmaya*."

Reb Meir, together with Reb Nosson and Reb Sheah, learned what it meant to shepherd a major project forward, translators to writers to editors to the graphics team to the production staff.

At the time, Rav Yaakov Kamenetsky made a comment that seemed unrealistic. "When are you translating *Shas*?" he asked. They were taken aback by the unexpected question, and the rosh yeshivah continued, "You can do it and you should do it and you will do it. If Hashem grants me the years, I'll give you a letter," he concluded.

A seed had been planted and it was starting to take root.

In 1978, another milestone was marked as ArtScroll moved its headquarters to Coney Island Avenue, in the heart of Brooklyn's Jewish community.

ArtScroll headquarters on Coney Island Avenue

Things continued to evolve when, in the summer of 1980, Reb Meir asked Shmuel Blitz to join the team. Blitz, with his background in sales and sharp business acumen, explained that ventures such as *Megillas Esther* could sell very well — but only to individuals; if the company would produce Siddurim and Chumashim, they could sell in bulk, to shuls and schools. It was a small shift in direction that would prove beneficial in generating the cash flow to keep the company afloat.

Stabilizing the business and directing the various projects had kept Reb Meir away from writing and he was hungry for a project of his own. He dreamt of an in-depth English *sefer* on Chumash, a translation of each *pasuk* presented along with a commentary incorporating the opinions and approaches of the classic *Rishonim* and *Acharonim*.

The next period was, by his own admission, the happiest time

With Shmuel Blitz at the *bris* of Shmuel's son

in his life. While preparing *Megillas Esther*, he had inhabited the joyous world of full-time immersion in Torah for a month, but writing *Bereishis* required years of sitting most of the day and night and just learning, then writing. Each concept and idea was analyzed, refined, and clarified before being written.

Six volumes on *Bereishis* would be released. Until the end of his life, Reb Meir kept the notes from those years of toil on the bookshelves near his desk, and would often show them to his grandchildren, a reminder of his happiest days, a period of near-total immersion in words of Torah. It was a sign of his humility and clear sense of mission that he stopped after *Bereishis* and didn't continue on to *Shemos*: although he had relished the opportunity to write, the market for that sort of work didn't justify the investment of his time and resources. He humbly accepted the reality that he was needed elsewhere, on the fund-raising and executive end; however, he would whimsically reflect that he hoped he would have time to continue working on the Chumash when things would quiet down. But

A Phenomenon of Torah Publishing

The ArtScroll Tanach Series, published by Mesorah Publications Ltd., was introduced to the Jewish public in January, 1976. It was met with a response that was totally unprecedented in the annals of English-language Judaica. The first book in the series, Megillas Esther, went into a second printing almost as soon as it entered the stores. In less than two months before Purim of that first year, over 22,000 copies were sold. A clamor arose from roshei hayeshiva, educators, scholars speaking Jews who thirst for unadulterated, unapologetically presented Torah knowledge.

The uniqueness of the ArtScroll series lies in its approach to commentary. Its editors describe it as an anthologized commentary implying that it offers a collection of comments. That is certainly true. Anthologies can be of many kinds. The key to evaluating and understanding a particular anthology is to know the philosophy and purpose of its author.

The Goals of the Commentary

The ArtScroll approach was in any language that so clearly Rashi by such major figures as the reader looking for interesting, undemanding insights may skim the footnotes. The sum total is a well-planned, variegated commentary that functions on many levels.

The Translation

Translation is a major concern of the ArtScroll Series. There was no available translation that served the purpose of the editors. The popular Jewish translations of the Jewish Publication Society did not consider themselves bound by the teachings of Chazal and they generally assign no more weight to the classic commentators than they do to secular sources. The Orthodox translations either reflected the particular, often original, interpretation of the translator, failed to rely primarily on Rashi, or lacked literary grace. An original

JEWISH PRESS • Page 58 • September 14, 1979

Rabbi Meir Zlotowitz (right) and Rabbi Nosson Sherman.

Jewish Press article (1979)

they never did, and until today, *mechanchim* and lay people alike regard the ArtScroll *Bereishis* as the consummate Torah work, and teachers bemoan the fact that the rest of *Chamishah Chumshei Torah* was never completed.

It wasn't only Reb Meir's undertakings that received this level of attention: each ArtScroll work was approached with the same level of commitment. Rav Avrohom Chaim Feuer — a son-in-law of Rav Mordechai Gifter — was completing his *Tehillim* translation, and he was spending long days at the ArtScroll office reviewing *every* single word. It was standard practice to order supper to the office, he recalls, and sit there until after midnight, assessing and analyzing, trying to refine each sentence and idea. After these intensive sessions with Reb Meir and Reb Nosson, Rabbi Feuer would often sleep in Reb Meir's home for a few hours, and then the three men were back at work again.

When the ArtScroll *Tehillim* was finally complete, Rav Feuer approached Rav Yaakov Kamenetsky for a *haskamah* and asked the rosh yeshivah what *sefer* he should work on next.

"Next?" Rav Yaakov asked. "Next, is to lock yourself in a room and learn!"

Rav Feuer understood the message. They weren't authors, but part of the process, the sacred chain of transmitters of Torah and as inspired as the writers would be, so too the final product. The job didn't entail only literary skills, but a vibrant connection to Torah.

Rav Feuer connected Rav Yaakov's directive with a story about the great pre-World War II Rebbe of Sokolov, Rav Yitzchak Zelig Morgenstern, a prolific writer, leader, and diplomat. The Rebbe met one of the prominent secular Jewish authors of the day, and the writer asked the Rebbe for the secret of his literary abilities.

"What do you do before you start writing?" the Rebbe asked.

"I fill my pen with ink," the author replied.

"Before I start writing," the Rebbe said, "I fill my pen with fire!"

"Rav Yaakov was telling me how ArtScroll would succeed, he was issuing a challenge," Rav Feuer reflects. "If we would become part of the message we were trying to convey, we would succeed."

The next frontier was the Siddur, introduced in 1984.

Reb Sheah, charged with creating the template for the Siddur, was determined to provide something new: the layout was fresh, user-friendly, and presented beautifully. Reb Nosson would provide translation, commentary, and his unique overview, making the translated Siddur a product the English-speaking public had never really encountered before. Reb Nosson's translation was so exalted that even in English one could feel the *kedushah* and beauty of each word of prayer.

The Siddur would ultimately sell over one million copies and change the shul experience for many Jews. In the words of Rebbetzin Malka Feinstein, "The Siddur was the great equalizer. It allowed a generation of women who hadn't been fortunate enough to attend a Bais Yaakov to come to shul and feel included. The Siddur was so simple, the format and instructions so clear, that everyone holding it suddenly felt that they could take part in davening."

On Rosh Hashanah, Reb Meir was sitting near his friend Rabbi Yehuda Levi in shul. There was some confusion in regard to a particular *minhag*, and people were peering into their *machzorim* in confusion, trying to figure out what should be recited next.

The two men looked at each other. "You need to do a *machzor*," Rabbi Levi said. Reb Meir nodded. "By next year, *im yirtzeh Hashem*," he responded.

Reb Nosson translated the *machzor*, adding commentary and creating a special Yom Tov overview, the comprehensive, panoramic view of what the *Yamim Noraim* really meant.

With Rabbi Yehuda Levi

The first *machzor* in the series, Rosh Hashanah, led to an interesting dilemma.

The standard *machzorim* didn't generally include the full text of *Kaddish*: rather, the word "*Kaddish*" was printed as a direction, an indication to recite the prayer. Rosh Hashanah in the year following the *machzor's* release was slated to begin on a Friday night, so congregations would be reciting *kabbalas Shabbos* before *Borchu*. The question was whether to insert the words "*le'eila ule'eila,*" an addition appropriate for the *Aseres Yemei Teshuvah*, following *Kabbalas Shabbos*, since accepting the Shabbos essentially means accepting Rosh Hashanah — or does the actual day of Rosh Hashanah start only following the recitation of *Borchu*.

There was no other *machzor* that clarified this issue, because the other *machzorim* simply said the word "*Kaddish*" without printing the text.

The editors understood the responsibility before them and knew they had to get it right. Reb Meir and Reb Nosson went to discuss their quandary with Rav Moshe Feinstein.

"I can offer *sevaros* to both sides," the rosh yeshivah said, "but to establish a *minhag* you need more than logic. I think you should approach a few veteran *shamashim* of big shuls and ask them what the *minhag* is."

Then they went to ask Rav Yaakov Kamenetsky, who essentially echoed Rav Moshe's answer, suggesting they consult with experienced *gabbaim*.

After embarking on a *gabbai*-interviewing tour, the decision was made to include the words *le'eila ule'eila*.

Over the years, Reb Meir would often wonder why both roshei yeshivah had offered the same suggestion, using a near identical phrase and stressing that they should ask more than one person. He was exhilarated when, after sharing the story in public, he was approached by a young *talmid chacham* who showed him a source. In the *Levush*, the Ba'al HaLevushim writes a particular halachah[3] and concludes, "This is the correct halachah, and I've even confirmed it with several *chazzanim yeshishim,* veteran *chazzanim!*"

The early 1980's saw ArtScroll release another of its core products: the very first biography with the ArtScroll imprint was Reb Elchonon, a tribute to Rav Elchonon Wasserman, *Hashem yinkom damo*, the rosh yeshivah of Baranovitch. To Reb Meir, it was a particularly meaningful choice. Rav Elchonon's son, Rav Simcha Wasserman, the rosh yeshivah of Ohr Elchonon, had been the first one to order the *Megillas Esther* in bulk, an encouraging voice from the start, and he had been a mentor to Reb Meir and Reb Nosson.

Rav Simcha Wasserman

Rav Simcha lived in Los Angeles, but when in New York, the rosh yeshivah

---

3. *Orach Chaim* 487.

would visit the ArtScroll office to purchase English books, which he saw as the perfect tools for reaching unaffiliated Jews and opening their eyes to *Yiddishkeit*. Reb Meir would always insist that there was no charge, but Rav Simcha was equally adamant about paying.

With the release of the book, Reb Meir felt he had finally managed to do something for Rav Simcha. The rosh yeshivah had seen the town of Baranovitch and its glorious yeshivah go up in smoke. Rav Simcha had lost his family, and he and his rebbetzin had never merited children of their own. With the book, even those not privileged to know Reb Elchonon from between the pages of his classic *sefarim* could also encounter his greatness, and this thought brought Rav Simcha a degree of comfort.

Invitation to ArtScroll's Tenth Anniversary Dinner

A decade had elapsed. There was much to celebrate and, in 1986, in honor of ArtScroll's tenth anniversary, a special *seudah* was held. Reb Meir sent airline tickets to Rav Mordechai and Rebbetzin Shoshana Gifter, honored guests at this festive celebration. Rav Gifter returned the tickets, along with a note. "We will join you, *im yirtzeh Hashem*, but this is our personal *simchah*, and we will pay for our own tickets."

At that event, a presentation was made to Reb Shmuel Blitz, who was moving to Eretz Yisrael to head ArtScroll's operations there. In his keynote *derashah*, Rav Gifter remarked that he too wished he was returning to Eretz Yisrael to live.

Another feature of that event was a *siyum* and speech by Reb Meir's oldest son, 19-year-old Gedaliah; a decade in, Reb Meir already envisioned the distant future.

In just ten years, the company had transformed Jewish life in America and across the world, opening up the world of Tanach and Mishnah, *tefillah* and halachah.

Now, the stage was set for the most ambitious project yet — but before embarking on the journey, Reb Meir had to assemble the perfect team to travel at his side.

6

THE ARTSCROLL FAMILY

A T A *SIMCHAH* TOWARD THE END OF HIS LIFE, REB MEIR was introduced by an ArtScroll employee. "This is my boss," the younger man said.

Reb Meir was visibly upset. "We work together," he said firmly.

From the earliest days of ArtScroll, Reb Meir created a culture that allowed every single staffer to feel part of what was going on, a partner in the accomplishments.

He had expectations from them: punctuality, dedication, pride, and efficiency. But he set the example, arriving first, staying last, and making sure that they never forgot how fortunate they were to share in the *zechus* of spreading Torah.

Even when money was scarce, recalls Rabbi Avie Gold, Reb Meir insisted that every employee receive a complimentary copy of each new book. "We expected an employee discount, and that would have been gracious; by giving us the books, he was conveying a message that we were all partners in each one. It did wonders for morale."

With Eli Kroen and Reb Gedaliah

In later years, Reb Meir would develop an appreciation for the writing style of *Wall Street Journal* columnist Peggy Noonan, and would sometimes recommend her pieces to budding writers. In one column, she used the term "genius cluster,"[1] referring to a group of gifted people who come together at the same place and time in order to solve a crisis. For the next few weeks, he would share the term with people around the office. "That's what we have here," he kept saying. "ArtScroll is a genius cluster, we have the best writers and editors and graphic artists; you are all geniuses that have come together at the same time in history!"

And tight as funds may have been on his end, he made sure his employees were paid on time. He prided himself on the fact that he was never late with a check. Over the years, there were occasions when he wasn't able to give a Yom Tov bonus to his staff. In those situations, he would pen a personal note of gratitude and appreciation to each one. *I wish that we had the extra money for the bonus,* he would write, *but unfortunately we don't. Please know that you're worth it and much more.*

One year, he was unable to provide his staff with the same pre-Yom Tov bonus as in previous years. He gave a smaller

1. "A World in Crisis, and No Genius in Sight," WSJ, July 2016.

bonus, and felt very badly about it. Then, a few days later, he gave another small bonus, since he had accessed more money, and then he managed a third bonus before Yom Tov. The total was still less than in the previous year, but he had shown his staff just how much they meant to him.

When the Israeli shekel rose in value, he gave a very generous, one-time bonus to the employees working in Eretz Yisrael. "Every month, they convert their US dollars into shekels and they get more or less the same amount, but now, because of the change, they're coming home with fewer shekels than usual. I can't handle the thought of our writers and editors having to cut back on what they're used to, so hopefully this will compensate them."

He conveyed his admiration not just with money, but with professional respect as well. One of the senior editors had worked on a manuscript, and he realized that Reb Meir wasn't pleased with the result. "But he had a way of sharing his opinion so that it didn't make you feel small, but big. He would compliment a phrase, then suggest a small change."

At his desk in the office

With Rav Chaim Zev Malinowitz

"He knew that some of us operated in a bubble, in our own offices off-site," says Rav Chaim Zev Malinowitz, who worked from his home in Yerushalayim, "so he made sure we appreciated the impact of our work, and the role we played in producing it. He shared every bit of positive feedback with all of us."

When Yisroel (Ira) Zlotowitz established his own business, he asked his father for advice. "Treat your employees like family," Reb Meir suggested.

He would use the term "the ArtScroll family," for the staff and contributors, and he took it seriously. He wanted to be called "Meir," rather than "Reb Meir" or "Rabbi Zlotowitz," because he felt the relationship in the office was that of family.

And, Mrs. Rachel Zlotowitz points out, he didn't use the term "family" lightly. "My husband cherished family above all else. That was his priority, always, so when he called the staff at ArtScroll his family, it meant something — and he wanted them to realize that!"

One of the writers came into Reb Meir's office and explained that he couldn't make ends meet on the salary he was making, so he was requesting a different payment structure.

Reb Meir immediately agreed and also offered him a raise — and then thanked the writer for bringing it to his attention. "I always tell my children that it's hard for me to keep track of everything they need, and they should tell me if they need something, so I appreciate your mentioning it to me."

When digital cameras were introduced to the market, they were very expensive, but within a short time, the price dropped and they became more affordable. Reb Meir bought several of these new devices — for his children, and for his employees.

One of the ArtScroll secretaries married and moved to Lakewood. She kept her job, commuting each day, and whenever possible, her new husband would try to come pick her up after work. On those occasions, Rabbi Zlotowitz would take the opportunity to invite the young man into his office for a chat, simply to get to know him better; he too was part of the family.

An employee wrote one night to say he wasn't sure he would be able to come in to work the next day, as he was in physical pain. Reb Meir acknowledged the note.

> I'm DISTRESSED to read that you're being challenged yet again with a new health issue. YOU might not be sure if you're up to coming in in the morning, but I AM sure: Don't come in in the morning. Sleep late and call me late morning and tell me how you're doing. Please be sure to get through to me after 10:30. As you know, I care. Refuah sheleimah
>
> Meir

When a hard-working secretary wrote him an email to say that she would be taking her vacation, he wrote back to say how happy he was. *It's so well-deserved — please make sure to relax and enjoy.*

Another editor received a larger than usual Yom Tov bonus along with a note. *Tell your husband this isn't for household expenses, it's for you to enjoy.*

A talented young *talmid chacham* had completed his work on one of the volumes of the *Shas*. He'd been paid for the total assignment based on the number of *blatt* he had translated: Reb Meir called him one day. "We recently reevaluated the structure, since we hadn't realized how much work went into each *blatt*, and now we pay the writers per hour, instead of per *blatt*. But you already completed your work and never got that raise; you were paid according to the old system, so we're going to give you the raise retroactively, back to the beginning of your work on the project."

Reb Meir felt that the names of the various writers, proof-readers, and editors who had helped with a *sefer* or book should be included in the acknowledgments section. He wanted them to feel proud of what they were doing and to realize that they were appreciated.

When a new *sefer* was released, he would ask the author and editors for the names and addresses of their parents and parents-in-law so that he could send complimentary copies along with a note sharing the *nachas* with them.

Enjoying a quiet moment on Chol HaMoed Pesach

One year, a few days before Pesach, Reb Meir stopped one member of the marketing staff. "You look very stressed, what's wrong?" Reb Meir asked.

The gentleman admitted that he was anxious about the upcoming Yom Tov: his wife wasn't feeling well and the task of making Yom Tov was overwhelming. Reb Meir didn't hesitate. "Okay, you're with us; you're joining us in the hotel where we are spending Pesach this Yom Tov."

And in case it wasn't clear, Reb Meir said, "I'm booking rooms in the hotel right now, it's a done deal. You're part of our family."

A valued member of the team had purchased his first home, and was clearly weighed down by the heavy financial burden. Reb Meir noticed, and called him in. "I know that there isn't much money for extras, but I'd like you to go on vacation with your wife. I'm booking two tickets to Eretz Yisrael and a week in the Plaza." When the employee came to say goodbye before leaving, Reb Meir handed him an envelope with spending money for the "forced" vacation.

An employee was working long hours, and Reb Meir noticed. "I see that you're here early and you stay late, it can't be easy on your wife. You don't see each other enough. From now on," Reb Meir ruled, "you must go out to eat once a month, on our account." Reb Meir listed some of the most elegant restaurants in New York. "That's where you should go, a real night out. And send us the bill."

A single young man joined the ArtScroll graphics team. Reb Meir drove him home from work a few days after he had started working, and asked him a question. "Tell me, does your father have ArtScroll *sefarim* at home?"

"Of course he does," the employee replied.

"Great," Reb Meir said, "then let's complete his collection. Over time, when you have a free minute, feel free to go into the stock-room and take different *sefarim* so that he'll have them all."

The new employee got the message: your family is our family.

Often, writers and editors who worked off-site would have checks hand-delivered to their homes by the ArtScroll courier, especially if it was before Yom Tov. Reb Meir understood that sometimes, the few days it took for funds to arrive in the mail could create unnecessary stress.

Employees were reminded again and again that he was available to talk if they needed a listening ear; if they were going through a difficult time, he wanted to know about it and help them.

A receptionist left early one day, confiding that her husband had a serious medical exam. Reb Meir called her at home that night to know how it had gone.

When one of the *talmidei chachamim* on staff passed away at a young age, Reb Meir continued to pay his salary and provide health insurance for the family. "In situations like this, the family has to step in, and we are the family," Reb Meir maintained.

When one of the senior staff members married off a child, an ArtScroll writer felt close enough to fly in from Eretz Yisrael to join in the *simchah*. Reb Meir was proud of the display of loyalty and friendship. At the end of the month, the writer received his monthly check, along with an additional check for $3,000. There was no explanation provided, but the writer understood that it was Reb Meir's way of showing appreciation for the gesture by covering the expenses of the trip and the associated extras.

A young girl from out-of-town came to live in New York, and she got a job working in the art room at ArtScroll. Reb Meir felt a special sense of responsibility for her well-being and happiness and arranged for various ArtScroll staff members to invite her for Shabbos. He asked one of the female editors to go make sure that the girl had a proper apartment, that it was safe and comfortable.

When an older single employee came to tell him that she was dating seriously, he insisted on meeting the prospective young man. "I need to make sure he's worthy of you," he said.

A young *ba'alas teshuvah* worked as a typesetter at ArtScroll:

Reb Meir and Rachel would invite her for Shabbos meals and she became close with them. When she got engaged, Reb Meir met the *chassan* at the *vort* and spoke with him.

The next day at work, Reb Meir called the *kallah* in for a meeting. "Listen, I met the *chassan*, and frankly, I don't think he's for you." He gently explained that he had had a bad feeling about the young man and then asked around and confirmed his suspicions. Reb Meir gave her the strength to break the *shidduch* and eventually helped her find someone more suited to her.

One of the employees asked permission to take a vacation: he and his wife were planning a trip to Eretz Yisrael and they were very excited. The day before he left, Reb Meir called him in to say goodbye and wish him a safe trip — and then handed him an envelope with $1,000 in cash. "Do something special," he said.

One of the junior graphic artists, a girl whose family didn't live in New York, got engaged: Reb Meir and Reb Nosson were the first ones at the *vort*. Reb Meir asked other ArtScroll staffers

In his office at ArtScroll headquarters

to come as well. "She doesn't have a lot of family or friends in New York, but if we come, the other side will see that she has people who care about her," he explained.

He demanded maximum effort and dedication to what he considered a holy calling. On Erev Shabbos, staff members would pass by his office to say "*Gut Shabbos*," as in a regular family. One week, a salesman passed by to say "*Gut Shabbos*" at 1:56 p.m. Reb Meir smiled and wished him a *Gut Shabbos*, but then took the inter-office public address system in hand and spoke to the entire staff.

"Please be aware that there are still four minutes left to the workday," he announced, a message to that salesman.

But just as he worked hard to inspire dedication, he tried to create an atmosphere that was pleasant and light: he loved to joke and appreciated it when he heard staff members sharing jokes. He had a standard routine he used to put new secretaries at ease. He would ask that his coffee be prepared by stirring the drink three times to the right, then twice to the left.

Inevitably, the nervous new secretary would bring him the coffee and Reb Meir would take a sip and frown. "You clearly stirred it three times to the left, and twice to the right, you didn't follow instructions," he would say — welcoming the new hire with the well-worn joke.

He would often interrupt meetings or call in passing staffers to share a good joke. He once entered the conference room and stopped an editorial discussion. "I need to tell you something important," he said with a serious face, "it's like this: Plagiarism is when you steal from one person. If you steal from many, it's called research!"

When employees remained in the office after hours, a routine occurrence in the early years during those frantic final days before a deadline, he would order a lavish supper for the office. Once, he overheard an editor making the order from a local eatery: Reb Meir took the phone from the gentleman and changed it, adding several other dishes and doubling the amount of food.

"I may have lost weight," he quipped, "but I still know how to order like I used to."

And just as he demanded dedication, so did he find ways to show dedication.

He called in a woman editor one day and asked, "What size shirt does your husband wear? I found these really nice shirts, they don't crease, and I think he'll appreciate them as well."

She understood that he wanted to give her a gift, something more personal than money, but wouldn't cross the lines of *tzniyus* — so he conveyed his appreciation by buying a gift for her husband.

One of the employees looked worried one day. "What's wrong?" asked Rabbi Zlotowitz. The young man replied that his car was in the shop, and the mechanic had informed him that it needed a new transmission, which didn't come cheap.

Reb Meir pulled out his wallet. "We'll go fifty/fifty," he said, handing over several bills.

Rabbi Berel Wein at an ArtScroll Retreat

When Rabbi Berel Wein initially became friendly with Reb Meir, Rabbi Wein had already led a flourishing congregation and a successful yeshivah, and he had worked as an attorney; he was also a sought-after public speaker and a published writer. Yet, Rabbi Wein recalls, he still found himself learning new things from Rabbi Zlotowitz.

Rabbi Wein's first ArtScroll work was a Jewish history series. He submitted the first book in longhand, on legal-size lined paper, in 1982. When it came time for the second book, Rabbi Zlotowitz gave him advice along with an expensive gift.

A brand-new computer was delivered to Rabbi Wein's Monsey home, and it came along with a tutorial — given by Reb Meir, who taught the rabbi how to use the word processing program.

Reb Meir joked that there were only two keys that Rabbi Wein had to master — one was delete, and the other was save. "Use them regularly and wisely," Reb Meir said.

Reb Meir understood that after working long hours in a high-pressure environment, some of the staff might arrive home feeling emotionally drained. Late one night, Chananya Kramer was getting ready to leave ArtScroll headquarters, after having spent many laborious hours working on the Mishkan DVD and computer program. Reb Meir, at the end of a long day, insisted on driving the talented producer to the train station in New Jersey, adding two hours to his own day: in the car, they chatted and laughed before bidding each other good night at the train station. On the way home, Chananya realized what Rabbi Zlotowitz had done — he had wanted to ensure that the Baltimore native would relax on the train back home, that he would allow the pressures of the long day to slip away and arrive home in a positive state of mind. So Reb Meir had driven him to the train station and made the experience as pleasant as possible.

Reb Meir didn't just tell his staff that they were extraordinary: he made sure they knew he believed it. The ArtScroll Retreat, a Shabbos getaway for donors and staff, was a special event. Reb Meir was intricately involved with every detail of the planning and schedule and was very much the host at the event, greeting each and every guest like family.

At the retreat, one of the guests — a wealthy and influential

ArtScroll donor — was upset about some detail of the service and he turned on one of the ArtScroll staff members who had been involved in the planning, insulting her for the job she had done.

Without hesitating, Reb Meir — usually, the quintessential diplomat — turned to the donor, eyes flashing. "It's not okay to speak that way to our staff members: they are great at what they do and we appreciate them. I'll ask you to please speak with respect toward them."

And just as he respected them, so did he demand that they respect themselves. One of the senior employees mocked an ArtScroll project, feeling that the new undertaking didn't meet the standards of the company. Reb Meir was furious at the disloyalty, and he didn't speak with the staffer for several days, conveying his disappointment and hurt.

Finally, he approached the employee and said, "You know that I love you and that this was hard for me, but I had to do what I had to do."

He once grew upset with an employee, and publicly voiced his displeasure. Later that day, with most of the staff gathered

together for Minchah in the on-site *beis medrash*, Reb Meir banged on the *bimah*. The room grew silent. "I got upset earlier and caused our friend public humiliation," he said, "and I'd like to publicly ask *mechilah*. I was wrong."

Reb Meir noticed a staffer wearing wrinkled cotton pants to work one day. "Remember where you work and what you represent," he said, "and please dress accordingly."

He was even able to dismiss employees with respect. When it was necessary to let a worker go, he would comment, "Some things you gotta do by yourself." He called in one young man for a meeting and looked him in the eye. "Look," Reb Meir said, "you have tremendous abilities and I have no doubt that you'll be successful somewhere else, but not here. And because I believe in you, I'm going to keep paying your health insurance and lend you seed money so that you can do something different."

Reb Meir once called in a successful *mechanech* and asked him how much money he made: he wanted to know how much *menahelim* and rebbeim were being paid and how often they got raises, on what sort of scale. Reb Meir apologized for asking personal questions, but explained that he needed to understand the market in order to ensure that the *talmidei chachamim* in his employ were being paid full market value.

With Rabbi Eli Herzka

A young writer, the wife of a *mechanech*, released a new book in late winter. The book sold well, but general company policy is that authors' royalties are paid semi-annually, which meant she would receive the money half a year later.

She wanted to know if she could collect her royalties earlier, since Pesach — with its daunting expenses — was fast approaching. She was too intimidated to ask Rabbi Zlotowitz, but people who knew him well assured her that he would be receptive to her request.

She sent a carefully worded email wondering if it would be possible to have a partial advance on the royalty check: his response was immediate and gracious, an assurance that he would take care of it. She assumed that a check would arrive at some point, and was amazed to see a UPS truck pull up in front of her house the next morning. The driver came bearing an envelope — a check from Reb Meir, and a personal note wishing her a good Yom Tov.

ArtScroll employees were often asked if they could help arrange for the donation of books or gift certificates for *tzedakah* campaigns: one of the salespeople was asked by her own mother-in-law if she could make the request from Rabbi Zlotowitz on behalf of a prominent *chessed* organization.

Reb Meir answered within minutes, seeing a chance not just to help a good cause, but to acknowledge a devoted member of the team. *The door is open. Tell me what you think is appropriate, and then let's go! Any shvigger of yours gets the attention she deserves!,* he wrote back.

He had several tense meetings with union representatives eager to unionize the workers at ArtScroll's bindery. After one heated exchange, Reb Meir looked the union leader in the eye and said, "Let me tell you a bit about myself. When we renovated this building, I insisted on air conditioning all along the production line and in the bindery, in the warehouse, and in the factory. The contractor told me it wasn't necessary, but I said it absolutely *was* necessary. I told him I couldn't sit comfortably in my office if the workers were sweating downstairs, so, with all due respect, sir, I appreciate your efforts, but our staff doesn't need a union leader to worry about them! I do that already!"

A young father and husband came home with a significant Yom Tov bonus: his grateful wife picked up the phone and called Rabbi Zlotowitz to thank him for allowing them to welcome Yom Tov with peace of mind.

Reb Meir was gracious with her, but the next morning, he called in the employee. "Don't ever let that happen again. That was money you earned and deserved, and there's no reason your wife should have to call to say thank you that way."

He was equally vigilant when it came to their spiritual comfort. Reb Meir insisted on building two separate kitchen areas at ArtScroll, so that both male and female employees could enjoy their coffee or lunch breaks without feeling uncomfortable. There were two microwave ovens, two toaster ovens, two coffee stations — so that all those involved in the *harbatzas Torah* could relax in an area that reflected their lofty calling.

It wasn't only the formal staff members whom he treated with respect.

Female employees would occasionally have to bring their own children in to work because school was closed, or if the child wasn't feeling well. Reb Meir would give these mothers a sense of pride, making sure they realized how much he appreciated the fact that their priorities were in order — and that their children, too, were part of the family.

One of the sales staff brought in her child and Reb Meir called the boy into his office. With a serious expression, Reb Meir offered him a job for the day. "I need someone good to seal envelopes," Reb Meir said, "and it's hard to find good workers. But you seem to have what it takes."

At the end of the day, Reb Meir handed the young man his salary for the day's work.

One of the senior editors was working long hours before Pesach and she relied on her teenage daughter to help run the house. "My daughter doesn't know why *I'm* the one getting the check," the woman commented, tongue in cheek, to Reb Meir.

When Yom Tov arrived, the mother received her own check and bonus — and another envelope arrived in the mail, a $300 check for the teenage girl who had helped out at home, courtesy of the grateful folks at ArtScroll.

A customer dealt with one of the ArtScroll sales staff and was deeply impressed with her courtesy and efficiency. He emailed Reb Meir directly to compliment the young woman.

Reb Meir forwarded the email to her manager, with a note of his own:

> *Dear Shaindy —*
>
> *I am happy and proud to share with you a beautiful email we received about you. Everyone recognizes your wonderful and courteous, efficient service. You can proudly add this email to the many accolades you've received over the years from people who appreciate your role-model efforts.*
>
> *Share this with your family. It's so well deserved. ArtScroll's image is enhanced because of you!*
>
> *Zei gebentched!*

In the final year of Reb Meir's life, the Mesorah Heritage Foundation was in financial difficulty, and it became painfully clear that it would be necessary to find ways to stretch the budget. Reb Meir sat down with one of the senior editors and calculated which writers were working more hours than absolutely necessary, and whose hourly wage could be cut. The editor, who had direct authority for those writers whose positions were in jeopardy, remembers two things from that difficult conversation. One is that Reb Meir took full responsibility for each decision, not trying to foist the unpleasant task of informing the writers onto anyone else. The second thing the editor noticed was that the thought of taking away *parnassah* from people was causing Reb Meir physical pain, the aggravation eating away at him during those difficult final months of his life.

It was as if, this editor reflected, Reb Meir's whole essence was being *meitiv*, giving; anything that worked against that nature was too hard for him to bear.

Reb Meir himself articulated it. When his son, Yisroel, established his own company, Reb Meir was very proud: the business was started at ArtScroll headquarters, under Reb Meir's watchful eye, and father and son had many conversations about how to proceed. "The best part of owning a successful business," Reb Meir told his son, "is the opportunity it gives to provide *parnassah*, a livelihood, to others."

7

THE MISSION

BUT EVEN AS ARTSCROLL ENTERED THE REALM OF *Torah Shebe'al Peh*, adding writers and editors, there were challenges.

"I remember being so tight on money that our drivers were hurrying around to pick up relatively small, post-dated checks from stores," a veteran ArtScroll staffer recalls. "There wasn't enough money coming in to cover payroll. Meir refused to compromise on quality or design, and of course the substance had to be perfect: we were in trouble."

In late spring of 1988, a reader sent a letter to ArtScroll offices. He expressed his profound gratitude for their having opened the world of sacred Jewish learning to speakers of the English language. He was moved to try to help them, he wrote.

A few weeks later, he received a letter saying that the rabbis would be happy to meet with him, and so it came to be that on an ordinary summer day, the tall, dignified gentleman came in to the ArtScroll offices at 1969 Coney Island Avenue; the open door would admit not just a visitor, but a new era along with him.

The gentleman asked to meet with the principals of the company, and was taken upstairs to meet with Reb Meir and Reb Nosson. He introduced himself as Professor Joel Fleishman, first senior Vice President of Duke University, and, in his soft Southern accent, he explained that he was an avid reader of ArtScroll's Torah publications, especially the ArtScroll Siddur and the first volume of *Bereishis* in the Chumash. The English translation of both the text and a broad spectrum of major commentators on the Chumash had never been available in English until that point; he had come in person to say thank you.

He complimented the quality and thoroughness of the books and, noting that college textbooks of similar quality sell for upward of $100, he asked how ArtScroll could produce such works at a moderate price. Reb Meir chuckled and answered, "With long hours and frequent borrowing."

Mr. Fleishman was surprised. "I've been at Yale and I'm now at Duke," he said. "You simply can't produce such literature without a not-for-profit foundation." This wasn't mere speculation; at the time, Mr. Fleishman was already a nationally renowned authority on foundations.

Not content to merely offer good advice, Mr. Fleishman offered to set up an IRS-approved foundation on ArtScroll's behalf. Reb Meir and Reb Nosson listened, and asked for time to consider his gracious offer.

A few weeks later, they came back with an answer. They would be grateful for his help.

He enlisted the assistance of Donald Etheridge, Duke's Director of Planned Giving, and, pro bono, they created the Mesorah Heritage Foundation and submitted the constitutive documents creating the Foundation along with the proposed by-laws to the Internal Revenue Service.

With Mr. Joel Fleishman and Reb Gedaliah

Being a perfectionist, Mr. Fleishman had Mr. Etheridge make sure that the new entity would strictly adhere to IRS guidelines and the laws of the State of New York, in particular to assure that the legally required arms-length relationship between the not-for-profit Mesorah Heritage Foundation and the for-profit ArtScroll Publications Inc. was meticulously maintained.[1]

His assessment that, "You can't produce such literature without a not-for-profit foundation," was accurate. Without his idea, it would have been impossible to fund the intense scholarship necessary to produce ArtScroll's edition of the Talmud, Mishnah, Midrash, and the many other works that so enhance Jewish life.

In later years, Reb Meir would often remark that Joel Fleishman had been a seminal figure in ArtScroll's history, not only

---

1. Specifically, the Foundation funds the scholarship and preparation of the manuscripts, providing a service to the Jewish community by keeping the books affordable. Then ArtScroll/Mesorah undertakes the responsibility and expense of publishing and distribution.

because of the idea he pitched, but because of the inherent confidence he expressed in the product.

Joel Fleishman didn't step back after providing this valuable favor. Until today, he serves as the hands-on chairman of the Board of Trustees, and is personally involved in the semi-annual review and oversight of the Foundation's activities.

For Reb Meir, making payroll each month meant reaching out to one of the generous Jews in his rolodex for a loan to keep the publishing house afloat. Now, with the establishment of the Mesorah Heritage Foundation, Reb Meir was finally able to focus on the dreams that had remained hidden for so long.

The staff had long since outgrown the company's offices, and even with many writers and editors working off-site, space was inadequate.

In conversation with his longtime attorney and confidant, Judah Septimus, Reb Meir mentioned that it was getting cramped. He wanted to buy a single building to house the bindery, warehouse, and editorial offices.

With Judah Septimus

The lawyer knew of just the place, a site near the Brooklyn waterfront. It was out of the traditional neighborhood, but it was just a short drive away — and it was available for a fair price; but ArtScroll had no funds available for the purchase.

Reb Nosson reached out to the Tisch family, with whom he had been studying Torah for years, for a loan. Larry Tisch put up the funds — nearly a million dollars — without asking for a single signature or document. He and his sons trusted Reb Meir and Reb Nosson implicitly, and within weeks, the property on Second Avenue was being outfitted to create history.

James Tisch speaking at a Mesorah Heritage Foundation Dinner
Seated (L to R): Stanley Wasserman, Reb Nosson Scherman, Reb Meir,
Jay Schottenstein, Joey Schottenstein, Jonathan Schottenstein,
and Jeffrey Schottenstein

Reb Meir's close friend, Nochum Silberman, was the architect, and he worked hard to incorporate each of Reb Meir's ideas. Reb Meir didn't just want the *talmidei chachamim* on staff to have offices; he envisioned a space where they would join together and speak in learning, as if in a real *kollel*. He wanted the workers along the production line, in the warehouse and shipping department, to be comfortable and warm.

In June of 1989, the ArtScroll staff moved into the beautiful, spacious new building, the Divine Hand providing them with the space they would need for the project perched just around the corner.

As a teenager, Meir Zlotowitz had told his friends that one day, he hoped to translate *Shas* into English.

The need for a translation was, in Reb Meir's opinion, obvious: not just because of the steadily increasing stream of *ba'alei teshuvah*, but also because the *Daf Yomi* framework had gathered many more adherents — including yeshivah graduates

With Rav Ahron Schechter

— who spoke English as a first language. There were hardworking men who longed to rediscover the joy in learning Torah they had experienced in yeshivah, and fathers who found it too difficult to learn with their children.

Before formally launching the project, the editors prepared a sample of what they envisioned and showed it to various roshei yeshivah. It was Rav Ahron Schechter who offered the precise terminology. "You can't 'translate' the Gemara," the rosh yeshivah of Yeshivas Rabbeinu Chaim Berlin remarked, "but you *can* elucidate it!"

Rav Gifter, ArtScroll's mentor since its inception, was confident that they were up to the task, and, as Rav Yaakov Kamenetsky had passed away, his son, Rav Shmuel, offered his blessings and encouragement.

The final seal of approval would have to come from Eretz Yisrael, heart of the Torah world: Rav Shlomo Zalman Auerbach gave his warm *berachos* and then Reb Meir and Reb Nosson traveled to meet with Rav Yosef Sholom Elyashiv in Meah Shearim.

With Rav Shmuel Kamenetsky

Rav Yosef Efrati, close *talmid* and confidante of Rav Elyashiv, reflects on what happened next.

"It was," he states, "completely unnatural, almost a miracle. It's clear that there was a Divine plan being carried out."

For the better part of eighty years, Rav Elyashiv had been closeted in the world of Torah and halachic *psak*, rarely venturing forth to take positions on communal issues.

"I feel like in *shamayim*, they were deliberating if the time was right for the ArtScroll *Shas*, and they looked to the *posek* of the generation to judge," Rav Efrati remarks.

Rav Elyashiv met with Reb Meir and Reb Nosson, hearing their vision for the Gemara, but Rav Elyashiv was looking past their professional vision and studying something else.

"The rebbi," says Rav Efrati, "was worried that someone would undertake to translate the *Shas* with less than pure

With Rav Elyashiv

intentions, with an agenda other than *ahavas Torah* and reverence for the Mesorah. He felt that Reb Meir Zlotowitz and Reb Nosson Scherman were *ehrlich*, sincere, and upright."

Along with asking several questions about the availability of other English language translations, Rav Elyashiv wanted to know about those people who would be involved with the actual writing; he wanted to ensure that everyone involved appreciated the *kedushah* of each word of Torah.

Rav Elyashiv gave his *berachah* and offered to remain involved should they have any questions.

"I can think of no other example of the rebbi offering support in such a fashion," says Rav Efrati. "It was unprecedented."

Rav Elyashiv did not read English, but he would keep English volumes displayed in his study as silent but eloquent testimony to his endorsement.

With the backing of these *gedolei hador*, the ArtScroll *Shas* project was underway. By that point, Reb Meir and Reb Nosson knew that to do it right, they would need to assemble an elite group of brilliant, talented, knowledgeable *talmidei chachamim* who would not only be proficient in English, but also blessed with the ability to "teach," to clearly explain each word and concept in the Gemara — what Reb Meir would come to call one of the finest *kollelim* on earth.

The project was launched with *Maseches Makkos* — sponsored by Mr. Marcos Katz of Mexico City — with the reasoning that the first *masechta* would also be the sample, the prototype by which others judged them. It needed to be a *masechta* that was short enough to produce in a realistic amount of time, but also a *masechta* that contains yeshivah-style *lomdus*, which would allow the full scholarship and skill of the ArtScroll staff to shine.

After the enthusiastic response to *Makkos*, Reb Meir wanted to meet the demand presented by *lomdei Daf Yomi*, the army committed to learning one *daf* a day. There was a new cycle of *Shas* about to begin: it was too late to start with *Berachos*, and *Shabbos* would need more than one volume. He wasn't sure that the first volume of *Maseches Shabbos* would be ready on time, and while the second volume was doable, Reb Meir didn't want to start with part of a *masechta*, because he hadn't yet built up consumer confidence. In time, people would learn that they could rely on ArtScroll to finish the job, but they hadn't seen that yet and he wasn't sure that they would invest in a volume that was only one quarter of a *masechta*. The people were doubtful, wondering about this fledgling company and its goals — who knew if ArtScroll would even be in existence long enough to ever finish *Shas*?

Eruvin seemed to be the obvious choice. There was enough

time to produce both volumes before *Daf Yomi* learners started the *masechta*, and Reb Meir also understood that if his staff could do *Eruvin* — an extremely complex *masechta* — properly and accurately, then the readership would know that no *masechta* was beyond the capabilities of the ArtScroll team.

In fact, the project was far more difficult than anyone imagined. During that final month before the deadline, the entire staff — writers, editors, typists, and typesetters — came in every Motza'ei Shabbos and worked for many hours to get the *masechta* out in time.

Editors recall clocking eighty hours a week during those final days, working from Motza'ei Shabbos until Erev Shabbos — and Reb Meir was there every moment that his staff was there.

Rav Hersh Goldwurm would sleep for a few of the overnight hours on the couch in Reb Meir's office so that he could recite *Birchos HaTorah* for the others upon arising.

"In retrospect," says Rabbi Yechezkel Danziger, one of the chief editors of the *Shas*, "releasing *Eruvin* was the best thing we could have done. Traditionally, a new *Daf Yomi* cycle sparked a new interest in joining. Almost everyone who joined could make it through *Berachos*. *Shabbos* was a bit harder and as many as 25 percent of new recruits dropped out by the end of the *masechta*. Then came *Eruvin*, which was simply too much for most people, and by the end of *Eruvin*, few new recruits would still be doing *Daf Yomi*. The Schottenstein Edition changed that dynamic. For the first time, most of the people who started *Eruvin* were able to

With Rabbi Yechezkel Danziger

finish it. *Daf Yomi* began to blossom — and so did our English Gemara. It was a mutually beneficial relationship."

After *Eruvin*, the goal was to continue to work with the *Daf Yomi* cycle, but in order to continue, Reb Meir realized that he needed more than individual sponsors for each *masechta*.

He sought a name grant — a single sponsor to dedicate the entire *Shas* project. A mutual friend arranged a meeting with one of the most prominent Jewish philanthropists; the potential donor heard the concept and seemed very intrigued by the prospect of perpetuating his family name in such a meaningful way.

A historic deal seemed imminent, but at the very last minute, the donor backed out, because his advisers had persuaded him that it was a "black-hat project" that would go nowhere and not have the impact on the Jewish future the publishers were envisioning.

Reb Meir was uncharacteristically disheartened. He shared his disappointment with Rav Dovid Feinstein. "*Nu*," the rosh yeshivah remarked, "he didn't have the *zechus*. Someone else will."[2]

Someone else did.

The seeds of the partnership that would change the Jewish world had been planted generations earlier.

Yehoshua Schottenstein had immigrated to the United States from Pilviskai (Pilveshok), Lithuania, a suburb of Kovno — a city where reverence for *talmidei chachamim* and the Torah they learned ran deep. He arrived in 1901, but refused to bring his wife and children to the new world until he was confident that he could raise them as committed Jews.

The Lithuanian immigrant peddled his goods from a horse-drawn wagon and was known to be fair and honest, a devout man who wouldn't work on Shabbos. The values and principles he lived by would guide him, his children, and their children.

---

2. As Rav Moshe had once remarked to Reb Meir, "Every project will get done — the only question is who will have the merit."

His son and daughter-in-law, Ephraim and Anna, would open the first Schottenstein store: that store and every subsequent store bearing the Schottenstein name would remain closed on Shabbos, reflecting the conviction of the founders.

Ephraim and Anna transmitted their ideals and beliefs to their children, four sons and a daughter. Respected as they were in the local synagogue, when they felt the spiritual climate in the synagogue was changing, a new shul was established within the walls of their home.

Their youngest son, Jerome — Yaakov Meir HaKohen — was sent as a young child to learn in New York's Yeshivah and Mesivta Rabbeinu Chaim Berlin, and later to Yeshivah University High School. The Torah educators in Columbus recognized that he had the potential to be a rabbi, so they took the unique step of sending him to New York. He succeeded in his learning, but the commercial streak of his parents and grandparents ran deep, and he was drawn to business.

Jerome, with his sharp mind and keen memory, remained infused with the spirit of the yeshivah and retained a lifelong love of learning. Along with his brothers, he expanded the family business and, together, they built a retail empire in the American Midwest.

In 1953, he married Geraldine Hurwitz and together, they raised a family with the very same values of *tzedakah* and kindness they had seen in their homes. Their children, Jay, Ann, Susan, and Lori, absorbed the message, and the family became known for widespread philanthropic contributions and involvement in education and Torah learning.

Reb Meir first heard about the Schottenstein family from his friend Rabbi Raphael Butler. During Rabbi Butler's tenure as executive vice-president of the Orthodox Union, he had worked on several projects along with ArtScroll, producing published works for use in NCSY (National Council of Synagogue Youth) programs. The Schottenstein family had sponsored several

(L to R) Jerome Schottenstein with Rav Reuven Feinstein and Rav Dovid Feinstein

adult learning initiatives, and Rabbi Butler thought they might be interested in underwriting a volume in this new English translation of *Shas*. At that point, Rabbi Alan J. Ciner, rabbi of Columbus's Agudath Achim congregation and the family's rabbi, mentor, and close friend, shepherded the relationship along. He felt that both sides — ArtScroll and the Schottenstein family — would benefit, and with his encouragement, Jerome Schottenstein spoke with Reb Meir and Reb Nosson. With the support of his wife, Geraldine, and his children, Jerome under-took the publication of the first volume of *Maseches Eruvin*. A few weeks later, he undertook to sponsor *Eruvin* II, paying for both upfront even though the first volume hadn't yet been completed.

Then Jerome Schottenstein became ill. A painful period fol-lowed, but during those difficult days of his illness, he derived comfort from holding the newly printed *Eruvin* Gemaros in his hand, his joy in the incredible merit he had been given easing the pain. As his condition worsened, a visiting rabbi made a

With Jerome Schottenstein at a Mesorah Heritage Foundation Dinner

suggestion. "You give so much *tzedakah*, to so many different people," he told his ailing host. "A person is allowed to make deals with G-d, so why not promise money in exchange for your being healed?"

Jerome Schottenstein looked at the rabbi. "I was raised in a home where you don't negotiate with Hashem. All that Hashem does is for the good. Whatever He chooses I accept."

Simultaneously, the sponsorship of the entire *Shas* project was available: there was a family interested in undertaking it, but Reb Meir felt drawn to offer it to the Schottenstein family.

On a spring day in 1991, Reb Meir and Reb Nosson flew to Ohio. First, they stopped in Wickliffe, where they visited Rav Gifter and received his blessings, and then continued on to Columbus for their meeting.

In Jerome Schottenstein's study, Reb Meir and Reb Nosson sat with the ailing host and his son, Jay. Appropriately, Rabbi

Ciner was there as well, watching as history was being made.

"I told him that Torah is the thread that binds all Jews together, but in truth, neither Jerome nor Jay needed prodding," recalls Rabbi Ciner of that fateful meeting.

"There is no greater honor for a Jew than to have his name associated with the Torah," Jay remarked to his father after Reb Meir made his offer. It didn't take a full day for the answer to come: on a spring morning in 1991, the agreement was reached.

The *Shas* project had a name: the Schottenstein name would find its way onto the shelves of shuls and yeshivos in every corner of the globe, onto the desks of those charged with teaching Torah to future generations, into homes where the word of the Living G-d is cherished and welcomed. At a festive dinner celebrating the partnership, the guest speaker, Lord Immanuel Jakobovits, Chief Rabbi of the British Commonwealth, would call the *Shas* project "One of the most momentous publishing

Meir presenting an award to Jerome and Geraldine Schottenstein at a Mesorah Heritage Foundation Dinner, with Joel Fleishman and James Tisch looking on

efforts gracing the entire length of Jewish history."

Mr. Jerome Schottenstein would live to see the dream as it started to unfold, and he had full confidence in the men he had charged with realizing its fulfillment. In the winter of 1992, on 5 *Adar Beis*, he passed away.

Rav Dovid Feinstein and Jay Schottenstein

Six weeks later, his only son, Jay, met with Reb Meir and Reb Nosson in lower Manhattan. The young Mr. Schottenstein already knew of the *Shas's* early impact, since people from all across the country had sent thank-you letters to Jerome Schottenstein, expressing their gratitude for allowing them into the world of *limud haTorah*. Jay had seen how much the project had meant to his father, and he also felt completely comfortable with the two rabbis from Brooklyn.

He understood both the magnitude of the project and the blessing of being able to spread Torah on such an enormous scale. He and his wife Jeanie enthusiastically took upon themselves to fulfill the commitment made by his father.[3]

"We all agreed that my father's wish was that it endure. We all wanted the same thing. We moved forward," Jay recalls, as if it were a simple, self-evident decision.

Reb Meir would remember it differently. Over the years, he would often point out that Jay Schottenstein was just 37 years old at the time, uncertain about what the future held. Even

---

3. Eventually, they would further the vision by underwriting the Hebrew translation of *Shas*, the translations of Talmud Yerushalmi and *Sefer HaChinuch* (The Book of Mitzvos), as well as the Interlinear Series, and numerous other projects.

With Jay and Jeanie Schottenstein, and Rachel

though he was a successful businessman, the financial commitment was daunting — but with his wife Jeanie's support
and encouragement, Jay was determined to honor his father's
legacy and continue.

There were times when it was difficult. "The completed
Schottenstein *Shas* is such a work of art, so precise and attractive, that people imagine that all the pieces just fell into place,"
remarks Reb Gedaliah Zlotowitz, "but my father told me it wasn't
so. As hard as the staff worked on the literary and production
end, my father would say, their heroic efforts were matched
by Jay and Jeanie, for whom it wasn't always simple to meet
the commitment. Jay and Jeanie had to make decisions along
the way, but ultimately, their resolve, and the determination of
the team at ArtScroll, joined to create the *Shas*. Torah is built
through toil."

The relationship between the Schottenstein family and
ArtScroll would flourish, growing deeper with the release of
each new volume: Jay didn't just safeguard his father's legacy,

(L to R) Jeanie, Joey, Jay, Jeffrey, and Jonathan Schottenstein at a Mesorah Heritage Dinner celebrating the completion of the Schottenstein Talmud

he built upon it. He would become chairman of the Mesorah Heritage Foundation's International Board of Governors, and one of Reb Meir's closest friends. Reb Meir and Rachel would join Jay and Jeanie for Yom Tov *seudos* in Yerushalayim, and the families would share *simchos* and personal events for the next twenty-five years. Reb Meir took personal pride as Jay and Jeanie's children — Joey and Lindsay, Jonathan and Nicole, and Jeffrey — became, in their own right, generous, committed supporters of Torah causes, following the family tradition. Jay would become a sounding board, an adviser, a confidant, and an ambassador for ArtScroll: when the latest ArtScroll catalogues would be printed, Reb Meir would send Jeanie a note, asking her to "feel free to pick flowers from the garden we planted together."[4]

---

4. Jay and Jeanie Schottenstein, along with their children, continue to see themselves as the recipients in their relationship with Reb Meir, Reb Nosson, and the ArtScroll family, feeling honored at being part of the journey. "The loss of Reb Meir," reflects Mrs. Jeanie Schottenstein, "is immeasurable within our family, experienced as only the loss of a true friend and partner can be. His memory will always be for a blessing and future generations will know of the love and admiration our family felt toward him."

With Reb Gedaliah, Jeanie and Jay Schottenstein

Jay and Reb Meir would speak often over the years. There were times when Reb Meir would call his friend and say, "Jay, I just wanted to hear your voice."

The Schottenstein edition team committed themselves to finishing the entire *Shas* within two *Daf Yomi* cycles — a commitment that they met, keeping to the precise timetable Reb Meir had given Jerome Schottenstein fifteen years earlier.

The project accomplished more than just providing help to those who had never formally learned Gemara. "What the Gemaros did," reflects Chanoch Weisz, a donor and close friend of Reb Meir, "was help people like myself, who had learned seriously in yeshivah years earlier, rediscover the joy of a *blatt Gemara*. Suddenly, the door was open again: fathers were learning with their sons again, older people were finding time they didn't know they had to learn through the *daf* a second or third time."

The sense of mission consumed all those involved in the

(L to R) With Jeffrey Schottenstein, Senator Joe Lieberman, and Jay Schottenstein
at the presentation of the Schottenstein Talmud to the Library of Congress

project. Reb Nosson Scherman recalls writing text for *Maseches Makkos* and including a very nice *peshat* in the commentary section on the bottom of the page. Rav Hersh Goldwurm looked at him. "That's a very nice *shtickel Torah*, Reb Nosson," he said, "but we're not here to write *chiddushim*: our mission is to explain the Gemara clearly according to Rashi."

Reb Meir would refer to Rav Hersh Goldwurm — who molded ArtScroll's approach to elucidation — as a master of clarity. Reb Meir would remark that both of his own rebbeim — Rav Dovid Feinstein and Rav Dovid Cohen — have a common trait: brilliant as they are, they can explain an obscure concept with such clarity that a child can understand it. Reb Meir would often rely on their insight in guiding the *Shas* writers, confident that they knew which expressions would simplify the ideas and make them accessible.

Mrs. Judi Dick recalls sitting with the other female editors for hours while the *talmidei chachamim* carried on intense arguments among themselves and with their colleagues in Eretz Yisrael regarding the precise wording in English that would convey the Gemara's meaning. The Gemara couldn't close and go to print — and the editors couldn't sign off and go home — until *every* last word was perfect.

Reb Meir realized something else as well: There would be a generation that would look to the ArtScroll *Shas* as to a "rebbi" or trusted *chavrusa*, the translation and notes guiding them through one *sugya* after another. To allow these people to feel comfortable with the Gemara, the entire project would have to have a particular flow, a style that would become familiar. That meant investing in writers and editors learned and talented enough to clarify complex ideas and topics, but capable of working as part of a larger team.[5]

Reb Meir was determined not to compromise on the clarity of the actual font, the quality of the paper and binding, and the beauty of the actual book; he was equally resolute about keeping the Gemaros affordable. To do this, he had to find new sponsors for each volume and *Seder* in addition to the Schottenstein dedication.

---

5. In one of the many letters of appreciation sent to the Zlotowitz family after Reb Meir's passing, the writer reflects: It hit me recently, after going through so many volumes of the Hebrew edition of the Talmud, that the same voice has been speaking from those pages volume after volume, *masechta* after *masechta*, year after year. I know that these works are prepared by many different rabbanim and yet the same style, the same voice, comes through every time to help me. I can't get over how if I didn't know better, I would think all these volumes were written by one person. The editors at ArtScroll have given me an opportunity to "break my head once" to accustom myself to the style and language in my first volume of the Hebrew Talmud, and every volume thereafter is a continuation. They have given me a rebbi I can refer to at any time of the day or night, whom I can consistently understand no matter what *inyan* I need to delve into. And that's the reason for my email. I couldn't do this if the Artscroll "rebbi" didn't have that same familiar voice page after page. If a rush job had been done on this masterpiece and I felt the differences between one section and another, I may never have continued using the Hebrew Talmud as my aid, and a lot of doors (and self-confidence) may not have opened up to me. I assume the delivery of such a refined production/publication is the duty of the editor, Rabbi Zlotowitz *zt"l*, and although I don't remember ever meeting him, I wish I could thank him.

During those years, Reb Meir made some close, cherished friends who would remain part of his inner circle until his last day. Chanoch Weisz remembers Reb Meir's comment to potential donors. "It costs real money to sponsor a *sefer*, it's true, but in the long run, this will be one of the best investments of your life. You'll see."

With Rav Dovid Feinstein and Chanoch Weisz

"I'm not asking you for money," Reb Meir would often remind his donors. "I'm *offering* you an opportunity to give money."

One day, Reb Meir visited two wealthy partners and asked them to join in sponsoring a *masechta*. The two men discussed it, and one remarked, "Even if our partnership falls apart and we get into a fight, this is eternal and we will always have this *zechus*."

In time, the two men did have a dispute that escalated: a bitter fight ensued and the business was disbanded. The two men stopped speaking to each other and had no contact at all. Many years passed.

In the summer of 2017, Reb Meir passed away and thirty days later, a public *sheloshim* gathering was held in *Gvul Yaabetz*, the Flatbush shul of Rav Dovid Cohen. Both those partners happened to be there: after the *hespedim* were complete, one man approached the other.

"You were right about one thing," he said, "that *zechus* we still have. We lost so much, but the *masechta* is forever."

A certain philanthropist had asked Rav Yaakov Kamenetsky for advice. This donor wasn't sure whether to invest his *tzedakah* funds with a particular institution, or in an ArtScroll project. Rav Yaakov told him to learn through the introduction of the Or HaChaim HaKadosh to the commentary on Chumash, and he would find the answer. Sometime later, the donor came back to Rav Yaakov, genuinely perplexed; he had studied the entire introduction, and seen nothing that would answer his question.

Rav Yaakov showed the gentleman how, at the very end of the introduction, Rav Chaim ben Attar thanks four wealthy Jews who sponsored the publication of his *sefer*. "Those four Jews likely supported other holy causes as well," Rav Yaakov said, "but it's due to their support of this publication, the *Or HaChaim al HaTorah*, that the world is privileged to benefit from this *sefer* until today. Their names live on through the *sefer*."[6]

Reb Meir didn't have to wait to see the impact of the ArtScroll *Shas* project: in a relatively short time, the demand overwhelmed the staff at ArtScroll. Reb Meir understood that the new Gemara was more popular than he had ever dreamt, but he wouldn't allow himself to exult.

He knew that not everyone saw the translation of *Shas* as a positive development. There were great roshei yeshivah who were concerned that the English translation and commentary would make Gemara learning too easy and take away the *ameilus*, the toil necessary for success in learning.

And Reb Meir understood this as well.

One evening, he met Rav Yitzchak Kleiman, a rosh yeshivah and outstanding *talmid chacham*, in Rabbi Frankel's shul in Flatbush. The two men had been close friends as teenagers in Camp Munk, but Rav Yitzchak had gone on to lead a yeshivah in St. Louis and they had parted ways and lost contact over the years.

---

6. Interestingly, a generation later, Mr. Sam Friedland of Monsey wasn't sure whether to dedicate an ArtScroll volume or earmark the funds for another *tzedakah*. He asked his rav, who shared the question with Rav Shmuel Kamenetsky, son of Rav Yaakov. The Philadelphia rosh yeshivah asked for a day to think about it, then replied that the *sefer* dedication took precedence.

Reb Meir offered to drive the rosh yeshivah to his next appointment and Rav Kleiman explained that he wasn't yet sure where he was headed. Reb Meir said that it was fine, he would drive the rosh yeshivah to wherever his destination would be.

In Reb Meir's car, the two men enjoyed a pleasant conversation, reminiscing about old times and catching up. Then Reb Meir turned to look at his passenger. "Reb Yitzchak, I know that you speak *emes* and don't compromise when it comes to truth. It's what makes you an effective rebbi. I've heard that you speak about the ArtScroll Gemara and you criticize it, that you're passionate in your opposition to it and tell people not to use it."

The rosh yeshivah nodded. "It's true. I want people to use the authentic Gemara, without a translation."

Reb Meir spoke softly. "I understand and I respect that. I only want to ask you one favor. When you speak against me, also remember that we were once such close friends."

It was quiet in the car: the rosh yeshivah contemplated Reb Meir's sincere request, a plea that the ideological difference not erase a shared personal bond.

He smiled broadly, and the two men embraced before Rav Yitzchak stepped out of the car, on to his next appointment.

The years passed. Rav Yitzchak Kleiman was *niftar* at the relatively young age of 71, leaving his family and devoted *talmidim* heartbroken.

A few months after the rosh yeshivah's passing, Reb Meir came into the *vort* of his granddaughter Shoshana Zlotowitz. The

(L to R) Baruch Ber, Rav Yitzchak, and Yechiel Kleiman

proud grandfather was visibly emotional as he approached the chassan, Yechiel Kleiman.

"Let me tell you about the last time I saw your grandfather," Reb Meir said, sharing the story of his conversation with an old friend and how they had parted in love.

And now, they had been reunited — not just friends, but family.

Rather than become haughty, the success of the Shas made Reb Meir more humble. He would often repeat his maxim that "Hakadosh Baruch Hu knows what He wants done in His world and He allows man to do it. If a person chooses not to accept the shelichus, Hashem can always find someone else." Reb Meir's attitude was that he was blessed to have been chosen and he wasn't about to relinquish that shelichus, to relax or take it easy.

Along with authoring several ArtScroll sefarim, Rav Eliezer Ginsburg, rosh kollel of the Mirrer Yeshivah in Brooklyn and rav of Agudas Yisroel Snif Zichron Shmuel of Flatbush, had an extremely close relationship with Reb Meir.

"There were some talmidei chachamim who did not support ArtScroll, and Reb Meir knew this," the rav reflects, "but I noticed something very unique. When Reb Meir would speak about these gedolei Torah, it was with tremendous reverence and respect, he never took their opposition personally. Most people would be hurt, but he wasn't, because he truly didn't see himself as anything more than a shaliach. Hakadosh Baruch Hu had given him a task and he would work to accomplish it — but it wasn't about him, and so he was able to feel real humility and reverence toward these talmidei chachamim."

Sometimes, there were signs of Divine grace, moments in which Reb Meir felt he was being encouraged by Heaven, shown that he was on the proper path.

In his written memoirs, Mr. Benny Fishoff — a dear friend and role model to Reb Meir — shares a story:

With Benny Fishoff

During the difficult winter of 1940, when I was separated from my beloved family, I received painful news from home. My beautiful, sweet younger brother, Yaakov Yitzchok, had passed away. I got the news on Chol HaMoed Pesach that he had been niftar on the 25th of Adar II, and I wasn't sure how to proceed in regard to shivah.

I was in Vilna, so I went to ask the gadol hador, Rav Chaim Ozer Grodzensky, who directed me to sit the seven days of shivah beginning right after Pesach. In time, the rest of my family would join little Yaakov Yitzchok in the Heavenly yeshivah; without knowing their yahrzeits, I marked their passing on this date, 25 Adar Beis.

It was the one date I could hold onto, to allow the emotions I kept in check all year to flow free, offering a resounding Kaddish — Yisgadal v'yiskadash Shemei rabba — for my beloved parents and siblings.

In 1982, I finally returned to Poland, to my birthplace of Wloszczowa, hoping to find a clue, some scrap that had endured and could connect me to my family. There was an old woman ready to talk, and I asked her if any Jews had remained. After I bribed her with a package of cigarettes, she led me to an old Jew named Benslovitch.

The elderly local looked at me suspiciously, his eyes darting in every direction, then motioned that I should follow him home.

He lived with his non-Jewish wife in a decrepit apartment, and when we were inside, I told him my name.

"Fishoff," he repeated, wide-eyed, "you look just like your father!"

He started to shout, "Yom Kippur, Yom Kippur, that's the yahrzeit."

He explained that the Germans had invaded tiny Wloszczowa — where my parents had been hiding out — and they had sent all the Jews to Treblinka. Only Benslovitch and his brother had managed to survive and be spared the same fate as the bulk of Polish Jewry.

"The Yidden were all captured and sent away on Yom Kippur night. They arrived in Treblinka, and they were led straight to the ovens, all of them killed that morning. That's the yahrzeit."

It was chilling testimony, but also valued information about my parents and family and their yahrzeit.

When I returned to New York, I shared the account with Rav Moshe Feinstein, and I asked when would be the appropriate time to keep my family's yahrzeit. Should I commemorate it on Yom Kippur instead of in Adar?

Rav Moshe thought for a while, and then asked me if Benslovitch was someone who could be trusted. "Is he shomer Shabbos?"

I recalled the symbols I'd seen in Benslovitch's home, indications that his connection with Yiddishkeit was weak, and I sighed. "I don't know," I finally said.

Rav Moshe instructed me to continue to mark the yahrzeit on 25 Adar II, as I had been doing for so many years, but he added that "it won't hurt to say a Kaddish on Yom Kippur as well."

Confident in the rosh yeshivah's psak, I left.

I didn't need reassurance that Rav Moshe's ruling was correct, but I took tremendous comfort in a Divine message.

My dear friend, Rabbi Meir Zlotowitz, the visionary behind ArtScroll, called me with a unique offer. He and his colleague, Rabbi Nosson Scherman, were overseeing the translation of Shas into English, sparking a genuine revolution. Through making the words of Gemara available to the masses, they were bringing Rav Meir Shapiro's dream of Klal Yisrael united through the daily daf so much closer to reality.

Rabbi Zlotowitz was kind enough to allow me to sponsor one of those masechtos, and I seized the opportunity: Hashgachah dictated that the next available masechta was Kesubos.

When the legions of lomdei Daf Yomi reached Kesubos 2, they opened the newly released Schottenstein edition, dedicated in memory of my parents and family, whose names were inscribed for eternity inside the handsome cover.

The date of that new beginning? The 25th of Adar II: yahrzeit of my beloved family, the one day in the year upon which I formally remembered their holy neshamos...

The Torah lives on...

Reb Meir reveled in that story and the message inherent in it. The nation was rediscovering the Torah it had lost fifty years earlier, and he was fortunate enough to be part of that renaissance.

One cold winter day, a close friend and donor, Joe Weiss, tried to persuade Reb Meir to take a short break. "We have a beautiful apartment in Florida, and it's empty now, just waiting for you to come down," he said.

This was during a period when Reb Meir was under tremendous fund-raising stress and he was in physical pain as well. Reb Meir admitted that he was tempted to accept the offer — but still wouldn't go. "Joe, I have a mission," he said. "There's no such thing as vacation when you're on a mission!"

"What was amazing," reflects Reb Meir's childhood friend Rabbi Burton Jaffa, "is that we saw a whole new side to him. I knew him for most of his life, and we'd never seen that sort of drive or ambition when it came to selling wedding invitations. Sure, he worked hard, but it wasn't the same. Once he started with the *Shas*, he was relentless, the most single-minded, motivated salesman I knew. It was as if he had discovered his destiny and he took his natural passion to the next level."

When a writer approached him with a proposal to publish a translation of a *sefer* that was already being worked on by

With Rabbi Burton Jaffa

another publishing house, Reb Meir was surprised. "We're on a mission to provide Klal Yisrael with access to classic *sefarim;* if they can get this from other publishers, and it's not a project that we can do better, then it's not what we're meant to do," he said.

A talented fiction writer had worked hard on the draft of a novel in which the protagonist was a young girl who had questions in *emunah.* The plotline saw her leaving the Orthodox framework before finding answers and coming back. The ArtScroll editor working on the book was worried that readers might identify with the questions, the doubts in *emunah,* and be negatively affected before reaching the conclusion.

She shared her reservations with Reb Meir, who immediately informed the writer that he couldn't publish the manuscript. The writer argued that the opposite was true: readers would be swept in and their *emunah* strengthened by the strong, joyous ending.

"Perhaps most readers will," Reb Meir said, "but if even one reader stops before the ending and their *emunah* is weakened as a result, then we'll have strayed from our mission."

Eventually, the ArtScroll brand would expand to include children's titles and even cookbooks. To Reb Meir, every facet of Jewish life was holy and relevant, and if he could provide titles that would elevate the process, then that too was part of the mission.

A new ArtScroll children's work became very popular in schools. Reb Meir saw its success as an obligation. "You know how kids treat their books, and how all school textbooks look after a few years?" he asked his staff. "We've got to change that. We need to make sure that the binding is so well-made that the books will remain fresh and new, because no child enjoys learning from a tattered book. No child is excited to read a book that is missing its cover."

"And," he reminded them, "make sure the font is large, because children like big letters."

It was all part of the mission.

And sometimes the clarity of what was the right thing to do came at great cost.

The first edition of the Succos *machzor* contained several errors. Reb Meir made the decision to do something that was virtually unheard of in the industry: he paid for ads in all the major newspapers announcing a recall. Anyone who had purchased a *machzor* could send it in and exchange it for a new one; and then, he had the flawed *machzorim* buried so that they would never surface again.

Another time, ArtScroll had invested money in a translation of Rav Chaim Volozhiner's *Nefesh HaChaim*. A respected rosh yeshivah called Reb Meir and discouraged him. "There are parts of that *sefer* that are real Kabbalah, the secrets of Torah, and not suitable for translation. Even if you get the words right, you cannot convey the spirit of that *sefer* in English."

Reb Meir countered that there was another publishing house working on the same *sefer*, and he feared that their version might be *hashkafically* flawed; as such, he felt it was his duty to offer an authentic translation.

"No," the rosh yeshivah told him, "your job isn't to provide alternatives. It's to translate those works that should be accessible to everyone."

Reb Meir thanked him for setting him straight. He immediately accepted the directive and cancelled the publication of *Nefesh HaChaim*, once again at significant financial loss.

In his *Mishpacha* magazine tribute to Reb Meir, one of ArtScroll's prolific biographers, Rabbi Yehuda Heimowitz, wrote:

> *Throughout the production of "Rav Nosson Tzvi Finkel"*
> *and the subsequent books, "Rav Elyashiv" and "Maran*
> *Harav Ovadia," Rabbi Zlotowitz personally led each*

conference call in which he and his team would share their feedback and discuss their concerns on every page of the manuscript.

These sessions were highly stimulating and challenging, as he would put the stories to the ultimate ArtScroll test: Would they serve to inspire readers to greater spiritual heights? He was unapologetic about what others derisively described as ArtScroll hagiographies, where only the good was presented. He would repeatedly remind me that ArtScroll never mentions any machlokes or other unnecessary derogatory details surrounding a gadol's court, because the audience does not grow from it. "We're aiming to inspire," was his unshakable approach to these works.

Menachem Butler, a son of Reb Meir's dear friend, Rabbi Raphael Butler, was himself close with Reb Meir. He once told Reb Meir about a colleague of his who was working on a biography of Reb Ahron Lichtenstein, rosh yeshivah of Har Etzion: the writer had found the ArtScroll biographies to be very well done and worth emulating.

Reb Meir thanked Menachem for the compliment, and added a request. *Please make sure to urge him to stress the human aspect, not just the academic aspect of Reb Ahron. He was a great, warm man, and when someone puts down the book he should be inspired to try to emulate that aspect of Reb Ahron in his daily life.*

There are sections in Reb Yonasan Rosenblum's biography of Rabbi Moshe Sherer that are heavy on public policy detail, accounts of various diplomatic campaigns and missions conducted by the Agudath Israel leader. One of the editors pointed out that including these accounts, which are somewhat heavy and complex, wouldn't add to the book's appeal or increase sales, but Reb Meir insisted that they remain. He felt that the book would be a handbook to *askanim* and activists for decades to come, and that there was an obligation to future leaders to provide them with as much context as possible.

Reb Meir once interviewed an illustrator who hoped to work with ArtScroll, and Reb Meir shared an insight. "I used to think that being an illustrator was about talent," he said, "but then I realized that it's also about *seichel*, intelligence. An illustrator has to feel whatever it is they're drawing if they hope to be successful."

He told the young woman he was meeting that he had once had an illustrator draw a Yom Tov table scene. The picture had been perfect, except for one detail: the participants at the *seudah* all appeared morose. Their mouths were turned up, as if in a smile, but they didn't look happy.

"And I realized," Reb Meir concluded, "that the illustrator was going through a difficult period in his life and was feeling unhappy, so that came through in his pictures."

As precise as he was with each word, Reb Meir had a very clear sense of what was — and what was not — important to the cause. A writer had a question about transliterating a certain word in a biography: Reb Meir responded, and the writer came back with another question on the same topic.

Reb Meir responded by email, sharing his own approach to the sensitive and important work of writing about a *gadol*.

> I think that you should proceed on the derech you are describing, but constantly remember one thing: this is not a document, a peirush al haTorah, or the passing on of a dikduk mesorah. It's not a methodology of transmitting Torah that will be scrutinized 500 years from now like some of our other classic works.
>
> Let's move forward. The further back-and-forth on this is not necessary. You have the keilim and the wise experience to do it properly. Be guided by your refined seichel, and by the admonition of the Chovos HaLevavos:

"Min hazehirus SHELO l'hizaher YOSER midei."[7]
Have a wonderful day.

The sense of mission that drove him led him to develop a unique perspective regarding who could sponsor ArtScroll projects.

"He genuinely believed that we were fortunate to be part of the *harbatzas Torah*," recalls a donor, "and that we had to be worthy of the *zechus*."

A donor once called Reb Meir after committing a considerable amount of money. He'd reconsidered, he said, and he wanted to back out. "Fine, then you've lost the *zechus*. That's your loss, not mine, because someone else will have it," Reb Meir said.

At the same time, another young man whom Reb Meir was close to had to back out on a commitment after experiencing a financial setback. He felt very badly about it, but simply could not imagine having the money to make good on his pledge. "No," Reb Meir told him, "you'll keep with it, and you'll pay us when you can. The *zechus* is tremendous and, as someone who appreciates you and knows your true worth, I feel like you deserve to be part of this. We're patient, but we want you as part of this."

Tobias Lefkowitz was inspired to dedicate a volume of *Shas* in memory of his mother, and he called ArtScroll's office to inquire about the possibility. He spoke with Reb Meir, who was non-committal.

The next morning, the Woodmere resident was stopped by his own rav on the way out of shul. "I got a call about you yesterday," Rabbi Heshy Billet told his congregant. "Rabbi Meir Zlotowitz called me for 'information.' "

With obvious admiration, the rabbi related that Rabbi Zlotowitz had wanted to ensure that the potential donor was someone

7. Part of being scrupulous is not to be more scrupulous than necessary.

whom ArtScroll could take pride in partnering with, that he was honest and upright in business. Only then would Reb Meir consider accepting his funds.

A well-known businessman went through an embarrassing personal situation, and his reputation was negatively affected. A few months later, he called Reb Meir and offered to sponsor a major project. Reb Meir turned him down.

One of the ArtScroll staff members was surprised and asked Reb Meir why he had rejected the offer.

"He's a fine person," Reb Meir explained, "but he doesn't want to give money because he believes in what we're doing and wants to share in the *zechus*, but because he wants to cleanse his own name. That's not what we're about."

Adam Sokol recalls what led him to become an ArtScroll sponsor. A dynamic businessman, he worked with various Jew-

With Adam Sokol

ish magnates, but there was one who seemed to exude a certain nobility. "I would look at Jay Schottenstein and wonder what it was, there are other wealthy people I know and they don't have that aura of greatness around them. I learned that it was ArtScroll, the association with so many holy projects, and I also wanted to be part of that. Jay inspired me."

"Reb Meir fused two gifts," recalls Rabbi Burton Jaffa. "He had this ability, inherited from his father, to see a person at a glance; it was as if he could see inside the person's mind and heart. And he also had this exceptional dedication to his work, to ArtScroll. So when he met a potential donor, he knew right away if this was someone he could join forces with."

On more than one occasion, Reb Meir rejected potential donors based on his own instincts. He once told Reb Nosson, "This person strikes me as someone whose behavior will not make us proud down the road and we cannot accept his money."

Reb Meir would remind his staff that he had once turned down a dedication worth three-quarters of a million dollars because the donors insisted on using phraseology in the dedication text that Reb Meir felt didn't properly reflect the Mesorah.

Gary Torgow of Detroit, Michigan received an unexpected message one day: Rabbi Meir Zlotowitz wanted to speak with him. The two men had never met, but being familiar with Rabbi Zlotowitz's reputation and accomplishments, Mr. Torgow immediately returned the call.

Reb Meir wasted no time in making a request. "I'd like you to join our Board of Governors," he told Gary.

Mr. Torgow explained that, while he was honored at the

(L to R) With Gary Torgow, Rav Dovid Feinstein, Stanley Frankel

thought, he knew several people who, he felt, were more suited to the role. Reb Meir explained that he wanted a representative of the Detroit community, and Mr. Torgow countered that he would be happy to sit down with Reb Meir and share a list of influential, committed Detroiters who would be appropriate choices.

They agreed to meet, and a few days later, Mr. Torgow informed Reb Meir that he would be coming to New York. They set up a time to get together, and Reb Meir welcomed Mr. Torgow to ArtScroll headquarters. The two men made small talk for a few minutes, then Reb Meir called over the intercom and requested that a new *sefer* be sent upstairs from the bindery: Reb Meir handed the fresh-off-the-press *sefer* to his visitor, who opened it up. Along with the other names on the Board of Governors there appeared one more: *Gary Torgow (Detroit)*. Reb Meir smiled. "I did my own investigations about Detroiters. Welcome to the family."

Yossi Melohn, an ArtScroll sponsor, recalls the conversations between Reb Meir and his own father, Yaakov Melohn, a visionary ArtScroll benefactor. "I remember thinking how those discussions would give a donor the sense of feel good and comfort. I work with investments all day, and with Reb Meir, the sponsors had a sense that they were investing well because he took what he did so seriously. Sponsors understood that the funds would be put to good use. We all felt like we were lucky that he accepted us."

Sometimes, when a fund-raiser comes into a room, donors step back and pretend to be invisible, remarks a longtime friend and supporter. "It's not personal, it's just that people don't always feel like they're able to give; but when Rabbi Zlotowitz came into a room, everyone just gravitated to him. We all wanted to be around him."

Even from a pure business point of view, says Asher David Milstein, supporters appreciated the opportunity. "The sponsors

Showing Yaakov, Yossi, Alexander, and Don Melohn the bindery

got off easy, because they just had to provide funding for the actual work. ArtScroll's reach is so wide, their distribution system so sophisticated, we knew that the *sefarim* in which he allowed us to partner would reach the widest possible audience."

And there was something else as well: the donors were confident that he viewed their money as holy, allocated for the benefit of Klal Yisrael.

A talented young writer came to the office to pitch a book he considered necessary. Reb Meir didn't agree.

"You're a wonderful person with good ideas, you're smart and creative," Reb Meir said, "and I'd love to take you out to Prime Grill and hear more about your vision. You have a bright future. But I'm not sure that I can invest the money I solicit from donors in this project; I have a responsibility

With Jay Schottenstein

to them to ensure that every penny is used in a way we consider prudent."

Once Reb Meir accepted a donor as part of the ArtScroll family, he viewed that person as a full partner. He would often invite donors visiting New York to "come see what you've created."

"What I find incredible," remarks Jay Schottenstein, whose family name is synonymous with ArtScroll's flagship project, "is that very often, when you donate and the organization does good things with the money, then they expect you to realize that, as if they did you the favor. With Meir, it was the opposite. He made us feel like it was all us, like he could never have done anything without us."

Reb Meir made sure his donors knew what they were accomplishing. In an email to Elly Kleinman as the Kleinman Edition Midrash Rabbah went to print, he wrote:

With Elly Kleinman

Dear Elly—

You accomplished with this work something that has never in history been done before and generations from now, it will still be learned and appreciated.

May we together have continued simchah, good health, nachas, and prosperity to continue our avodas hakodesh together mitoch kol tuv...

With love and gratitude for making this monumental work possible,

Meir

Chanoch Weisz recalls reading a book about Apple founder Steve Jobs. "And you, Meir, are the Steve Jobs of the Jewish world," he told his friend.

Reb Meir's face colored and he looked down in obvious embarrassment. "What are you talking about?" he asked. "By us, it's the donors who change the world, not me."

More than once, he was asked to involve himself in business discussions with his donors, either making connections or providing references. Often, he was invited to join in business deals by donors who liked him and wanted to see him succeed. "We need someone with your brains, insight, and people skills," a donor recalls telling him. "You'll invest with me and you'll end up rich. Think how much more you can do for Klal Yisrael if we let you in on this deal."

Reb Meir rejected the offer outright. "I have a mission in life, and if donors become business partners, then they see me differently and I won't be effective in my real job. Thanks, but no thanks."

To another donor who extended the same offer, Reb Meir explained. "Imagine I join you in a deal and it fails — our relationship will sour, and then Klal Yisrael will lose out. How can I take the chance?"

Reb Meir's appreciation for the donors, speculates Asher David Milstein, wasn't just an expression of his innate *middah* of *hakaras hatov*; it was because they enabled him to fulfill his

(L to R) With Rabbi Jeff Seidel and Asher David Milstein

own mission. When Milstein sponsored thousands of free Siddurim and pocket-sized *sifrei Tanach* to be distributed through Rabbi Jeff Seidel's Jewish Student Information Center, he could see how excited Reb Meir was. "It was as if this was his own dream, to make the Siddurim available for free to Jews everywhere — so a donor sponsoring Siddurim for others was, to him, the perfect realization of that dream."

"You could see," reflects Milstein, "that even though he lived in Brooklyn, he identified with the lonely Jew in middle America, the backpacking student who would pick up a Siddur or Chumash somewhere in the Far East."

The Jewish nation, Reb Meir told Asher David, is a symphony and *every* last instrument needs to be heard for the music to be perfect. "Reb Meir loved music and when he made that comparison, I felt his passion," recalls Milstein. "He really meant it that way."

"Every organization, every Jewish center, every synagogue is making music and we're all partners," Reb Meir told him. "We need all hands on deck in the fight against the fraud being perpetrated by those who try to undermine the Torah."

(L to R) With Joseph Chaim Shenker and Asher David Milstein

Although he would never sit back and reflect on his own accomplishments, those closest to him heard his satisfaction in what had been accomplished in other ways. He would often discuss the incredible merits of the Romm family, reflecting on the immeasurable *zechus* of having printed the Vilna *Shas*, their enduring legacy. Every year, on Erev Shabbos *Parashas Chukas*, Reb Meir would remind his children of the sad significance of the day.[8] The passion and heart with which he

---

8. The *Magen Avraham* (*Shulchan Aruch, Orach Chaim* Chapter 580) says that it is "worthwhile for every Jew to cry for the burning of the Torah" and relates how on Erev Shabbos *Parashas Chukas*, in the year 1242, twenty wagonloads filled with Gemaros and Talmudic literature (including many works of the *Baalei Tosafos*) were burned in Paris by agents of the church and of King Louis IX. Each of these volumes was a priceless, handwritten manuscript, in the era before there were printed *sefarim*. This was such a national tragedy that the *Maharam M'Rottenburg* composed a *kinnah* about the event, "*Sha'ali Serufa Ba'Aish*," which is recited on Tishah B'Av.

The great men of that generation asked for Divine answers, by way of a dream. The Heavenly message was just three words: "*Da Gezeiras Oraysa*," the Aramaic translation of the first *pasuk* in *Parashas Chukas*, "*Zos Chukas HaTorah*, This is the decree against the Torah" (*Bamidbar* 19:2, as quoted by *Targum Onkelos*). It was understood from the cryptic reply that the burning of the Talmud was Heavenly decreed.

With Rav Dovid Feinstein and Ezra Marcos of the Edmond J. Safra Foundation

discussed the tragedy — words of Torah lost to Klal Yisrael! — made it clear to them that he saw his life's work as a personal mission.

When ArtScroll would eventually translate the *Shas* into the French language for the Edmond J. Safra French Edition, the very first meeting between Reb Meir and the team of *talmidei chachamim* supervising the work on the edition took place in Paris, the city where the wagonloads of holy *sefarim* had been burnt by the church in 1242. The editor took Reb Meir and Reb Nosson to the actual site of the burning of the holy books: they were deeply moved, for it reinforced the importance of this new project, one which would allow Jews to connect with the light of *Torah Shebe'al Peh* in the French language.

Asher David Milstein would check in from his frequent travels to let Reb Meir know in which remote locale he had seen ArtScroll books and *sefarim*. There were communities he visited in which the shul did not even have an active rabbi — just some old-timers, holding onto the memories and dreams

— but, thanks to Milstein's vision and generosity, they would have ArtScroll *sefarim* and Chumashim, guides to Jewish living and knowledge. Then there were shuls with dynamic rabbanim, but no past at all: just dreams for the future. Milstein sponsored Siddurim, Chumashim, *sifrei Tanach,* and sets of the Yerushalmi for Chabad Houses across the globe, and he would often share emails from grateful *sheluchim.* The emails would come from Madrid and New Zealand, from Wyoming and Cuba. Reb Moishe Halpern, the rosh Beis Medrash LeRabbanim in Berlin, acknowledged the receipt of several sets of ArtScroll *sefarim* with a particularly moving email.

Dear Asher

I hope all is well with you.

I sat down on Shabbos and opened the Midrash to say over to my boys, and learned from the beautiful Chumash, and now I sit here with the Yerushalmi open in front of me, and I must express to you some of the feelings that I have when learning from the beautiful sefarim you so kindly sent to me.

I must tell you that with all the various obligations of learning and teaching and preparing Shiurim etc., it is hard to find time to learn lishmah, just for the sake of learning, even though we know of the obligation. However, when having an opportunity to open a new set of sefarim, to explore new horizons, to venture into the world of Yerushalmi where I have never been before, or the deeper understanding of the Midrash, this gives me so much more excitement and interest; I cannot describe to you my happiness.

I must add a short story that I heard as a child, one which remains with me to this day. The Ponevezher Rav used to say over the story, describing the moment when his own heart was first filled with the desire to learn and know the whole of Shas.

In the Lithuanian village in which he grew up, there was a minhag that on Purim, the kehillah would send mishloach manos to the rav on behalf of the entire town. The parnas and the rosh hakahal would bring the gift to the rav's home, and each year, two little boys were chosen to carry the gift in to the Rav.

One Purim, he was chosen to carry the gift into the rav; it consisted of two innovations which had been introduced to the world during that year. New dripless candles had just been made available: until that point, candles didn't give clear light and left a bad smell. The other novelty was the newly printed Vilna Shas, the clearest print yet. The gift was a new Shas and these candles. The boys brought it into the Rav.

The Ponevezher Rav would describe the joy of the rav's face, his exclamation that he couldn't imagine Olam Haba as being anything other than a new Shas and clear, clean candles to learn by: there was no bigger delight. The Ponevezher Rav said, "At that moment a desire to know all of Shas entered my heart."

I heard those words over thirty years ago, but when I saw and opened these boxes, I must say it was one of the only times I really think that I felt that happiness and that cheishek of the rav.

I look forward to learn volume after volume im yirtzeh Hashem. My appreciation knows no bounds.

Along with expressions of thanks from those who had received *sefarim*, Asher David would also keep Reb Meir updated on his own travels.

One winter day, he emailed from Venice.

Dear Rabbi Zlotowitz and Rabbi Scherman,

Celebrating the first ArtScroll siyum of Talmud Yerushalmi (on Maseches Rosh Hashanah) in Venice, Italy. It is fair to assume there has not been a siyum in Talmud

Yerushalmi for at least 70 years, maybe longer, in Venice.

May we merit the coming of Moshiach in our time,

Your friend, Asher

Reb Meir wrote back.

Dear Asher—

Beautiful! What a zechus.

What comes around goes around.

Venetzia was the printing capital in the Middle Ages when printing was first introduced. Magnificent works were printed there.

Reb Meir attached an article that noted that the first edition of the Talmud Yerushalmi was printed in Venice in the 16th century. This was more than mere trivia, or a historical footnote. Reb Meir saw the fact that a *masechta* of Yerushalmi had been completed in the city of Venice as noteworthy: Torah is

A set of Talmud arrives at Chabad in Vietnam — a gift from Asher David Milstein
(L to R) Rabbi Menachem Hartman, the *shaliach* of Ho Chi Min City, and Zvi Perl

the thread that runs through the ages, the only true reality, and printing Torah works is part of the sacred mission of keeping the flame alive.

It was this sense of obligation that drove many of the decisions at ArtScroll.

For a few years, ArtScroll published a daily calendar, a *luach* with dates and relevant information.

Eventually, Reb Meir decided to stop printing it. "We're not spreading Torah and it doesn't generate income," he told Rabbi Avie Gold, "so there's no reason for us to be doing it."

That summer, a fellow called ArtScroll's office and asked where the annual *luach* was. "It's almost Rosh Hashanah and it hasn't yet arrived," he said in agitation. The receptionist informed him that the *luach* wouldn't be printed that year, and the caller got upset.

"You can't do that," he exclaimed. "Let me tell you a story."

One morning, he'd been at work and when he checked the *luach*, he noticed that it was a Jewish holiday, Shavuot. He called the office at his Reform temple to inquire about Shavuot and they informed him that it wasn't a significant day and there were no special services. He read in the *luach*, however, of its importance and was directed to the relevant Torah sources. "So I read all about it, and now I know what Shavuot is: otherwise, I'd never have known. How can you stop printing it?"

Reb Meir heard the story and turned to Reb Avie. "Please get to work on this and have it ready on time, just as you have every other year — and make sure that gentleman gets a copy."

At the *shivah* for Reb Meir, Rav Eliyahu Essas came into the house. In the 1970's, the former Refusenik had been one of the leaders of the Russian *teshuvah* underground, teaching Torah and leading the spiritual resistance until he was eventually allowed to leave in 1986. He recalled how each ArtScroll *sefer* that arrived would spawn new lessons, open new frontiers of

Jewish thought and inspiration for these valiant soldiers of faith.

The sense of duty that drove Reb Meir meant that he never really stopped to sit back and revel in his accomplishments: it was never about what he had done, but what he would do next. After having successfully completed the *Shas* in English and Hebrew, Reb Meir decided to embark on the next great project, the translation and elucidation of the Yerushalmi. He immersed himself in the new undertaking — and could have been forgiven if he had excused himself from taking on other monumental projects until it was complete.

But his dear friend, Reb Zvi Ryzman — not just a business man and donor, but a published ArtScroll author and *mechaber* of several *sefarim* as well — encouraged Reb Meir to consider a new frontier in teaching Torah: the internet. Zvi suggested that this too was part of ArtScroll's mission.

The issue was raised at a Board of Governors meeting. Reb Meir listened as the members of his "brain trust" weighed in: The

With Rachel, and Zvi and Betty Ryzman

Board of Governors Meeting (2003):
Seated (L to R): Andy Neff, Rabbi Mayer May, Sol Teichman, Reb Meir Zlotowitz, Jay Schottenstein,
Reb Nosson Scherman, Hirsch Wolf, Ezra Marcos
Standing (L to R): Elliot Schwartz, Nochum Silberman, Bernard Shafran, Reb Gedaliah Zlotowitz, Steve Savitsky, Jay Tepper,
Rabbi Raphael Butler, Howard Tzvi Friedman, A. George Saks, Gary Torgow, Moshe Talansky, Zvi Ryzman, Fred Shulman, Asher Stahler,
Reuven Dessler, Yosef Davis, Judah Septimus, Kalman Renov, Elliot Tannenbaum, Chanoch Weisz, Steve Adelsberg, A. Joseph Stern

overwhelming sentiment was that ArtScroll had the staff, experience, and professionalism to do it right. He was convinced.

"When Meir invested in a project, it wasn't just a question of money; it meant his single-minded attention and involvement as well," recalls Reb Zvi. "And the digital app became one of those projects. Once he believed that this was what the generation needed, he was determined to do it flawlessly."

Jay Schottenstein was there when Reb Meir took the first few steps on this new path. "Generally, when a person is very successful in one area, he is hesitant to embrace change, to evolve, because he isn't sure if he will be able to replicate his success. Meir was different. I was amazed at the way he approached this, totally confident that the ArtScroll app would be as effective as the ArtScroll published works."

Yitzchok Saftlas had made this observation decades earlier, when the industry was on the cusp of switching technologies. "When I worked at ArtScroll, we used something called the Bedford System. Reb Meir had traveled to Bedford, Massachusetts to purchase the machinery, and he had mastered it. It was

(L to R) Jay Schottenstein, Rav Dovid Feinstein, Mendy (Edward) Czuker, Reb Meir, Gary Torgow

the most sophisticated typesetting equipment," Saftlas recalls, "but in the early 1990's, desktop publishing was becoming a trend. Reb Meir didn't agonize about his investment, the significant time and money he'd spent on the equipment; he moved quickly to buy computers and learn the new programs. He had no time to waste, because he was on a mission."

In an email sent after Reb Meir's passing, Binyamin Jolkovsky, editor of the *Jewish World Review*, shared a story.

> *In the fall of 1993, I was attending journalism school at the University of Maryland, just outside of Washington. I simultaneously had a job at the local Jewish weekly.*
>
> *The High Holy Days were one of the paper's biggest profit generators, with the expanded issues prepared weeks in advance.*
>
> *During a "down time" period at work, I began reading the issues' galleys.*
>
> *The staff managed to fill most of the space around the ads. But as I progressed through the issues' many pages, I noticed there was hardly any content that reflected the awesomeness of the season.*
>
> *The paper's owner was the friendly sort and at my interview, he told me twice that he was open to suggestions on improving his product.*
>
> *So that is what I did. I ever-so-politely told him that I noticed that despite the paper wanting to be the collective voice of the entire community, there wasn't a single article from an Orthodox rabbi.*
>
> *(Washington, and nearby Silver Spring, had more than a dozen frum shuls in those days.)*
>
> *The owner conceded that I was correct. But, he said, I shouldn't take it the wrong way.*
>
> *"It's not that I'm against including Orthodox rabbis," he explained. "It's that I haven't found any that write effectively enough to engage our readership."*

I asked if he would consider using material if I would get content that met with his approval, and the owner said that yes, he would publish it.

I used to learn and daven in Stolin and used to schmooze with Rabbi Scherman when he'd join us. I gave Rabbi Scherman a call and while he thought it would be a great idea to have his work excerpted in a secular Jewish paper, ultimately, he explained, it wasn't his call, and he transferred me to your father.

Your father was friendly and intrigued. Half-jokingly, he asked why I was becoming a journalist if I could help Klal Yisrael by working for ArtScroll. I told him if I should ever change my mind, I would give him a call. Just to prove that he was serious, he gave me his direct number.

Your father granted the paper permission to use an excerpt — and told me which piece he thought would be the most stirring.

He was clear about his intentions. "This isn't about business," he said. "It's unlikely I'm going to make many sales from it. This is about Klal Yisrael."

The article was a hit. The paper actually received letters about it, something, the owner said, which rarely happens for religious-oriented pieces.

Yes, the paper finally found an Orthodox rabbi who can write — with substance and style.

It was a kiddush Hashem. And while it was Rabbi Scherman's prose, it was your father who made it happen. He did it for Klal Yisrael.

The sense of responsibility to Klal Yisrael shaped his relationship with others in the industry: they might have been termed competitors, but not to Reb Meir. He enjoyed a close relationship with Reb Yitzchok Feldheim of Feldheim Publishers; they were once at the same convention, and Reb Meir manned the

Feldheim booth for a moment when Reb Yitzchok was called away. He liked to joke that he had once been a Feldheim employee.

He would send copies of his books to the Feldheim family, and for years, the two companies would exchange boxes of children's books — so that the Zlotowitz children could enjoy Feldheim books as well.

When people would stop him to thank him for what ArtScroll had done, he would cut them off, barely able to listen. He couldn't tolerate compliments and effusive thanks and would certainly never talk about what he had achieved. He felt that such talk would distract him from what still had to be done.

Reb Meir supported a night *kollel* in Lakewood, led by his son-in-law Rabbi Yehuda Munk, husband of his daughter Tzivi. Called *Nachalas Ahron*, in memory of Reb Ahron Zlotowitz, Reb Meir ensured that the *yungerleit* were paid generously and on time (including for the *bein hazemanim* period, when the *kollel*

Rav Yeruchem Olshin speaking at a Nachalas Ahron Kollel *siyum*

wasn't in session). He wouldn't allow Reb Yehuda to fund-raise for the *kollel*, sending the money himself each month. As committed as he was to carrying the burden alone, he was equally determined not to receive any sort of formal recognition, and very few people even knew of his involvement.

Busy at work, in frequent physical pain, nevertheless he made it a point to come to Lakewood for the *siyumim*, sharing in the joy of the Torah and *talmidei chachamim*. Once, at a *siyum* for a *masechta* completed by the *lomdei hakollel*, Reb Meir agreed to speak. He stood up and shared something he had read in the writings of Rav Aryeh Leib, son of the Chofetz Chaim.

Reb Leib overheard his sainted father engaged in one of his conversations with Hakadosh Baruch Hu, speaking in plain Yiddish, as if to another person. *Ribbono Shel Olam,* the Chofetz Chaim was saying, *You've given me so much. You've allowed me to write the Mishnah Berurah. You've allowed me to write the Shemiras Halashon and Chofetz Chaim ... Ribbono Shel Olam, after all You've done for me, what have I ever done for You? Nothing... Please, allow us the zechus to find a way to repay You...*

Reb Meir said that he got emotional every time he thought of that story.[9] "We all live life trying to *shteig*, to accomplish and grow, and when we actually succeed, we feel good, like Hashem owes us something now. Really, it's the opposite: the more He allows us to do for Him the more we owe Him..."

A Lakewood *mechanech* had to be in Flatbush for Yom Kippur: as a friend of Rabbi Duvie and Dvorah Morgenstern, he asked if he might eat the *seudah hamafsekes* with them. They graciously welcomed him, along with their other guests — Mrs. Morgenstern's parents, Reb Meir and Rachel Zlotowitz.

---

9. In a *hesped* at Reb Meir's *levayah* in Eretz Yisrael, Reb Meir's dear friend Rav Eliyahu Meir Klugman said, "We always heard Meir say the story about the Chofetz Chaim, but we knew he was also talking about himself!"

Reb Meir was in a quiet, pensive mood, but at one point in the meal, he looked around his children's table and asked that every participant at the meal share their own personal Erev Yom Kippur feelings, their mindset and approach to the holiest day.

Unprepared, the Lakewood visitor remarked, "We say every day in *Birchos HaTorah* that Hakadosh Baruch Hu is the *Melameid Torah l'Amo Yisrael*.[10] I can think of no greater *zechus* on Erev Yom Kippur than to sit with the person to whom such a description could be attached." The others seated around the table nodded in agreement, but Reb Meir frowned. "Please cut it out and say something real," he said.

While working for Yisroel Zlotowitz, Chana Rothstein was asked by her boss to take off from her regular job and help with the ArtScroll dinner instead. The efficient young woman got to know his father, Reb Meir, and they developed a warm, respectful relationship. She would reach out to him for advice, and when she experienced personal challenges, she found him a voice of *chizuk* and wisdom.

Her 8-year-old daughter, Adina, was assigned a school project, to "interview" a person she admired. The girl chose to write about Rabbi Meir Zlotowitz, and she asked for some of his time: Rabbi Zlotowitz made himself available for a phone interview the very next day, at 7 in the morning. Speaking with a child, Reb Meir was unusually frank in assessing his own impact.

Name of person: *Rabbi Meir Zlotowitz*

Where were you born: *Brooklyn*

Where do you live: *Brooklyn*

Describe a typical day in your life: *Wake up, wash negel vasser, go to my office and read many sefarim that people translated from Hebrew to English. If it's good we print it. If it is not good, we fix it so people can read it better.*

---

10. The Almighty teaches Torah to His nation, Israel.

Name a hobby or outside interest you enjoy: *Reading and doing art.*

Name something you did in your life that you are proud of and would like people to know about you: *Because of our work, thousands of people all over the world come to learn Torah in a way they never did before.*

At a massive public event, the organizers saved Reb Meir a seat on the dais with the rabbanim and dignitaries. Reb Meir was perfectly content in the dense crowd, looking up at the dais. When one of the hosts came down to persuade him to come sit among the dignitaries, Reb Meir said, "Listen, I sell books, that's all I do."

A deferential young man stopped Reb Meir and started gushing about how ArtScroll — and its founder — had changed his life, how Reb Meir was his rebbi, the defining influence in everything he did. Reb Meir stopped him. "Tell me, my friend, when you put on your shirt in the morning, how do you go about it?"

The young man was confused by the question, and he was quiet.

"Do you first do one arm, then the other? Because I do it the same way, so we're really the same sort of person," Reb Meir said, satisfied that he had diffused what was, for him, an uncomfortable situation.

If he came into a room and people stood up in his honor, he would be overcome by embarrassment. "President Truman once said," Reb Meir would quip, "that when he walked into a room and everyone rose, the hardest thing to remember was that they were standing up for the presidency, not for him."

When he asked people for favors, the request came as if from a simple person, with no expectation or sense of entitlement. He once asked Rabbi Pinchos Lipschutz, publisher of *Yated Ne'eman*, to publish in the newspaper a tribute piece authored by one of the Zlotowitz grandchildren.

With Rabbi Pinchos Lipschutz

Dear Pinny

I hope I'm not overstepping — even in our close friend-ship. My granddaughter expressed her dream that her piece be published in Yated. I didn't say anything; I just asked her for a copy.

Do you have a place in Yated for such things? Would it be possible to get it in this week?

You'd really make me a hero if you'd be kind enough to include it.

(What we don't do for our kids — especially grand-children.)

If it's something you don't do, or have no place for, please just forget it. And accept my apology.

B'ahavah,
Meir

There was no mention of the good turns Reb Meir had done for Rabbi Lipschutz or the fact that ArtScroll had been a major advertiser since the *Yated's* inception. No acknowledgment that Reb Meir was already a legend to a great part of Klal Yisrael, and certainly in his own family — just a sincere plea, with the addition that "You'd really make me a hero..."

A magazine featured a glowing portrait of ArtScroll and its founders. Reb Meir left a message for the writer expressing his appreciation for the piece. "Thank you for making us famous," he said.

Reb Yaakov Herzog of Toronto once referred to Reb Meir as a *"tzaddik,"* in an email. *No*, Reb Meir wrote back, *it is Klal Yisrael that owes YOU gratitude for what you make possible*, insisting that the generous supporter who enabled Torah to be shared with the public was the true *tzaddik*.

With Yaakov Herzog

Yaakov countered that after 120 years, in the Next World, Reb Meir could use whatever terms he'd like — but in this world, such labels as *tzaddik* were irrelevant.

I must tell you a story about my father, Reb Meir replied:

> *My father was an old litvishe rav; he learned in Lomza Yeshivah for 13 years, was a chavrusa for one year with Rav Yaakov Kamenetsky, and he knew Shas, Yerushalmi, and Shulchan Aruch literally be'al peh, with every se'if kattan. Before he was niftar at 94 years old, he warned me not to write any "titles" on his matzeivah, just Harav Ahron ben Reb Meir Yaakov z"l. I asked him why — because he was truly a gaon olam and we were writing the matzeivah, not he.*

He answered me in one phrase, that if we write on his matzeivah excess shevachim, zei vehlen mohnen fuhn mir in himmel, veil zei veisen der emes...[11]

Reb Meir cherished a thought shared with him by Rav Avrohom Pam, the rosh yeshivah of Torah Vodaath, and would often repeat it.

With Rav Avrohom Pam

"When I see a large crowd listening as I speak," the rosh yeshivah confided to Reb Meir, "I remind myself, 'It's not because you're such a wonderful speaker,' and when I notice the crowd around me as I dance with the *chassan*, I tell myself, 'It's not because you're such a great dancer.' It's hard not to take yourself seriously if there are always people around, but the trick is to remind yourself that it's all a bluff, a joke. The *yetzer hara* creates the illusion that you're something and you'd better not start believing it. It's not about you."

Reb Meir knew what ArtScroll had accomplished and understood its impact; he just didn't see himself as a major part of the story. He disdained compliments and praise because of the inference that he was the cause of ArtScroll's success. It was only when people that he revered shared compliments that he had no choice but to listen, because respect obligated him to allow them to speak.

---

11. They will hold these titles against me in the Next World, because they know the truth.

With grandson, Shmuli Zlotowitz, and Rabbi Shalom Gold

His close friend, Rabbi Shalom Gold, was rosh yeshivah of a unique institution. Yeshivas Rabbi Akiva, in the Old City of Yerushalayim, was founded specifically for those who discovered Torah later in life — after the age of forty, just like Rabbi Akiva had.

Even with extraordinary determination to grasp the fundamentals of *Torah Shebe'al Peh*, reading *lashon kodesh* — and certainly Aramaic — was near impossible for *talmidim* starting at that age. "It was obvious that without ArtScroll, we would have no yeshivah. They enabled us to exist," says Rabbi Gold, "and I told this to Reb Meir. It meant something to him."

Reb Meir would often visit the yeshivah, and though he would never agree to speak to the *talmidim*, he would sit in the *beis medrash*, surrounded by walls covered in ArtScroll volumes (which he had happily donated), and revel in the atmosphere created by men toiling to find truth.

Reb Meir traveled to Eretz Yisrael with his son Reb Gedaliah and grandson Tzvi when the 12-year-old boy put on tefillin

With Rav Shimon Galai in the van

for the first time. Along with Reb Meir's son Yisroel and their close friend Jack Jaffa, who were also there, they went to meet with various *gedolim*. After hours of crisscrossing the country, Reb Meir was physically exhausted and in pain. They ended the day in Bnei Brak, where they had several meetings with *gedolim* scheduled. The first stop was at the home of Rav Shimon Galai, but the building had no elevator, and Reb Meir — who knew that he would soon have to walk up the staircase to the home of Rav Chaim Kanievsky — felt that he simply couldn't make the climb. Reb Gedaliah and Jack left the van and went to meet Rav Shimon.

The *tzaddik* welcomed them to his apartment, and when he heard Reb Gedaliah's last name and about the ArtScroll connection, he inquired about Reb Meir; though they had never met, Rav Shimon appeared familiar with Reb Meir's accomplishments. They told him that in fact, Reb Meir was downstairs in the van, in too much pain to climb the stairs — and Reb Shimon didn't hesitate. He immediately stood up and led them back downstairs, where he hurried to greet Reb Meir. "I must say 'shalom' to a Yid with so many *zechusim*, that's a Yid I like to meet!" he said.

Reb Meir was a great admirer of the current Belzer Rebbe, Rav Yissachar Dov Rokeach, and would often go into the Rebbe for *berachos* or advice. After one audience, the Rebbe said to him, "Come, I want to show you something."

Sets of Schottenstein Hebrew Talmud in the Belzer *beis medrash*

The Rebbe took Reb Meir by the hand and led him down the stairs and into the hallways outside the large *beis medrash*: the shelves were filled with hundreds of blue ArtScroll 'Schottenstein' Gemaros — over sixty sets. The Rebbe pointed to what he called, a "*bloi'eh vant*," a wall of blue, and said, "See the people learning here — it's all yours!"

A prominent Belzer *askan* lost his wife to illness. His Rebbe called him in one day and said, "Would you like to do something special for her *neshamah*?" The husband was eager to hear the Rebbe's advice.

"There is a person who is saving other Jews, allowing them access to Torah, letting those who

Presenting the Belzer Rebbe with a new *sefer*

never learned understand and those who have learned understand it more clearly. His name is Reb Meir Zlotowitz and the
Gemaros he published will change the world. I want you to buy
the Schottenstein Shas for the *beis medrash*."

Of course, the husband acted immediately, purchasing many
sets of the *Shas* for the great Belzer shul in Yerushalayim.

Rav Dovid Feinstein shared an interesting halachic *shailah* he
had received.

There was a secular Jewish woman who kept a single custom
from her parents' home: she would go to the local shul on Yom
Kippur and fast all through the long day. Her husband mocked
the practice, telling her it was hypocritical to express repen-
tance when she had no plans to actually change, but she was
tenacious about holding onto this tradition: she always came
home after Yom Kippur feeling inspired and cleansed.

The day meant a lot to her, and eventually, she asked her

With Rav Dovid Feinstein

husband to come to shul as well. At first he refused, but she was so persistent that one year he agreed to come to the synagogue for a few minutes.

In order to reassure himself that it was merely an act of generosity to his wife and nothing more, the husband first went to the local Burger King, where he devoured a nonkosher hamburger; only then did he wander into the shul for *Neilah*, the final prayer of the holy day.

He picked up one of the *machzorim* and, bored, he started to flip through the book. He started to read the Yom Kippur overview, penned by Rav Nosson Scherman, and found himself swept into the narrative, feeling the power and potency of the day. He experienced a rush of remorse, and was overwhelmed by a single thought: What am I doing with the life G-d has given me?

That night, he and his wife sat down for a long, honest conversation.

They embarked on a road to full return, and, with the guidance of Rav Dovid Feinstein, they celebrated their marriage with a *chuppah* and proper *kiddushin*. Rav Dovid would tell the story in Reb Meir's presence and add, "And do you know why this man called me recently? The man who became *frum* through ArtScroll called to ask a *shailah* about fasting on Shivah Asar b'Tammuz!"

Reb Meir once told his close friend Rabbi Michoel Levi about a gentleman who had called the office and admitted that he had finally allowed his grandson to go to a Jewish day school — thanks to ArtScroll. The caller had explained that he was a marginally religious Jew who

With Rabbi Michoel Levi

didn't allow his grandson to attend a real Torah school out of worry that the child would know more about Judaism than he.

But then he had discovered the world of ArtScroll. "Now," the grandfather said, "I feel comfortable in my Jewish learning and I'm confident enough to let my grandson go to a Jewish day school."

Reb Meir carried a letter with him from a gentleman in New Zealand. *I couldn't help it*, the man wrote, *when I saw the Gemara, I felt compelled to reacquaint myself with it, and now, as a result of learning using the translation, I have undertaken to move back to Australia and enroll my son in yeshivah.*

A respected individual was once discussing the translation of the Gemara with the Skverer Rebbe, an unyielding protector of the Mesorah. The visitor was complaining about what he perceived as ArtScroll's breach with tradition: the Rebbe invited the man to stand up and look outside into the busy waiting room.

The long table outside the Rebbe's chamber was lined with waiting petitioners — many of them learning from the blue ArtScroll Gemaros. The Rebbe didn't say anything else, his answer abundantly clear.

Jack Jaffa, son of Reb Meir's lifelong friend Burton Jaffa and a close friend in his own right, was standing in a Brooklyn electronics store one day when a teenage boy came in on a skateboard. The boy had a trendy haircut and wore a tight pair of jeans: Jack noticed a copy of the ArtScroll *Mesillas Yesharim* peeking out of the boy's pocket.

"Why do you have that *sefer* with you?" he asked the teenager.

The boy's face lit up. "My yeshivah gave it out to us when we graduated and since I discovered it, I take it everywhere with me. It's my guide to life, I like to have it nearby always."

Jack Jaffa smiled. "That means a lot me," he said, "because my family sponsored this edition."

With Jack Jaffa

The boy's eyes flew open. "Really? Would it be okay if I gave you a hug?" he asked.

When the boy had gone, Jack called ArtScroll headquarters.

"Uncle Meir," he said, "I need to tell you what just happened."

Reb Meir listened as Jack related the story. Finally, Reb Meir spoke. "Jack," he said, "we have no idea whom we're reaching or how we're reaching them, but this is why we do what we do. Thank you for telling me the story."

Several times a year, Reb Meir would share thoughts with an intimate group of ArtScroll supporters via email. Before his last Rosh Hashanah, he shared a *dvar Torah* that revealed so much about what drove him.

> *In instituting the order of the weekly Torah readings, the Sages ordained that Parashas Nitzavim should always be read the Shabbos before Rosh Hashanah. We submit that one reason for this decision can be found in Moses's opening words, as he spoke to his people on the last*

day of his life. He began by addressing the nation in its entirety: "all of you," and enumerated different categories of Jews, from the most revered leaders and scholars down to the most menial, seemingly insignificant laborers. Then he went on to give his inspiring charge for the millennia-long future of the nation. The message is clear. Moses was not making demands only from Israel's greatest. He made the same demands of the porters and woodsmen as he did of the leaders and scholars. Every Jew has the potential to excel, and no one is predestined to fail. As Rambam writes, every Jew can be as great as Moses our teacher. Of course this is not meant literally. What it does mean is that just as Moses reached his complete potential — which is the most anyone can do or is expected to do — so can every Jew, whatever his lineage or level of ability.

The first Rebbe of Gur, the Chiddushei Harim, spoke at the inauguration of the new synagogue built by his followers in the Polish town of Gora-Kolvaria. To the many thousands of chassidim from throughout Poland, he cited the story of Rabban Gamliel, who was the Nasi, the temporal leader and also the leading Talmudic sage of the Jewish community. Rabban Gamliel had high standards for his academy; he admitted only scholars whose inner sincerity and piety matched their outward appearance. To him, clothes and outer appearance did not make the man, and he appointed a gatekeeper to ensure that unqualified students were not permitted to enter the study hall.

When Rabban Gamliel stepped down from his position, his successor, Rabbi Eliezer ben Azariah (who is prominently mentioned in the Pesach Haggadah) removed the gatekeeper, and the study hall was flooded with hundreds of new students. Rabban Gamliel was anguished

— not over the loss of his position, but because he realized that his policy had prevented so many Jews from studying the Torah.

But why was Rabban Gamliel upset? He felt that it was important to maintain high standards. What happened to disabuse him of this sincerely held notion?

The Chiddushei Harim explains that Rabban Gamliel saw something that astounded him and caused him to regret his earlier conviction. The swarms of new students were not qualified when they were allowed into the once-restricted study hall. But when they became students and were exposed to their new teachers and colleagues, when they were infused with the challenging and sacred atmosphere of the study hall, they were transformed. As time went on, they attained the standards Rabban Gamliel had demanded of his new students. That phenomenon made the great leader realize that Torah and Judaism can transform people. It shed light on Moses's final speech and Rambam's codification, that ordinary people can elevate themselves if given the challenge, the tools, and the opportunity.

Reb Meir Zlotowitz was the one who gave them that opportunity.

The first time Rabbi Chaim Zev Malinowitz came to the Brooklyn office to meet the ArtScroll leadership, he had trouble finding the address. It was the era before GPS and Waze and he drove through the unfamiliar streets near Second Avenue feeling completely lost when suddenly, the building appeared in front of him.

He parked and came into the lobby, where Reb Meir greeted him.

"Reb Chaim, I see you made it," Rabbi Zlotowitz remarked.

"Yes," Rabbi Malinowitz said, "but I have no idea how I got here. Hashem led me here."

Reb Meir didn't hesitate. "Reb Chaim, none of us understand how we got here, but Hashem led us and here we are!"

Even when Reb Meir accepted praise, he was quick to deflect the credit to others.

A close friend and ArtScroll writer sent him an email from Eretz Yisrael. *I was in the large Satmar shul in Bnei Brak this afternoon. There were many more blue ArtScroll Gemaros there than any other sefer... You will never know the magnitude of your harbatzas Torah, as it's impossible for a human to make an accounting of what you have done.*

Reb Meir responded: *Thank you; I'm blushing. Jerome Schottenstein z"l always wanted to fund something that will unify Klal Yisrael; he was zocheh to it. I never boast, but I'm grateful to the Ribbono Shel Olam that the Shas is one of the few things that transcend the lines that divide us. It's found in Satmar and in Bobov, in Meah Shearim and Gush Etzion. I am humbled by the zechus.*

And if it wasn't for the chizuk of Rav Elyashiv zt"l, Rav

Video message at the 2012 *Siyum HaShas*

Shlomo Zalman zt"l, Rav Gifter zt"l, Rav Dovid Feinstein shlita, and other visionary gedolim, our work would have been suffocated in its infancy.

And of course, Reb Meir signed off with his customary *I love you.*

When the ArtScroll *Shas* was finally completed, Reb Meir shared a personal sentiment with his dear friend and partner Jay Schottenstein. "I feel like we've worked so many years to assemble the perfect team: we were careful with whom we selected. Some joined us and then moved on and some had to refine and develop their skills, but at this point, we have it just right. We have *talmidei chachamim* who aren't only knowledgeable, but also eloquent and precise, and they know how to convey ideas in a clear way. How can I disband a team like this when they can do so much for Klal Yisrael? We have to find new projects not because we owe it to them, but because we owe it to Klal Yisrael!"

Reb Meir's dear friend, Rav Yaakov Bender, rosh yeshivah of

(R to L) Rav Dovid Feinstein, Reb Meir, Rabbi Moshe Bender,
Rabbi Yaakov Bender, Rabbi Avrohom Bender

Darchei Torah, traveled to Chicago on behalf of the yeshivah. He spoke several times, and being comfortable with his own Chumash — an ArtScroll Jaffa edition — he preferred to use a similar format Chumash in his many *derashos*: he was happy to see that the various shuls and yeshivos in Chicago had copies of that Chumash, and when he returned home, he emailed Reb Meir sharing his appreciation. Reb Meir acknowledged the compliment and thanks by deflecting it, passing it back, then drawing the relevant conclusion:

L'maaseh, people want to learn, as you well know, so we try to supply the tools. Kids want to learn, and you provide the rebbeim and the atmosphere to make it possible. You and I have to be very grateful to the Ribbono Shel Olam for allowing us to be His shelichim. We can't stop for a moment; there are a lot of people who would like to jump in if we don't take the privilege and do our hishtadlus...

8

LET'S GET IT RIGHT

R EB MEIR WAS A MAN OF DETAILS, OF PRECISION AND
exactitude.

In his personal life, he had always been punctual and focused. When it came to ArtScroll, his natural meticulousness was put to good use.

He saw each word of each book or *sefer* as eternal, and would often say that when a rocket is launched, the coordinates have to be perfect; if it's only a little bit of a degree off at launch, it would miss its mark by thousands of miles at the end of the journey.

"We need to get it right now, at printing," he would remind the staff, "or be way off the mark later on."

He felt that when it came to spreading Torah, precision was more important than in any other area, and would often retell a story involving his rebbi, Rav Moshe Feinstein.

Rav Moshe once quoted a halachah in a *shiur* and one of the listeners challenged the source, saying that the rosh yeshivah was off by a *se'if*. After the *shiur*, Rav Moshe went to check and was relieved to see that he'd been proven right.

"It's just one *se'if*, the rosh yeshivah was right there either way," a *talmid* remarked, wondering why Rav Moshe had been so determined to ascertain that he had been correct.

"No," Rav Moshe said emphatically, "it's not like that. I *pasken shailos* and advise people all day based on memory, and if I would have gotten this wrong, even if to you it appears that it's an insignificant mistake, it means I forgot something — and then who knows what else I might have gotten wrong?"

"And so," Reb Meir would complete the story, "we cannot have a single mistake. We teach Torah, and if there's even one small inaccuracy, then everything else is suspect as well."

Reb Meir was determined that not only would the actual text and commentary be flawless, the books would look beautiful as well. He designed the fonts himself — along with Reb Sheah Brander — and was constantly upgrading the materials used in the binding, looking for the best methods so that the books he produced would last longer and remain in good condition.

"Remember how in yeshivah, you'd buy a Gemara and have to immediately get it bound?" he once asked a close friend. "I would look on and think, why not just make Gemaros with better binding so that you can get right down to work and start learning."

Reb Meir once sent fourteen hundred volumes of a particular *sefer* directly to *sheimos*, refusing to ship them to stores, because the binding was faulty. It was a financial loss and a waste of energy.

"Big deal," a friend remarked, "is it so bad if the binding isn't perfect?"

"When people pick up our *sefarim* in five hundred years from now," Reb Meir said earnestly, "they will still see that if it's an ArtScroll *sefer*, it's done right."

Reb Meir once called Phil Martino, who was in charge of the

downstairs bindery, and asked him to come up to the office. Reb Meir lifted a book off the table. "Watch," Reb Meir told Phil as he began to open and close it, repeating the motion several times. "Now," Reb Meir said, "a regular book gets opened a few times, but once it's read, it's put away. Not our books. These books get opened again and again and again. They have to be able to withstand this sort of use." Only when Reb Meir was satisfied that Phil could visualize what lay in store for *every sefer* did he allow him to get back to work.

Reb Meir's close friend Asher David Milstein received a shipment of ArtScroll books: in one of the copies of *Sefer HaMitzvos*, the content was upside down to the cover. Asher notified Reb Meir, whose response is indicative of both his pride and his sense of humor.

> *Dear Asher—*
>
> *Thanks for bringing the incorrectly bound book to my attention. We hand-checked hundreds of other copies here, and it seems that the copy you received was an aberration. You now own a "collector's item." Who knows how much Sotheby's will auction it off for someday?*
>
> *All the best!*
>
> *Meir*

When ArtScroll published its edition of *Perek Shirah*, Reb Meir insisted on using the finest images possible, because the book was meant to pay tribute to the Creator and the magnificence of His work: Reb Meir decided to use images taken by a National Geographic photographer whose pictures were celebrated for their beauty and luminosity, feeling confident that the pictures could complement the sacred text.

Whoever said you can't judge a book by its cover, he would quip, clearly never tried to sell books.

Reb Meir took great pride in the fact that at the ArtScroll

bindery, they sponge-paint the edges of the pages of the *Shas* to create a marbled finish. Not because it is necessary — in fact, it isn't. The colored edges of pages in the many editions of *Shas* throughout the years had been essential because the paper was of poor quality; editions of the ArtScroll *Shas* are sponge-painted only to underscore the authenticity, to make it clear that it follows the tradition of the very *Shas* from which Jews have always learned.

In 1984, Rabbi Paysach Krohn had the idea of publishing an English language book on the halachos and *minhagim* of *bris milah*. As a *mohel*, he wanted to write it, and he approached Reb Meir and Reb Nosson with his idea.

They liked the concept, and told him to write a trial chapter before they would commit to publishing it. Rabbi Krohn prepared the draft and they approved it and gave him the go-ahead.

Rabbi Krohn asked for a deadline.

"I'll never forget his answer," Rabbi Krohn reflects. "ArtScroll

(L. to R) Reb Sheah Brander, Reb Nosson Scherman, Reb Paysach Krohn, Reb Meir, Reb Gedaliah, Shmuel Blitz

With Rav Zelik Epstein and Chaim Zlotowitz

wasn't yet the superpower publisher it would become, but Reb Meir said, 'There is no deadline, but you have to write a book that people will refer to for many years to come, an authoritative work.' Even then, he had that vision."

Reb Meir would repeat with pride how, when he had thanked Rav Zelik Epstein for writing a *haskamah* to the ArtScroll *Shas*, Rav Zelik had said that he was the one who should thank Reb Meir. "If you look in the *haskamos* on the *Mishnah Berurah*," the rosh yeshivah of Sha'ar HaTorah explained, "you see the names of unfamiliar *gedolim*. Now clearly, these people were *gedolei olam*, as evident from the fact that the Chofetz Chaim sought their approval, but their names are known to us only because of their inclusion in the *Mishnah Berurah*. So I have to thank you, because people will remember me only because of my *haskamah* in your *Shas*."

Reb Meir heard about a new adhesive substance that would hold the pages in place better. Determined that the ArtScroll bindery would have the best quality glue available, he put all his appointments on hold and immersed himself in trying to acquire some to test. If there was a chance that he could upgrade the quality of his product, then that became the priority.

When commissioning images to be used as visual aids in perek *Eilu Tereifos* in *Chullin*, Reb Meir hired a professional with experience in photographing animals, so that the images would provide maximum insight into the relevant halachos.

An industry colleague once pointed out that some publishers preferred to create books that would eventually rip, so that customers would be forced to buy new ones. "That makes sense if you're running a business," Reb Meir said, "not if your mission is to give someone a Siddur that can become their best friend."

Elliot Schwartz was standing at a public event with Reb Meir when someone approached and started to shout. His ArtScroll Siddur had torn, he said, and he criticized Reb Meir for the poor workmanship.

Reb Meir remained calm. "That's so upsetting," he said, "and I take personal responsibility. Please send me a copy of the cover page so that we can immediately replace it for you."

"It was a novel attitude for the industry," Schwartz points out, "because along with the sense of mission, Meir understood that he would be more successful through honoring the customer and reinforcing ArtScroll's image than through negotiating whether or not the Siddur was really torn."

Reb Meir came to the office one day and called in some of his salespeople. "I had a hole in my shirt, a tiny little hole, but it bugged me so I called the company. They were so apologetic and said that the new shirt was already on the way." He paused. "*That's* what we need to be like: they didn't ask for pictures of the hole and make me crazy about where I bought it. They know that if I wear their shirts and I feel good, then they've won!"

He once called Rabbi Pinchos Lipschutz, publisher of the *Yated Ne'eman* newspaper, on a Motza'ei Shabbos. "Pinny, you ruined my third shirt this year," Reb Meir told his friend. "I don't like the ink you're using for the *Yated*, it's cheap and it comes off on my fingers and shirt. Change it."

"If this happens again," Reb Meir continued, "I'm sending you the bill for my dry cleaning." Then he laughed delightedly — joking with a friend even as he delivered real advice for perfecting the product.

Reb Meir reminded the writers and editors that the same precision applied to which word or phrase they chose to use. He would remind the writers that he wanted a translation that wasn't distant, clinical, or academic.

"Webster's dictionary is constantly updating and evolving," he said, "so of course our vocabulary has to evolve: people should recognize the way that they speak in our text."

And yet, the contemporary feel could never come at the expense of the timeless truths he was marketing.

Reb Meir was once seated next to an intelligent gentleman who challenged him regarding ArtScroll's translation of *Shir HaShirim*, which is based on Chazal's allegorical interpretations of each word.

"How can you claim to be authentic when you ignore the actual translation?" the man asked.

Reb Meir reminded the gentleman of a term that had been used a few years earlier, when the Watergate scandals rocked Washington. "Do you remember the 'White House Plumbers'?" Reb Meir asked.

The term had been coined by the media as a nickname for a covert White House Special Investigations Unit, established by President Richard Nixon in 1971. The president had formed the unit to combat the leaking of classified information to the news media, and in time, it was this group that would carry out the Watergate break-in.

For months, the media focused on these Plumbers, discussing their exploits and methods.

"Now," Reb Meir continued, "imagine if someone would have listened to the radio for those few months and only for those few months — they would have believed that the word 'plumbers' refers primarily to that unit. They would never have considered that the real meaning of the word has nothing to do with governmental intrigue, because they didn't see the bigger picture.

"But then time passed and people forgot about Watergate and the term 'plumbers' went back to its real meaning, not a covert unit, but professionals who repair drains and unclog pipes.

"And so," Reb Meir concluded, "we believe that the ultimate interpretation of a word or *pasuk*, its essence, is judged by Chazal. They are the ones who see the bigger picture, the past and present and future, and they told us what each word *really* means."

Reb Meir would review manuscripts and drafts that came in; to him, the very worst assessment of a submission was that it was carelessly written.

He reviewed a book and saw that one of the sources provided by the author didn't check out. He rejected the whole work because he felt that it was done sloppily, and that a writer who doesn't check sources isn't trustworthy on anything else.

He had no tolerance for messiness or laziness, both of which reflect a lack of seriousness about the mission at hand. Too much talk made him nervous, because he believed that sometimes, talking lulls a person into a false sense of accomplishment. He wouldn't share news of exciting new projects, even with donors, until the work was near completion.

He once misplaced a set of car-keys and was unusually

irritated. His grandson wondered if he didn't have another set. "It's not that," Reb Meir said, "what's bothering me is that I never lost anything in my life. Everything has a place — and Ahron, I will find it!"

Late that night, he called his grandson. "Ahron, I just wanted to tell you that I found the keys," he said happily.

It was important to him to ensure that every email or message that came via the ArtScroll website was addressed, and he personally reviewed copies of the correspondence. He once noted that a young boy had won an ArtScroll gift certificate in a raffle, but hadn't yet cashed it in. Reb Meir worried that perhaps there was a technical problem preventing the boy from accessing his prize, and he got personally involved in finding out why.

When people called or emailed ArtScroll requesting permission to make copies of printed materials, he wanted to know about it. He generally granted permission if he felt the request was reasonable, but it was important to him to understand how and why those materials were being used.

One of the earlier ArtScroll dinners was scheduled to be held at the Waldorf Astoria Hotel, but as reservations flowed in, it became clear that a larger venue was needed. Less than two weeks before the event, it was decided to switch the dinner to the New York Hilton. In those pre-email days, it wasn't simple to notify hundreds of confirmed attendees that the dinner location was being changed, but Reb Meir was determined that each and every guest would find out.

The staff worked the phones and succeeded in reaching nearly every guest — but that wasn't enough for Reb Meir. The night of the event, he had three limousines parked outside the Waldorf, drivers waiting at the wheel, and an ArtScroll representative standing at the hotel entrance in case any guests would arrive.

Reb Meir ingrained the importance of deadlines and schedules in his staff. He once asked Yitzchok Saftlas to draft a

With Reb Nosson Scherman at a Mesorah Heritage Foundation Dinner

sample of a particular project. "I can have it for you at twelve o'clock," Yitzchok said. Reb Meir shook his head. "No. Better guarantee it for one o'clock and come in early than promise twelve o'clock and deliver it late."

An ArtScroll staffer remembers those frantic weeks before the Stone Chumash was slated for release and the deadline loomed larger by the moment. Reb Meir turned to Reb Nosson and said, "Listen, you don't worry about ad copy or phone calls or the other *sefarim*: just stay in your office and write and I'll take care of all your other responsibilities." It was a lesson in focus and prioritizing — a deadline isn't negotiable, and Reb Meir would do whatever it took to free up Reb Nosson.

After leaving ArtScroll to establish his own firm, Yitzchok Saftlas wanted advice from his mentor, Reb Meir. He hesitated for a few days, then finally made the call and began by saying, "I really wanted to call sooner."

Reb Meir spoke. "The world is filled with people who just

wanted to make the call," he said. "Yitzchok — always just make the call."

When a new writer wondered if Artscroll was capable of releasing his work on deadline, Reb Meir smiled. "We put out a seventy-three volume *Shas* in fifteen years. Do the math — that's about nine weeks per volume. I think we can handle your book."

Barry Schwartz is CEO of RustyBrick, the web service firm that Reb Meir used to develop the ArtScroll digital app.

In a written reflection after Reb Meir's passing, Barry, who — along with his brother Ronnie — worked closely with Reb Meir, shared his feelings.

The Artscroll content on digital devices brings a level of detail and clarity that is above and beyond. You could click on a phrase and instantly see all the sources and commentary around that phrase. Visualizing in three-dimension the construction of an Eruv that you can virtually walk through to fully grasp the detail of how our sages instructed us to build the

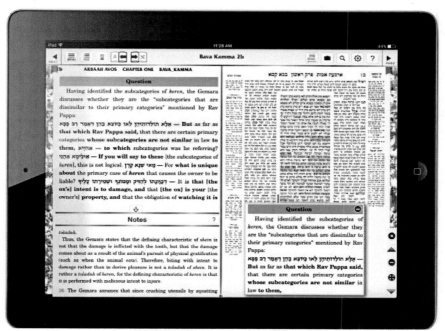

An ipad with the ArtScroll Digital App

structure. Color-coding the Talmud allows those new to Talmud study to quickly learn how to do the "Daf." The list goes on and on. These were all visions of Rabbi Zlotowitz and the ArtScroll team, based on his mission to make Torah study more accessible with a level of perfection that is unprecedented.

And then Schwartz spoke not about the product, but the person.

We at RustyBrick had the privilege of working directly with Rabbi Zlotowitz and experienced firsthand how important it was to him and the whole ArtScroll team that everything be 100 percent perfect. Everyone we worked with under Rabbi Zlotowitz stressed the same requirement — there was absolutely no acceptable level of imperfection for any ArtScroll release, even a digital representation.

Throughout the process of developing the ArtScroll Digital Library, Rabbi Zlotowitz was involved every step of the way. Despite the challenges of having high-level data encryption, we had to make the app work, smoothly and instantly. Time and time again the Rabbi pointed out imperfections that he demanded we fix. We tried to explain that we can release the app now, with some small bugs, and then release quick and rapid fixes and upgrades along the way — which users appreciate. But no, it had to be perfect on release.

Finally, Schwartz closed with a very personal observation. *This perfection and deep level of care can be seen in Rabbi Zlotowitz's eyes. Talking to Rabbi Zlotowitz, he always looked directly at you and there was something deep and meaningful that one cannot fully explain. His eyes made everyone he ever spoke with feel that this conversation was the most important conversation he had that day.*

Mayer Pasternak, ArtScroll's Chief Technology Officer, oversaw the building of the company's website, and then presided over the "expansion" from page to screen. The process of taking the ArtScroll product — with its aesthetic beauty, accuracy, and precision — and digitally adapting it, took over a decade of tedious work.

Reb Meir was intrigued by e-books, and he charged Mayer with finding a device capable of displaying ArtScroll books and *sefarim* — but he didn't simply want the text to appear. Reb Meir needed it to look perfect — he wanted the ArtScroll look, with the crisp layout and the trademark font, and of course, the Hebrew-English interface and *nekudos*. At one point, the two men traveled to meet Joseph Jacobson, the professor who invented E-Ink. He was acquainted with ArtScroll and eager to work with them, but ultimately, the technology wasn't realistic for what Reb Meir wanted. No device was capable of really displaying Hebrew properly until the iPod was released.

At that point, Reb Meir, with the generous support and encouragement of the Wasserman family, launched the Wasserman Digital Initiative.

"He didn't give me a budget," Mayer recalls, "he just told me

With Stanley Wasserman

what he expected. We had a huge team working on this and together, we did something unprecedented, reconstructing the entire Vilna *Shas*. You can tap on any phrase and get the translation, hyper-links, sources, and images."

"Reb Meir was determined that the look would be clean and attractive, but he was equally determined to keep the precise *tzuras hadaf*, every single letter. He wanted it to be clear that even as he reached into a new frontier, he wasn't selling something new, just using a new means."

To that end, Reb Meir made a decision with which many disagreed. He insisted that digital app users see a message, a note that *gedolei Yisrael* had discouraged internet use for recreational purposes and suggested that devices be filtered.[1] Others on the development team felt that the disclaimer took away from the sleek, modern feel of the app, but Reb Meir felt just the opposite: the modern, innovative app was an effective way to reach the younger generation, but the end goal was to connect them to the most timeless wisdom of all.

And like every project he did, it would be done right. "Reb Meir understood his place in history," Mayer Pasternak reflects, "and he knew that the work had to be done perfectly. We literally invented technology to do it the ArtScroll way — classy, clear, and faithful to the holiness of each and every word."

Perhaps no one heard more about the right way to do things than Benjy Seror, who was Reb Meir's "right-hand man" — a trusted ArtScroll employee who became so close to his boss, Reb Meir would refer to him as a son. It wasn't just talk: on Erev Shabbos, Benjy would drive by the Zlotowitz home to pick up Mrs. Rachel Zlotowitz's fresh lukshen kugel, which she prepared for him as she did for her own children.

---

1. "Note," the screen reads. "This app does not require the internet for daily use. Following the ruling of leading rabbinic authorities, web devices should be used only with filters."

Reb Meir once gently corrected the way Benjy was performing a particular task and quipped, "If Hashem gives me enough time in this world, then I'll make you perfect."

Benjy laughed. "But what would you do all day if we were perfect? You'd be bored."

"No," Reb Meir countered, "then I could show you that even perfection isn't enough — it also needs to be perfected."

With Benjy Seror

9

TO UPLIFT AND ENCOURAGE

A MASTER OF WORDS AND HOW TO USE THEM, REB MEIR learned, early on, the power of words to encourage. He understood that a heartening message could change a life, and he would often use his own story as evidence. "If, when I showed Rav Dovid Cohen the manuscript on *Megillas Esther*, he would have just said 'very nice,' then there would be no ArtScroll today. But because he reacted with excitement, telling me that it was something special and that we must print it, we felt like we were onto something great."[1]

Reb Meir would often recount that, along with the support of *gedolim*, ArtScroll received encouragement from an unexpected source. Feldheim Publishers had been the pioneers in

---

1. On Erev Rosh Hashanah, Reb Meir would call Rav Dovid Cohen to wish *a gut yohr*, and also to say thank you. "Imagine," Reb Meir would say, "if when I first brought you the manuscript of *Megillas Esther*, you would have said, 'It's nice,' but not encouraged me and told me how great it was — I would likely have given up. I just want to say thank you!"

translating *sefarim* into English, and shortly after *Megillas Esther* was released, Reb Meir received a hand-written letter from Mr. Yaakov Feldheim; the veteran publisher saw the potential and wished his friends — and competitors — well.

Reb Meir would say that along with the graciousness of it, it was the most effective reminder that they all shared a common mission.

"Reb Meir," reflects Rav Elya Brudny, "was a master in the *umnus*, the art, of giving a compliment. What's the secret? A compliment," Rav Elya explains, "means to find a trait that a person already believes he possesses, and then strengthening it; it allows a person to identify with that *middah* and use it in a good way. Reb Meir had the eyes to see that attribute right away, and the eloquence to express it. One sentence from him could change your day."

Mike Lerman from South Bend, Indiana would contribute to the extended Lerman family newsletter by sharing words of inspiration and uplift. For his column in the family periodical, he once wanted to use a story that appeared in an ArtScroll book, so he faxed a written request for permission to the ArtScroll office. The answer came not from a secretary but from the boss: Rabbi Zlotowitz himself called Mike to grant him permission — and tell him how wonderful it was that the family remained in touch, especially in such a meaningful way!

A young *talmid chacham* wasn't sure whether or not to accept the *rabbanus* position offered to him: he went to discuss his options with Reb Meir, whom he considered a wise man. Reb Meir encouraged him to take the job. Reb Meir told the visitor that he had the learning, the leadership skills, and the emotional depth, and assured him that he'd be a great success.

The young man listened and accepted the job. In honor of his first Shabbos as rav, a shipment of *sefarim* arrived at the

With Rabbi Yechiel Spero

shul, a gift from ArtScroll — and a message that Reb Meir believed in him.

On the very first Shabbos after Rav Shimshon Sherer assumed the position as rav of Khal Zichron Mordechai, Reb Meir — along with his son, Reb Gedaliah, and his son-in-law, Rabbi Duvie Morgenstern (husband of his daughter Dvorah) — made the walk to the shul, a means of showing support and encouragement for the new rav. Reb Meir's feet were hurting, recalls Reb Gedaliah, and the walk wasn't easy — but the opportunity was one he wouldn't pass up.

A dynamic young *mechanech* had an idea for a book of short, inspiring stories. He knew very little about the process, and submitted a rough, half-baked manuscript to ArtScroll, just a few sample stories. Reb Meir accepted it, raw and imperfect as it was, telling the writer, "We believe in you."

When the book was ready for publication, the author was astonished to see the advertisement announcing that ArtScroll was *"Introducing a brand-new series."*

And with that, Rabbi Yechiel Spero — author of several best-selling volumes and an extraordinarily impactful series — joined the ArtScroll family.

Mrs. Aviva Gluck flew to Florida for the annual Torah Umesorah President's Conference, a gathering for activists and lay leaders of Torah institutions and organizations. Her husband had flown earlier in the day and she arrived late Thursday night, well after midnight.

She came into the hotel, but was immediately overwhelmed. The spacious lobby was completely empty and the hallways were eerily silent: she wasn't sure where to go. She peered into a conference room where she saw Reb Meir in conversation with a revered rosh yeshivah — and she dared not interrupt.

But he looked up and saw her, and with a courteous nod to her, he stood up and turned to the rosh yeshivah. "Rebbi, this woman is Mrs. Gluck, her husband is Zvi Gluck and he's saving lives: is it okay if I just help her get settled?"

In fact, Reb Meir didn't generally go to conventions or conferences, regardless of how much respect he had for their sponsors. He felt that ArtScroll was a Klal Yisrael organization and couldn't be associated with any single demographic: the Torah Umesorah Presidents Conference was the lone exception. He very much appreciated Rabbi Zvi Bloom's vision in creating a gathering specifically to provide encouragement and training to those charged with responsibility for communal *mosdos*, and he was eager to be part of giving them *chizuk*.

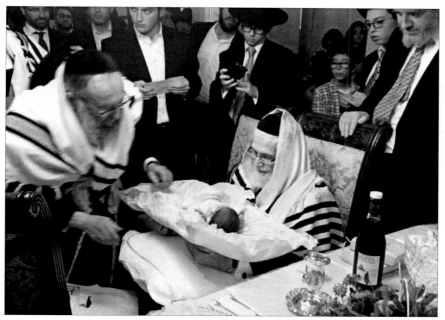

Sandak at the *bris* of a foster child

One of his children took a foster child into their home: once *askanim* saw that it was a home blessed with an abundance of love and warmth, they asked the family to accept other children in need of a home. Reb Meir was deeply moved at the selflessness of his children, who gave not just money or time, but actually allowed others to share their lives. He would tell his daughter-in-law, "I will get to *Olam Haba* by holding onto your coattails."

Reb Meir had changed the world for hundreds of thousands of people, but he was telling his children that their having changed the world for one anguished child would be the merit that he would grasp as well.

He and his friend Reb Shloime Werdiger had the *"minhag"* to walk home from shul together on Shabbos, after davening. Reb Shloime davens at the Gerrer *shtiebel*, and the davening at Rabbi Weinfeld's shul, which Reb Meir attended, would end about the same time; the two men would meet near the corner of East 22nd Street and catch up on the preceding week.

When Reb Shloime accepted the chairmanship of Agudath Israel's Board of Trustees, messages of support came from all

(L to R) Mendy Klein, Howard Tzvi Friedman, Jordan Slone, Reuven Dessler, Meir, Shloime Werdiger, Yosef Davis

over. "But I can tell you that no one, no other person, gave me the sort of *chizuk* that Reb Meir gave me," he recalls. "No one else was able to convey encouragement like he could."

In general, Reb Meir had an "eye," an ability to identify young people with potential to serve the *klal*: he drew them close, encouraging and guiding them. In his final years, he had a large circle of influential *askanim* who regularly consulted with "Uncle Meir," each of them certain that he was their personal cheerleader and mentor.

One of these young men was Rabbi Yehiel Kalish.

That relationship started when Rabbi Kalish was a member of the Cincinnati Community Kollel. In 2000, one of the local shuls asked Rabbi Kalish to deliver a daily *Daf Yomi shiur*, but the young man had a quandary. The *Daf Yomi* cycle was in the middle of *Maseches Kesubos*, and it seemed more logical to give the *shiur* participants a clear starting point, such as the beginning of *Berachos*. Being bold, Rabbi Kalish — who had never met or spoken to Rabbi Zlotowitz — had a sense that the ArtScroll founder would have insight as to how to proceed, and sent him an email.

Reb Meir replied within hours to the unfamiliar young member of the Cincinnati Kollel, and offered very clear advice: start from the middle of *Kesubos*, he said, and join with the rest of Klal Yisrael, since this way the *shiur* would have an identity and attachment with something bigger. Eighteen years later, that *shiur* has gone through *Shas* two times because of Reb Meir's accessibility, wisdom, and willingness to find time for a young man looking to serve the *klal*.

A close friend opened a new yeshivah, and Reb Meir wrote him a letter.

> *It seems like only yesterday that you confided in me this wonderful aspiration, and today, all of us witnessed the fait accompli. We all had the greatest confidence in your expertise, proficiency, and competence in executing the*

*project, but to have completed the multitude of facets —
spiritual and financial — so thoroughly and so flawlessly
in so short a span of time is truly a profound achievement...*

Reb Meir's close friend, Mr. Gary Torgow, chairs a dinner
each year in his native Detroit, to benefit the local yeshivah,
Beth Yehuda. At one of these dinners, Mr. Torgow was making
his way through the crowded ballroom when he noticed Rabbi
Zlotowitz — who had never even indicated he was coming, let
alone take a more prominent seat — in the audience.

"Rabbi Zlotowitz!" exclaimed Mr. Torgow. "Why didn't you
tell me you were coming? I would have seated you at the dais!"

"I just came to observe and have *nachas*," Reb Meir replied,
with a warm and loving smile.

The Weinberg Foundation in Baltimore approached a local
industry executive about publishing a large-type edition of the
Siddur for elderly people with failing eyesight or those with
vision problems. The publisher, not familiar with printing
Hebrew *sefarim*, called Rabbi Meir Zlotowitz for advice. Three
days later, Reb Meir boarded a plane to Baltimore and met the
publisher. Reb Meir grasped the vision and graciously offered
to publish the Siddur, eventually publishing a similar edition of
the *machzor*.

But Reb Meir saw more than just the publishing opportunity:
he drew the young man close, sensing that there was much they
would accomplish together. In time, Howard Tzvi Friedman
would become a leading *askan*, justifying Reb Meir's vision.

During the fortieth anniversary celebration at ArtScroll, Rabbi
Yonah Weinrib was moved to share a letter of congratulations,
nostalgically reflecting on his beginnings with ArtScroll Printing
in the early years and expressing his amazement at how the
company had grown to impact world Jewry.

Reb Meir was deeply moved — and typically, he returned
the conversation not to the growth of ArtScroll, but to the rise

With Rabbi Yonah Weinrib and Reb Nosson Scherman

of the young man in whom he had seen such talent decades earlier as a foremost artist. *My dearest, dearest Yonah,* he replied, *I didn't respond earlier to your beautiful and nostalgic email because I was so touched and moved by it, and I frankly didn't know how to reply. You know that I've always had special regard for you, and it's heartwarming to read your memories of the early days at ArtScroll when I had sefarim scattered over my dining room table on East 14 St. It's especially gratifying to see how you've grown over the years and have become a respected household name worldwide...*

Rav Ahron Kaufman was a vibrant young *talmid chacham*: before there were formal programs for youth at risk, he was pulling teenagers off the Brooklyn street-corners on Friday nights, inviting them to a private *minyan* and *seudah*. Reb Meir encouraged him, lauding the young *talmid chacham's* vision and heart — and sending a box of Siddurim to the informal *leil Shabbos minyan*, as if it were a real *kehillah* and shul.

When Rav Ahron eventually went on to found and lead Yeshiva Ateres Shmuel of Waterbury, there were pessimists who wondered if the concept — a yeshivah that would accept and believe in each and *every* *bachur* — made sense. Reb Meir was certain that the yeshivah would flourish and send forth successful *talmidim*, and would often remark to Rabbi Kaufman, "Waterbury is the ArtScroll of yeshivos. Torah belongs to *every* single Jew and if we can help them access it, we must!"

As positive and encouraging as he could be, Reb Meir's perception and insight enabled him to guide people away from opportunities as well. Adam Mirzoeff had been tapped by a major Klal Yisrael organization for a leadership position. The young man was honored by the request but unsure whether to accept it: being close friends with Reb Gedaliah, he knew Reb Meir well and thought that the older man might be able to direct him.

"Do you feel passionate about the cause?" Reb Meir asked. Adam admitted that he didn't feel enthusiastic about it.

"If your heart is not in it," Reb Meir said, "then you can't do it. People see you as a leader, and you need to love what you're doing and believe in it in order to influence them."

Reb Gedaliah reflects on that piece of advice. "The end of that story is the way Adam has subsequently emerged as such an *effective* *askan* — because my father understood what it would take for him to be successful in the service of Klal Yisrael."

When Reb Meir heard that Yeshivah Toras Emes in Flatbush had hired a gifted young rebbi as *menahel*, he was overjoyed: before calling the new *menahel* to say mazel tov, he called the school's president to make sure he knew how fortunate the school was at having retained such a "superstar."

On a visit to California, Reb Meir had some unexpected free time: he used it to send an email to a friend.

> *I'm in Los Angeles now for a simchah and I was thinking about you. I can't BEGIN to tell you how much nachas I have from you and your so many accomplishments*

— and specifically the visionary growth of your son's yeshivah which has become such a "shem dovor"[2] in such a short time. It's on everyone's tongue.

I'm really proud to be your friend. And I'm proud that your son is following in your innovative footsteps.

B'yedidus rav,

Meir

P.S. When's the last time you ever got such an email without someone following up with a request for money or to get some kid into the yeshivah? I'm not even reaching out for you to lend me a nickel! This email is pure devorim hayotzim min halev.[3]

One afternoon, he was on the phone with his friend Joe Weiss, who shared a joke. Reb Meir laughed heartily. A few minutes later, Reb Meir called him back. "I have to thank you, Joe. I was having a particularly stressful day and that laugh was exactly what I needed, so thanks for turning my day around."

Rabbi Leibel Karmel would compile a collection of witticisms and jokes and send them to a group of friends in honor of Purim: over the years, the mailing list grew bigger and a wide audience enjoyed the good humor — but only one person called Reb Leibel to share his appreciation. Reb Meir thanked him for the work that went into producing it and said, "You made my *simchas Purim!*"

Reb Meir was frequently in pain from his arthritis. He rarely complained, but once, after he sighed deeply, he looked at his son-in-law, Reb Efraim Perlowitz, husband of his daughter Faigie. Reb Efraim's mother, Goldie, had withstood several challenges in life with dignity and faith and Reb Meir was a great admirer of hers.

That day, he apologized for giving in to his pain, and said, "Look Efraim, I'm not like your mother. I sometimes complain."

---

2. "Noteworthy and celebrated."

3. "Words that emanate from the heart."

Reb Efraim stood there in silent awe, appreciating how his father-in-law had managed to turn his own pain into an opportunity to make someone else feel good.

People close to Reb Meir were often asked to solicit him for donations of ArtScroll *sefarim* or books to be used as prizes in *tzedakah* campaigns. One close friend apologized for the constant requests, and Reb Meir reassured him. "Look, I can't always say yes, I have to be responsible — but you should never stop asking, that's *your* mitzvah and you should keep doing it!"

The child of one of his friends made a similar request. The school her children attended was hosting a Chinese Auction,

Writing an inscription for Kalman Wartelsky, with his father, Reb Ezzy, looking on, together with Rav Dovid and Rebbetzin Leah Cohen

and after describing what a wonderful school it was, she asked for books — and expressed her apology for prevailing upon the friendship. Reb Meir wrote back, "Your enthusiasm comes through your email" — ensuring that she knew that it was all right to ask, and also that he appreciated her passion for the institution.

A manager at the Yerushalayim hotel where Reb Meir would stay was deeply distressed when he learned of Reb Meir's passing. He told the Zlotowitz children how, over the years, Reb Meir would conduct meetings in the hotel lobby: there was ample opportunity to observe the goings-on in the busy reception area and see how the manager, in the course of a day's work, dealt with all sorts of irate customers, enduring insults and criticism. Inevitably, Reb Meir would approach and say, "I've been sitting here all day and watching. You're doing a fantastic job. People are stressed, they don't mean to attack you. Please don't take it to heart."

An email he sent to one of the ArtScroll staff members received an auto-response in return, a note informing the sender that the recipient was taking an email break for several days. *I'm in awe,* Reb Meir wrote back to his employee, *and I hope you're successful.*

Reb Meir and his grandson once stepped into an elevator: an unfamiliar man took advantage of Reb Meir's proximity to tell him about a project he was engaged with. Reb Meir listened and said, "Keep doing what you're doing, you're holding up the whole world." The man's face lit up at the compliment and they parted as the elevator doors opened.

"Aron, do you see," Reb Meir asked his grandson, "how little time and energy it takes to make someone feel good? How easy it is to give *chizuk* to someone, a little push that helps them to keep accomplishing?"

Reb Meir had a special knack for finding the right words to encourage children: not just his own grandchildren, but all

Seated (L to R): Chaim Morgenstern, Ahron Perlowitz, Shmuli Zlotowitz,
Reb Meir, Ahron Morgenstern
Standing: Chaim Tzvi Perlowitz, Ahron Zlotowitz, Eliezer Perlowitz

children. An employee brought her son into work one day when the child didn't feel well enough to be in school. Reb Meir noticed and approached the young boy, who was sitting there aimlessly.

"Hey, would you want a job? You want to work for us?" Reb Meir asked.

The boy nodded. "Okay."

Reb Meir sat down with the boy and assigned him various small tasks, charging him to report back when he'd completed them all. At the end of a busy day, Reb Meir again sat down with the boy and paid him his salary — $25 for a job well done.

A high-school girl, a granddaughter of a friend, loved graphic art and wanted to know if she could hang around the ArtScroll office during her summer vacation. She wouldn't get in the way, she promised, and would simply observe: she wanted to learn more about graphics by watching the professionals.

She enjoyed her few weeks on site. On her last day of vacation, Reb Meir called her in and handed her a check. "Thanks for being part of what we do," he said. "You'll be great at this one day."

Reb Meir was sitting at a *simchah* with a respected rav when a mutual friend approached. "You should publish a book of the rav's articles, they're always on the mark," he said, indicating the rav.

It was uncomfortable for both Reb Meir and the rav. Later, Reb Meir approached the rav and explained that, while he really enjoyed reading the articles, they weren't of a genre that sold well enough to justify the expense of producing a book.

From then on, whenever one of the rav's articles appeared in print, Reb Meir would call or send a personal note commending the piece — his way of making sure the rav knew of his admiration, even if he didn't see the book idea as realistic.

One of the ArtScroll graphic artists had to inform the boss that she would be moving away, as her husband had gotten a position in an out-of-town *kollel*. Reb Meir relied on her heavily, and she came into his office with some trepidation about sharing the news.

"Of course we'll miss you," he said, "but I'm so happy for you that you're going to make a difference for Klal Yisrael."

Reb Meir's son-in-law Rabbi Asher Dicker, husband of his daughter Estie, is a popular rebbi. When he would ask for books to distribute as prizes to *talmidim*, Reb Meir didn't simply allow him to take them. "Asher," he would say, "we are in this together!"

Reb Meir's son learned in Long Beach, in the same *shiur* as the son of Rabbi Pinchos Lipschutz. Reb Meir would often call his friend. "Pinny, I just wanted to tell you that I heard from my son that your son is learning well!"

His former employee, Yitzchok Saftlas, who had launched his own marketing company, was featured in a popular magazine.

With Yitzchok Saftlas

You have no idea how much nachas I had reading about your success, Reb Meir wrote to him. *I relish the fact that I always saw great potential and talent in you — from the time we first met when we worked together at ArtScroll.*

He would not only personally call new writers to welcome them to the ArtScroll family, he would also call their parents, allowing them to share the *nachas.* When Mrs. Chaviva Pfeiffer, daughter of Rabbi Paysach Krohn. He published her *Maggid Stories for Children*, Reb Meir called her grandmother, Mrs. Hindy Krohn. He wanted to wish her mazel tov on the accomplishment and inform her that she, her son, and her granddaughter had made history as the first family with three generations of published ArtScroll writers.

Reb Meir admired the work of Rabbi Aaron Kotler, CEO of Lakewood's Beth Medrash Govoha. Once, they were working together on a project, and Reb Meir shared a story about Rav Aharon Kotler, the founding rosh yeshivah of Beth Medrash Govoha, with the rosh yeshivah's grandson and namesake.

During the years that Rav Aharon Kotler led his yeshivah in Kletsk, he was approached by a *talmid.* The *bachur* was facing forced military conscription, and was urgently awaiting papers that would ensure his release. In desperation, the *bachur* decided to travel to the post office in the next town to see for himself if the papers had arrived. He received the rosh yeshivah's blessings, and set out on his journey.

As the *talmid* sat on the train, ready to depart, he was startled to see Reb Aharon himself, racing around the platform and knocking on the windows of the compartments, searching for his *talmid*. "*Bachur'l, vu zent ihr?*"[4]

The *bachur* opened the window and called out to his rebbi — who had run for a full hour's time to the train station in order to catch him — and wondered what the emergency was.

"After you left yeshivah, a telegram arrived from the post office saying that the papers have arrived!" the rosh yeshivah exclaimed joyfully.

"That is wonderful," replied the *bachur*, "but why did the rosh yeshivah have to run all this way to tell me the good news when I would have found it out eventually?"

"*Bachur'l*, I wanted to tell you '*ihr zolt nisht zorgen,*' that you shouldn't be worried on the way there."

Reb Meir was deeply moved by the story — and he conveyed that emotion to Reb Aaron, who had an idea.

He went to a local artist and asked him to create a depiction of the key words in the story, "*ihr zolt nisht zorgen,*" as a gift for Reb Meir, seeing how Reb Meir had appreciated the message.

Reb Aaron picked it up when it was ready, and brought it to the post office, where he sent it off to Reb Meir.

Within a few minutes, a package arrived at Reb Aaron's own office: a framed rendering of those very words, "*ihr zolt nisht zorgen,*" a gift from Reb Meir that had been sent out the day before.

Two close friends, each carrying so much public responsibility, sharing the identical message of hope, in the very same fashion! Both gifts were treasured, kept in places of honor in their respective offices: one in Brooklyn, the other in Lakewood.

Reb Meir was honest enough to share sincere criticism when he thought it constructive, but even those words were laced with *chizuk*. On a visit to Yerushalayim, he ate dinner at a

---

4. "*Bachur*, where are you?"

new restaurant and was disappointed with the service. After the meal, he approached the manager and detailed the ways in which the service staff had failed the customers. Then he shared his suggestions about how to make the experience more pleasant.

When he was finished, Reb Meir handed the manager several hundred shekels as a tip and said, "This is your *parnassah* and I want you to succeed. Thank you for listening to me."

After leaving the restaurant, Reb Meir explained himself to the grandchild who had accompanied him. "People can't take criticism unless they feel you're a friend; we parted as friends, so maybe he'll listen."

Reb Meir would be the first to compliment a rav after a *derashah* — and never in an artificial manner. "He would let me know if I spoke too long, or if a point hadn't been clear," Rabbi Meir Platnick remembers, "but when it was good? Boy, did he let me know it. And because I knew that he was always honest, his positive feedback meant so much more."

He called the head of a major organization and said, "You know that I love you and want you to succeed. I have a graphics background and I feel you should know that, in my opinion, the advertisement you ran in the papers this week doesn't do justice to your organization. You guys are classier than that, and could do better."

Someone used inappropriate language in conversation with him. Reb Meir placed an arm on the man's shoulder and held his gaze. "You know that you can't talk that way, right?" he said.

"Never," the gentleman in question reflects, "did someone manage to make me feel more cared about while giving me *mussar*!"

In a telephone conversation with a young rav, Reb Meir responded to the rav's perfunctory question of "How are you" by saying that in fact, he felt unwell. The rav wished him a *refuah sheleimah* and got down to the reason for the phone call. Several minutes later, when they had concluded their business, Reb Meir asked the young rav for permission to say something personal. "My father was a rav, and I observed him. I feel like I should share this with you because you're a young rav, just getting started, and can benefit from hearing it. If someone says they don't feel well, a rav has to do more than say, '*refuah sheleimah*': he has to show genuine interest and show that he cares. Your *mispallelim* will appreciate it."

"When Reb Meir praised your work," recalls Rabbi Yechiel Spero, "you floated on cloud nine, but when he felt it necessary, he was pointed and direct in his critique. When he was disappointed, he clearly expressed that he felt that I was capable of better: there was no sugar-coating things when it came to the exactness of Torah!"

"On more than one occasion," Rabbi Yissocher Frand recalls, "I received a phone call or email after a speech — Rabbi Zlotowitz telling me that he'd heard I had spoken well. It made me feel great — because I knew it was sincere.

"I knew it because if he himself was at a speech and I would say something he felt was imprecise, not right, he would tell me. That's a true sign of friendship."

In a printed tribute in the *Hamodia* newspaper following Reb Meir's passing, veteran ArtScroll author Rabbi Shimon Finkelman remembers: *In one book that was a collection of stories on the parashah, I had put particular effort into writing a*

With Rabbi Yissocher Frand

certain story, calling the protagonist for exact details, writing and rewriting until it was perfect — or so I thought. A few days after its publication, Rabbi Zlotowitz spoke with me by phone. He had read part of the book over Shabbos and was not happy with this story. He felt that it ended too abruptly and somewhat sadly, and that the reader would not appreciate it. He asked that I correct it before the next printing and if I could make the revised version fit on the printed page.

I felt very bad, but he was right. I worked very hard on adding the missing piece in a few sentences. Before the next printing, I sent the revised version for his approval. I was not expecting a phone call from him this time; he was a very busy man. I would have been happy with a note, or even just to see the correction appear in the next printing. But Rabbi Zlotowitz did call, because he was a very caring person and he knew that I had felt bad when he had expressed his displeasure. He wanted me to know that he was very happy with the revision and that it would be included in the next printing.

A friend, a respected public *askan*, happened to mention that he had ordered a new car. Reb Meir politely asked what model it was, and the gentleman replied that it was a BMW. Reb Meir didn't react, but the next day, he shared an article with this friend, a report on the BMW Company having expressed regret for having Nazi ties.[5]

Along with the link to the piece, he sent a personal email:

Dearest —

I'm only sharing this with you because I never knew how deeply BMW was involved with the Nazi regime. They

---

5. During the Nazi stranglehold between the 1930's and 40's, the auto magnate functioned as the regime's military supplier and forcibly retained some 50,000 forced laborers and concentration camp prisoners... BMW manipulated political pathways in the National Socialist Party in order to secure highly profitable bids to manufacture weapons, ammunition, artillery, and U-boat batteries (*The Jerusalem Post*, March 08, 2016).

were the primary armed vehicle manufacturer. See link below. I thought only Mercedes was involved in the Nazi war machine.

Let's go for a Rolls.
With true adoration —
Uncle Meir

It was classic Reb Meir — a call, especially for someone associated with a public organization, to examine every decision and make sure that there are no traces of corruption or *chillul Hashem* — but a message delivered with obvious love and good humor.

His "no" was given was so much love, it felt like a yes.

A yeshivah student emailed to request permission to make photocopies of segments of the Stone Chumash for use at an upcoming Shabbaton for students, faculty and roshei yeshivah.

Sweet... Good hearing from you. You know how much I love your father, and how there's nothing I wouldn't do for him or his children. But in this case, I must apologetically decline because of various internal restrictions and precedents.

When we entered into the arrangement of publishing the Stone Chumash, the only exceptions made were the Agudah convention and the OU convention. We get this request from others all the time and we always have to regretfully decline. Please try to understand and forgive me.

If you wish Hebrew-only, I can grant you permission to reproduce from our Jaffa Edition Hebrew Chumash with the proper credit. Much hatzlachah to you, and best wishes,
Uncle Meir

P.S. Please call me about the Stone Chumash for your aufruf Shabbos!

True to his word, when the young student was engaged, Reb Meir sent a box of Chumashim for use at the *aufruf*, as he had promised.

Reb Meir perceived that it takes more generosity of spirit to offer honest criticism than to give artificial compliments. A prominent activist was once working with him on a communal matter: Reb Meir had asked him for help, and it was taking longer than Reb Meir would have liked.

Reb Meir phoned him and said, "Listen, my dear friend. If you can help me, please do so — and if you won't be able to, do me the service of telling me straight that it won't work. That's also a favor!"

And Reb Meir shared something personal. "At ArtScroll, we get submissions from aspiring writers. We'll accept some of them and work with the writers, and we'll have to reject some of the others. I once read that the common practice among publishers is to delay answering as long as possible, because no one wants to turn away a writer and then see them produce a best-seller with another publisher, so publishers try to buy time to decide. I accepted upon myself never to do that: if we're going to take it, I'll tell them right away, and if we're not — then I'll also tell the author right away, so that they can go to another publisher without delay. No is also an answer, but don't push me off please."

In the early years of ArtScroll, Reb Meir called a bookstore owner to collect an outstanding debt. The bookseller didn't want to take the phone call, because he knew what Reb Meir wanted, and he didn't have the funds available to pay.

Finally, he swallowed hard, picked up the phone and said it straight-out. "I don't have the money. I can't pay what I owe you."

Reb Meir was upset. "We sent you the books on time," he said, "so that you can run your business properly. We also need to make payroll and we expect our customers to pay us on time so that we can run our business!"

The bookseller apologized again and hung up.

The next day, the phone rang. Reb Meir on the line again. The store owner took the phone with apprehension, wondering if he was going to get another lecture.

"I just wanted to add one thing to what I told you yesterday," Reb Meir said. "I told you what I did not appreciate — and now I have to say how special it is that you had the courage to say, 'I don't have the money and I can't pay you.' That's rare. Most people would either avoid the phone call or give a million excuses about where the money is. Your honesty is impressive."

After Minchah at the office one day, Reb Meir emailed the ba'al tefillah.

> *Please forgive me, but you know that I love and care about you. I was worried about your out-of-breath intensity at Minchah during your chazaras haShatz. It was scary watching you. Consider being less intensive, and catch your breath. May the nachas of your tefillos be efficacious.*
>
> *Kol tuv!*

Reb Meir was able to speak with such honesty and candidness because he created the familial atmosphere in the office, the sense that there was always an open line of communication. "It wasn't a one-way street," Yitzchok Saftlas remembers, "but a real connection."

A relatively new editor joined a meeting in Reb Meir's office. Feeling intimidated, he was too bashful to speak up and share his opinion. Reb Meir didn't appreciate it, and suddenly stopped talking mid-sentence. "I don't need a meeting to find out what I think — I already know that," he said. "I want to hear what *you* think. Please talk."

The ability to communicate, to instantly connect with people, wasn't limited to work.

"You can learn one thing from every person," he would often say, and he cherished the opportunity to be around others. Reb Meir once attended a banquet, and the hosts were insistent that he accept a seat on the near-empty dais. He refused their offers, but they persisted. Finally, he said, "I'll be totally honest with you; this has nothing to do with humility — I just need to be around other people, speaking, listening, schmoozing — that's where I'm happiest."

Phil Rosen, a close friend and donor, would ask Reb Meir to join him when attending secular Jewish affairs. "I would ask him to accompany me to events for high-ranking Israeli government officials, or unaffiliated Jews, because I knew no better ambassador for the Orthodox community. Reb Meir came in his black hat, with his full beard — and one by one, they would be swept into his orbit, wanting to continue speaking with him. His warmth, his humor, his genuine interest in their lives and, of course, his sense of responsibility to Klal Yisrael, won them over every time."

After Reb Meir's passing, the many Matmid reward points he had amassed as an El Al frequent flyer had to be formally transferred to his wife's account. The travel agent forwarded the documentation to El Al and the email response came back from the faceless bureaucracy: *The points are now in her account. Please send her our condolences — her husband was a mentch! We all thought very highly of him.*

One of the newspapers ran an obituary on a man Reb Meir considered as close as a brother, his beloved friend Ronnie Greenwald. The pictures in the article were somewhat blurry, and the managing editor felt very bad, especially as he knew how much Ronnie's honor meant to Reb Meir.

He apologized, and Reb Meir — who wouldn't release a product until it was perfect — responded with great warmth and reassured the writer that there was no reason to feel bad:

Ronnie has enough zechuyos and he always played it low key anyway, Reb Meir wrote.

The easy acceptance is especially remarkable against the backdrop of another email, which Reb Meir sent to Rabbi Pinchos Lipschutz of *Yated Ne'eman* a few hours after Ronnie's passing. *I LOVED him. Do him justice in next week's paper...*

Reb Meir knew how to use his quick wit to cut through tension. He had once fainted in shul, and there was panic all around him: when he came to, the first words out of his mouth were, "*Kohanim arois,*" the traditional announcement for Kohanim to exit the premises in the presence of a deceased person — Reb Meir's innovative way of making a joke out of his own situation and putting people at ease.

He enjoyed good-natured teasing and banter. Reb Meir was visiting Lakewood, and he davened in an unfamiliar shul. The Siddur he removed from the shelf wasn't an ArtScroll product. "People will think that you like this Siddur better," someone remarked. "No," Reb Meir retorted, "they will think that the regulars grabbed all the ArtScroll Siddurim first so there was none left for the guest!"

A friend received a UPS notification that a shipment of ArtScroll *sefarim* was on the way to his house. He emailed Reb Meir his thanks, and wrote, "I ordered more *shranks.*"[6] Reb Meir responded a moment later, "We don't need more *shranks* — we need more *shrinks.*"

Reb Meir and his friend Gary Torgow were attending the same *simchah* in Cleveland: both would be there for Shabbos, and Reb Meir asked Gary if he would be amenable to being hosted in the same home. Reb Meir explained that because of his leg ailments, it took him some time to walk to and from shul: he looked forward to having Gary's company over Shabbos in order to accompany him on these walks.

Mr. Torgow instantly agreed, assuring Reb Meir that it would

---

6. Yiddish for bookshelves.

be a great honor. Over Shabbos, Reb Meir was in pain, and he needed assistance from his friend, Gary. Each time Reb Meir asked a favor, he would apologize again. "Gary, I am so sorry for being a burden to you."

"No, Rabbi Zlotowitz, it's a great honor to be able to keep you company," Gary assured him.

This exchange repeated itself several times over Shabbos, Reb Meir apologizing for being a burden and Mr. Torgow reassuring him that it was an honor. Finally, near the end of Shabbos, Reb Meir stopped walking for a moment and his eyes narrowed. "Okay, listen Gary, we're going to compromise: I'm going to agree that it's not such a big burden, but you'll concede that it's also not such a great honor!"

The sense of humor was one of his most effective tools: Reb Meir's quick wit allowed him to create an instant rapport with all sorts of people.

The very first time he went to meet Rav Elyashiv, he was warned by *talmidim* not to make small talk. Rav Elyashiv, they told him, wasn't like Rav Yaakov Kamenetsky or Rav Gifter, who would engage in pleasant conversation with him before turning to more serious matters. Rav Elyashiv's schedule was rigidly protected, every moment earmarked for his learning: there was no time and no interest in jokes.

The meeting was scheduled for five minutes to four — at four o'clock sharp, a delegation of politicians from the Degel Ha-Torah party were to arrive for consultation.

Reb Meir and Reb Nosson came in and started to describe their vision, sharing some of their previous *sefarim* and telling Rav Elyashiv what they hoped to accomplish. The rav was clearly intrigued by their presentation — so much so, that when the next group of visitors came, he asked Reb Meir and Reb Nosson to remain in his room so that they could continue speaking, and then excused himself to receive the politicians outside, in the hallway.

Presenting Rav Elyashiv with the latest volume of the Hebrew Schottenstein Talmud

As Rav Elyashiv stood up, he apologized for making them wait for him and assured them that he would be back shortly.

"It's no problem," Reb Meir said, and indicated the piles of *sefarim* all around them, "*ergsten fahl*, in the worst case, we can learn something."

He had made a joke. To Rav Elyashiv!

The *gabbai* looked on in dismay, but Rav Elyashiv broke into a wide smile and laughed. From that moment on, he would smile whenever Reb Meir came in.

Years later, Reb Meir would show Rav Elyashiv a French-language translation of the *Shas* and Rav Elyashiv joked, "*Nu*, when are you translating it into Turkish?"

"If you knew my zaide then you can appreciate how unusual that is," says Rav Aryeh Elyashiv. "He didn't joke; besides the fact that it took time, he wasn't that comfortable around most people who came to him. He didn't really know them. That he would joke with Reb Meir is the ultimate sign of esteem, it meant that the zaide was totally at ease."

Along with several volumes of the ArtScroll Gemaros — Bavli and Yerushalmi — there was an English-language Gemara on the shelf in Rav Elyashiv's home. Rav Elyashiv once pointed at it and jokingly told Reb Meir, "I use it to learn English!"

Rav Elyashiv would occasionally go to Telshe-Stone for a "vacation" — the only change from his regular schedule being that there was no public reception time and he didn't deliver the daily *shiur*: he could simply learn uninterrupted.

Only family and the closest *talmidim* were admitted during those days — and Rabbi Meir Zlotowitz, whom the rav would greet with a glowing smile.

Reb Meir once remarked, "Every rav needs a friend like me: who else tells them jokes?"

Reb Meir heard that one of his donors had completed a successful business deal, and he called to wish mazel tov and ask if they could meet that evening.

"Of course I want to share my success with ArtScroll, but tonight I'm tied up, let's meet tomorrow and I'll give you a nice check," the donor said.

"Listen," Reb Meir told his friend, "tonight you still know that the money isn't yours, it's Hashem's — tomorrow, once it's in your account, you'll forget all that and think it's your money. I want to meet tonight!"

The donor laughed heartily and agreed.

When the Torgows were making a wedding and Reb Meir was called up to recite a *berachah* under the *chuppah,* he walked up the aisle toward the canopy; as he ascended the steps, he looked over to Gary and said, "*Nu,* who didn't show up?"

A prominent, well-regarded individual made a very poor decision, and people close to him asked Reb Meir to intervene. In his email response, Reb Meir wrote with his classic wit: *Even smart people do stupid things. One thing you never see, however, is stupid people actually doing smart things. They just luck out every once in a while.*

A young man approached Reb Meir in a Lakewood shul with a suggestion. "*Shir HaShirim* is already printed in the Siddur," he said, "so if ArtScroll would just print *Koheles* and *Rus* in the back of their Siddur, then people wouldn't have to purchase *machzorim* for the *shalosh regalim*." Reb Meir met the man's gaze and said, "Right." Then they both burst out laughing.

One Shabbos, Reb Meir gently chided a young man in shul. "When you wear a tie, you have to keep the top button of your shirt closed, otherwise it looks sloppy," Reb Meir said. The man explained that he had put on weight and the shirt no longer closed properly. "Ah, in that case, you're *patur*," Reb Meir said, "because Chazal say *Kabed es Hashem m'groncha*.[7] You need your throat to daven."

Reb Meir was checking in for a flight to Eretz Yisrael and the ticketing agent informed him that his luggage weighed too much and would have to be opened up, and heavy items removed. Instead of arguing, Reb Meir smiled and removed a picture from his jacket pocket.

"Look," he told the agent, "this was me a few years ago, before I lost all that weight. I flew then as I fly now, so I think it's okay if my luggage weighs a bit more, since I weigh a bit less." She laughed heartily and allowed him to proceed.

"I always thought the sense of humor was just that, another one of his gifts: he was very funny and liked telling — and hearing — jokes," says Reb Meir's close friend Rabbi Yehuda Levi, "but one day I overheard a conversation that changed my perspective. It was *Parashas Zachor*, and we were sitting next to each other in shul. Before the *ba'al korei lained* the special *kriyah* for *Zachor*, Reb Meir leaned over to my 8-year-old son and asked him, with a serious expression, if the correct pronunciation of the word was '*zecher*' or '*zeicher*.'

---

7. *Mishlei* 3:9. "*Kabed es Hashem mei'honcha* — Honor Hashem with your wealth." *Al tikri* "*mei'honcha*," *elah* "*migroncha*," do not read it as "wealth," but "with your throat." Honor Hashem with whatever He has given you, even a pleasant voice (*Rashi* ibid.).

"My son answered that his rebbi had told them it was a *shailah*, a halachic debate."[8]

"Reb Meir whispered, 'Well, I work at ArtScroll and I know the answer — but I'm not telling you!'

"And then I realized," concludes Rabbi Levi, "that the jokes were all part of something greater, something holier. I always knew him as a tremendous *mechazek*, looking to encourage and lift spirits: that day, I realized that the good humor was part of that same mission. It was important to him to make sure that everyone around him was smiling, even the 8-year-old child."

Just a few weeks before Reb Meir's passing, a very close friend came to visit him in the hospital. Reb Meir had just endured a medical scare, and the visitor saw all the Zlotowitz children conferring in the hallway outside the room. The expressions on their faces led him to believe that the situation was very serious, and he entered Reb Meir's room with a similar demeanor.

Reb Meir was lying in bed, and he looked up to face the visitor. "No," he said with a smile, "please don't come into this room with that expression: in here, we're always upbeat. Thank you."

---

8. See *Mishnah Berurah* 585:18.

10

ONE WHO GIVES HONOR

THE ARTSCROLL PRODUCT, REMARKED ONE OF REB Meir's grandsons, was just an expression of Reb Meir's own personality; respect for the written word, for its appearance and layout, reflected Reb Meir's essential *middah* of *kavod*.

He exuded respect and gave respect — and, as Chazal teach,[1] this made him into a person who commanded respect.

The respect was part of his story from the very beginning; childhood friends recall little Meir's reverence for his own father.

Reb Meir would often tell his children that his father, Rav Ahron, was the first "*gadol*" he knew, and that imbued him with a lifelong awe and love for *talmidei chachamim*.

It wasn't just the way Reb Meir spoke about his parents — his reverence showed itself in practice as well.

Rav Ahron would frequently visit the ArtScroll office on Coney Island Avenue and Reb Meir would stop whatever he was doing

---

1. *Avos* 4:1: *Who is honored? One who honors others.*

and greet his father like a dignitary. Rav Ahron would avail himself of different services at the office and Reb Meir made it clear that there was no bigger honor for the staff at ArtScroll than to be of assistance.

One of the bigger mistakes made by a new secretary was not putting Rav Ahron Zlotowitz through immediately when he called for his son. Reb Meir was incredulous. "You kept my father on hold?" he asked in astonishment.

The secretary innocently explained that Reb Meir had, in fact, been tied up on another phone call.

He shook his head in wonder and made it clear that there was no situation that would make it correct for her to have placed his parent on hold.

Reb Meir once confided that he wouldn't drive along the block where his parents lived if he didn't have enough time to stop in and pay a brief visit. He was unable to simply pass by their home, as if it were just another house on the block.

One day, he came into his father's home and noticed a plate of cookies on the table. Rav Ahron didn't generally snack, and Reb Meir asked what the cookies were for. Rav Ahron didn't answer at first. "It's a *siyum*," he finally said, indicating the Gemara, *Maseches Niddah* — the last *masechta* in *Shas* — in front of him

"Papa, is this a *siyum* on *Shas*?" Reb Meir asked.

Rav Ahron acknowledged that indeed, it was so.

This picture, an elderly Jew seated at his table with a plate of cookies and the entirety of *Shas* before him, was one Reb Meir never tired of describing to his own children and grandchildren, as if he lived with the image before his eyes.

There were humorous moments too.

At the hat store, Rav Ahron once selected a new hat. The salesman quoted a price of $50, and Rav Ahron, who lived frugally, was astonished. "There's no way that's the correct price, I paid $20 for this exact hat last time I was here."

The salesman was about to explain that the price had risen over the years, but Reb Meir motioned to him to let it go. The salesman agreed to Rav Ahron's price, and Reb Meir returned later in the day to pay the difference.

The next day, Rav Ahron wore the impressive new hat to an Agudas HaRabbanim meeting. His fellow rabbanim complimented the new hat, and Rav Ahron proudly told them how much he had paid. "It was $20, a good price. You should all go get new hats!"

If someone showed respect to his father, Reb Meir remained eternally grateful to them and looked for ways to show them *kavod*. When his grandson became a *talmid* of Rav Shlomo Avigdor Altusky, rosh yeshivah of Darchei Torah in Far Rockaway, Reb Meir was doubly pleased. In addition to the fact that his grandson was close to a rebbi, it meant a lot to him that it was Rav Altusky, whose grandfather, Rav Yehuda Leib Kagan, had shown respect to Rav Ahron Zlotowitz.

Reb Meir and his family were planning to spend Pesach in a hotel, and Reb Meir urged his parents to join them. Rav Ahron steadfastly refused. One day, a few weeks before Pesach, Reb Meir had an idea.

He took a day off from work and asked his father to come for a drive. They headed up to "the country," driving through the Catskills until they reached Zucker's Glen Wild Hotel. "Come, Papa," Reb Meir led his father to the hotel kitchen, where the elder Rabbi Zlotowitz — a veteran *mashgiach* — stood and observed the staff.

Finally, he gave his verdict. "*Gut, m'kehn doh essen*, one can eat here," he said.

That year marked the first of many years that Rav Ahron and his wife Fruma joined their son and his family for Pesach — because Reb Meir had understood his father's hesitation and figured out a way to put him at ease.

The publishing of *Nachalas Ahron*, his father's *sefer*, was a

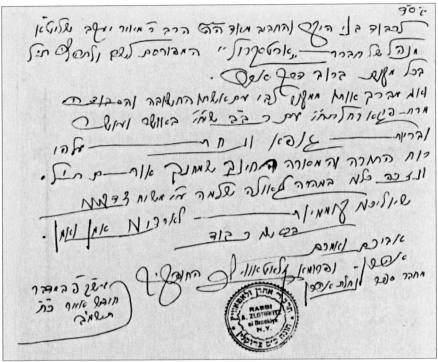

R' Meir's copy of *Nachalas Ahron* inscribed by his father

major project for ArtScroll. Reb Meir personally devoted himself to printing the *sefer* with an attractive cover and layout, ensuring that his father's *chiddushei Torah* would be presented in the most respectful fashion.

After his parents passed away, Reb Meir was just as deferential.[2] He would travel to Eretz Yisrael for their *yahrzeits*, even though the two dates fall less than two weeks apart — too long for him to remain in Eretz Yisrael, but close enough that the back-to-back trips were extremely taxing. Even in his final years, when he was often in great physical pain and overwhelmed by work responsibilities, he tried to go for both *yahrzeits* — to show his enduring reverence for both his father and his mother.

---

2. The obligation to honor parents pertains even after their demise (*Shulchan Aruch, Yoreh Deah* 240:9).

At the *kevarim* of his parents

He never tired of telling his own children and grandchildren who their grandparents were. Those grandchildren who carried the names of his parents, Ahron and Fruma, were reminded at every opportunity of the inherent obligation that came with their names.

Reb Meir kept his father's *Shas* in his own home, and would often show the worn volumes to his grandchildren. "Have you ever seen such a worn-out *Shas*?" he would ask. He would challenge them to pick up any volume and see the margins filled with notes, ensuring that they would see a living example of their zaide's diligence.

Ultimately Rav Ahron Zlotowitz was *niftar* in his son's home. Following the passing of his wife, Rav Ahron would spend most Shabbosim with Reb Meir and Rachel, but he was generally in a hurry to leave after Havdalah. "I would prefer my children ask *why* I'm leaving," he would joke as he packed up to go, "than my children asking *when* I'm leaving."

He spent Shabbos Chanukah of 1989 with his children, but

he didn't hurry out after Shabbos was over, as he did most weeks. He felt unwell, and said that he would spend the night at their home.

Early the next morning, Mrs. Rachel Zlotowitz sensed that something was amiss: she didn't hear the predictable early-morning sound of Rav Ahron learning at the dining-room table. Worried, she went to check up on her father-in-law. He asked for a cup and a basin, and after washing his hands, he fixed his yarmulke and sat up straight.

Then he passed away, a "*misas neshikah,*" a painless, easy death. Reb Meir's beloved father was gone. The grieving son would continue to revere and honor his father's memory, repeating *divrei Torah* and sharing stories about "Papa" at Shabbos *seudos* and *simchos*. Reb Meir cherished his copy of *Nachalas Ahron*, his father's *sefer*, and would keep papers and documents that had sentimental value to him inside its covers.

During the *shivah* for Rav Ahron, Reb Gedaliah and Daniella Zlotowitz were blessed with their eldest son. At the *bris* of Ahron Zlotowitz, Reb Meir shared a thought he would often repeat. In *Tehillim*, Dovid HaMelech says, "*Hafachta mispedi l'machol li, pitachta saki vate'azreini simchah,* You have transformed my lament into dancing for me; You undid my sackcloth and girded me with gladness."[3] Reb Meir would say that sometimes, one merits seeing how the *pesukim* literally express the reality and experience of life, and this was one of those occasions. "Hakadosh Baruch Hu lifted my *bigdei aveilus*, wiped away my tears, and replaced them with the extraordinary joy of holding a grandson who carries my father's name."[4]

Reb Meir didn't show respect only for his own parents; he inspired others to *kibbud av va'eim* as well.

---

3. *Tehillim* 30:12.

4. Ten days after Reb Meir's passing, the wife of this beloved grandson — about whom Reb Meir had recited that *pasuk* of *Hafachta mispedi l'machol li* — gave birth to a boy. The child was named Meir Yaakov ben Ahron, a new generation bringing joy in the face of mourning.

A veteran ArtScroll employee recalls how important it was to Reb Meir that staff members show up on time and work full days. "There wasn't much tolerance for slacking off or unexplained absence at ArtScroll; he worked long days and expected the same from us. But if I ever had to leave because one of my parents needed any sort of help — even something relatively small, like a ride to the doctor — there was no one more anxious to see me leave work. When my mother was hospitalized, he was always pushing me to leave work and get back to where I belonged, at her bedside."

When a senior member of the ArtScroll team sent the email announcing the *levayah* of his own father, Reb Meir replied.

> *He is being accompanied by the love and exceptional kibbud av his children had for him. Avrohom — your mesiras nefesh for him and your mother z"l — which was incessant for several draining years — under the most extreme circumstances — is extraordinary. May it*

With Rabbi Avrohom Biderman

be a zechus for all of you. And may he be a further mail-
itz yosher to you and your extended family.

Biydidus v'hakara,
Meir

Upon reading about a donation made by the children of his close friends Jay and Jeanie Schottenstein, he wrote to the young couple, commending not just their generosity, but the message they had sent along with the gift:

Dear Joey and Lindsay —

Shalom!

I had a lot of nachas reading about the gift you made to Hatzalah in Israel. It's very needed and very special. **The attribution you gave to your parents for instilling in you the values of giving was very appropriate and inspiring,** *and I'm proud to be your family friend.*

Meir and Rachel with Jeanie, Lindsay, Joey, and Jacob Schottenstein

May Hashem bring peace to Klal Yisrael, and may we share good tidings together always amidst health.

With warmest best wishes,
Meir

He would remind his children to call his own parents on Erev Shabbos — and also their maternal grandparents, for whom he insisted they show equal respect.

He expected his grandchildren to call him from yeshivah, seminary, or camp on Erev Shabbos, but inevitably, he would end the phone call by reminding them to call their other grandparents as well.

"The respect he showed his parents would define him," a lifelong friend remarked, "and it shaped the way he dealt with all sorts of people; he was always on the giving end in any relationship, leaving whomever he was speaking with feeling a bit taller."

Along with selling *chametz* to his own rav, Rav Chaim Yisroel Weinfeld, Reb Meir would sell the *chametz* in his office and bungalow to other rabbanim, because he felt that the tradition of *"mechiras chametz gelt,"* giving the rav money in exchange for this service, was a rare opportunity to give money to *talmidei chachamim* without compromising their dignity.

He was at a *chasunah* reception where a respected rav received the *kibbud* of reading the *Tenayim* document — an honor considered less prestigious than that of reciting a *berachah* under the *chuppah*. Reb Meir approached the rav later that evening and said, "That wasn't a suitable *kibbud* for you."

With Rabbi Chaim Yisroel Weinfeld

"And that was something only Reb Meir could say," the rebbetzin of that rav reflects, "because my husband was fine, he didn't mind the *kibbud* he received. But on some level, it wasn't what he was accustomed to, but only Meir Zlotowitz perceived that and had the ability to articulate it without making it into more than it was. He just 'got' people and understood their needs."

A young acquaintance once called to invite him to a *simchah*. Reb Meir apologized and explained that he wouldn't be in town that evening. "Okay," the caller said, "have a safe trip."

"No!" Reb Meir corrected him, "that's not how you respond. What you ought to say is, 'Are you sure you can't reschedule the flight so that we can have you at our *simchah*? It would mean so much to us,' and then, when I tell you that it's impossible, you should say, 'In that case, we will miss you very much. Have a safe trip.' That's how you show respect to another person."

Reb Meir called an out-of-town donor to make an appointment. "There is no reason that you and Reb Nosson have to waste all those hours," the donor said. "Wait until my next trip to New York and I'll come to you."

Reb Meir wouldn't hear of it. "We are the ones who need your help, so we'll come to you."

"But I have to be in New York anyway," the donor argued.

"Don't 'anyway' me," Reb Meir said. "*Derech eretz* dictates that we come to you, so we're coming."

When cell-phone use became commonplace, dropped calls were frequent: conversations were often interrupted in the middle if either party was in a low-coverage area. Once, a young associate of Reb Meir lost the conversation in mid-sentence and wasn't sure whether or not to call back. Reb Meir called him back and, characteristically, he explained that he had developed a rule for such situations. A conversation between people was significant, and each one owed the other the courtesy of treating it with respect; as such, whoever had originated the call was responsible to see it through and call the other one back.

The son of a close friend was in Brooklyn and paid a spontaneous visit to ArtScroll headquarters. Reb Meir greeted him warmly, but later that day, he emailed the visitor: "Thank you for coming, it was so wonderful to see you. I would only ask that next time you call or email to let me know before coming so that I can free myself up to greet you the way you deserve to be greeted."

Reb Meir enjoyed learning how to use new gadgets, and when upgrading his computer or phone, he would read through the manual and master the technology. There was one technological innovation he rejected: caller ID. He reasoned that if he knew who was calling, he might be tempted to ignore another person. He didn't feel that was correct, and so he never had the feature installed.

At a wedding, he saw his granddaughter in conversation with an older person. "I noticed," he later told her, "that you remained seated even while speaking to someone who was standing. The proper thing to do is show respect and stand up as well in that situation!"

Reb Dovid Scharf, a close friend of his son Reb Gedaliah and a leading *askan* on behalf of Yeshivas Mir-Yerushalayim, welcomed Reb Meir at the annual Mir dinner. He wanted to bring Reb Meir over to greet the Mirrer rosh yeshivah, Rav Eliezer Yehuda Finkel, but Reb Meir desisted.

The next day, he emailed Dovid.

Dear Dovid:

When some people wanted to bring me to him and introduce me, I knew it meant jumping the line so I demurred. I NEVER jump a line. It lacks kavod for all of those who had patiently been in line and I always avoid it. Even when I get a first-class upgrade I never let the VIP staff walk me past the people waiting in the jetway to board the plane. It's not right.

That's why I didn't want you to bring me to the Rosh Yeshivah when so many people were waiting there.

So Dovid, continue your wonderful askanus gezunteheit, and may your entire family benefit from the zechuyos accrued for your support of the largest Mossad HaTorah in the world.

Biydidus,
Uncle Meir

He would constantly remind his children that it's improper to enter or leave a room without acknowledging others. "You say hello when you come in and goodbye when you leave," he would tell them, and gently rebuke a child or grandchild who had left the dining room after a *seudah* without saying goodbye. A person in a room with other human beings, he taught them, has an automatic obligation to respect them; greeting each one when he or she comes and goes is an expression of that respect.

He once emailed an editorial note to a writer. "Okay," the writer emailed back. "Don't 'okay' me," Reb Meir responded; the message was clear. You can agree or disagree, but you have a responsibility to acknowledge my point in a courteous way.

Reb Meir was reviewing the travel expenses submitted by one of the salesmen. The employee was proud of the way he had kept travel costs down, but Reb Meir wasn't impressed. "Listen," he told the salesman, "you're not doing me a favor by renting a cheap car and eating in cheap restaurants and staying in cheap hotels. Know who it is you represent and show respect for us, show respect for yourself. Treat yourself with respect, stay in normal hotels and drive a decent car and eat like a *mentch*, and then," Reb Meir smiled, "you will do your job like a *mentch*!"

A grandson accompanied Reb Meir to the hat store. They parked and headed to the store, but then Reb Meir stopped. "Please leave your hat in the car," he instructed the young man.

"You didn't buy the hat from this store, and to walk in with it is a sign of disrespect to the proprietor."

He saw every person as deserving of respect, and that vision was never clouded, even when he faced potential loss. A businessman committed to sponsoring a major ArtScroll project: after making the initial payment, he appeared to be struggling to fulfill his pledge. He accepted Reb Meir's offer of more time, and then asked for even more time to come up with the promised donation.

It was difficult for Reb Meir, because he had to keep paying the many staff members involved in the project without the benefit of the sponsorship money. He asked a lawyer friend, who was close with this businessman, to offer an expert opinion: Was there any point in waiting for the funds?

The lawyer got back to Reb Meir with the report that unfortunately the donor meant well but he was in financial distress and would likely never make good on his pledge. The lawyer did have an idea. He had found another donor interested in taking over the project — he wouldn't pay the original price, but as a secondary buyer, he was prepared to undertake a good part of the production costs.

With Rav Dovid Feinstein

Reb Meir didn't hesitate. "There is no way we can do that. We've already released a volume of this edition and advertised it with the name of the first donor, so it would disgrace him if we replaced his name with that of another donor."

"Yes," the lawyer argued, "but at the same time, you need funding to pay the *talmidei chachamim* and you're not obligated to take such a heavy loss to protect him. Please, at least ask Rav Dovid Feinstein if you can do it," the lawyer urged.

"I don't have to ask Rav Dovid a *shailah* if it's *muttar* to be a *rotzei'ach*, permissible to spill blood; publicly humiliating another person is murder and it's never allowed."

The respect showed itself in the way he dressed.

Reb Meir would say that he had learned how to carry himself from Agudath Israel leader Rabbi Moshe Sherer, whose shoes were always gleaming and who wore cufflinks every day of the week. Reb Meir admired that, and he expected similar stateliness from his staff as well.

He would bring a barber to the office every few weeks to provide haircuts, free of charge, to the staff. In addition to ensuring that the ArtScroll team looked as impeccable as the product on which they labored, Reb Meir reasoned that sitting at the barber waiting was a waste of precious time; this way, each moment was maximized.

On a flight back from Eretz Yisrael, Reb Meir — returning from having been *menachem avel* the children of Rav Elyashiv — met a respected *mechanech*.

After greeting him, Reb Meir politely pointed out that it was unbecoming for a respected educator to be seen with such a wrinkled shirt. "I know that you're traveling, but they make non-iron shirts these days that don't get creased. You represent the honor of Torah."

He once met a young *talmid chacham*, a close family friend, in Lakewood. Reb Meir was happy to see the younger man and greeted him warmly. After they spoke, Reb Meir reached into his pocket and handed him a $20 bill. "Please," Reb Meir said, "get your suit pressed. You're a *talmid chacham!*"

Reb Meir once called Rabbi Paysach Krohn aside and said, "Reb Paysach, you are a well-known figure. Between performing

With Yisroel Besser

brissen and delivering lectures, you're in the public eye; your shoes should be polished better than they are."

After meeting the writer of this book for an interview that appeared in *Mishpacha* magazine,[5] Reb Meir asked him to wait in the office for a moment after the conversation had concluded. Reb Meir returned with a moist washcloth and began to wipe away a stain on the writer's coat. "You represent a Torah publication," Reb Meir said, "and you have to look the part."

A friend of his happened to see Rav Dovid and Rebbetzin Malka Feinstein in the Woodbourne pizza shop[6] and he brought his children over to receive a *berachah* from the rosh yeshivah. The proud father sent a picture of his family with the rosh yeshivah to Reb Meir.

Reb Meir emailed his thanks, but added a line. *How could*

---

5. "Guardians of the Book," *Mishpacha* magazine, June 29, 2016.

6. The pizza shop in the Catskills was owned by the proprietor of a similar establishment on the Lower East Side, so when visiting the mountains, Rav Dovid and his rebbetzin would try to visit their friend and neighbor and wish him well with his summertime business as well.

you approach the rosh yeshivah without first going to the car and putting on your hat and jacket?

Reb Meir once emailed Rabbi Pinchos Lipschutz to take issue with a picture that had appeared in the *Yated Ne'eman* newspaper: the image of a well-known American philanthropist visiting the *gedolei Torah* of Bnei Brak. Reb Meir was disturbed by the implications of printing it — because the American donor wasn't dressed appropriately for a visit to a *gadol!*

Reb Meir's respect showed itself in his attitude toward time: he valued each moment of his own time — and the time of other people as well.

His wife, Rachel, recalls how difficult it was to find gifts for him. "He wasn't a taker, he enjoyed giving much more," she reflects, "but there were two presents that I knew he would love."

One was a large, shul-sized digital clock with precise *zmanim* and other halachic details pertaining to the day. It wasn't very attractive, but Reb Meir cherished it, hanging it across from his desk at home.

The second was a small clock with a pendulum whose chime

With Rav Dovid Feinstein and Reb Gedaliah at a family *simchah*

was heard across the whole house on the hour. Reb Meir liked the idea that his family would always be reminded that time was passing and would personally wind the clock.

The problem with being on time, he would joke, is that there is no one there to appreciate it.

Guests at Zlotowitz family *simchos* knew that the schedule would run precisely as it said on the invitation. Along with a list of who would be receiving *kibbudim* under the *chuppah* of his children, Reb Meir always prepared a second list in case any of those on the first one wouldn't be present when called up.

Wedding Reception of Chaim and Shira Zlotowitz (final)
November 25, 2007

2:45	Arrival for Photographs (ends at 4:45 promptly)
4:15	Family Shots -- *full family must be present at this time*
4:45	Family Maariv in Kabbolas Panim Room
5:00	**Smorgaboard reception begins = Chassan's reception**
5:15	**Music Begins**
5:15	**Kallah enters Ballroom**
5:30	Kabbolas Kinyan of Tenoyim and Reading / M'chuteinestas present
5:40	Kabbolas Kinyan of Kesubah & signed
6:03	****** Chosson Procession to Bedeken***
6:10	**Bedeken**
	[Remember to have someone take along kesubah]
6:25	**Chupah begins**
	[no children marching down]
6:50	Chupah over / Chosson & Kallah into yichud room
	** All family members who are going to be photographed
	MUST IMMEDIATELY GO BACK TO LOBBY UPSTAIRS
**	
7:05	Chosson-Kallah join photo session
	[During this time, appetizer is eaten]
7:40	**Chosson Kallah enter Ballroom / 30 minute dance [promptly]**
	Salad served during this dance
8:10	**Main course is served**
9:00	2nd dance / 25-30 minutes Promptly [desert now served on tables]
9:30	Dance ends
9:40	**BIRCAS HAMAZON AND SHEVA BERACHOS NOW**
9:45	Last short dance
10:15	**Music Ends Mazel tov!**

Schedule from Chaim and Shira's wedding

Someone asked him if he didn't feel it disrespectful not to wait for a particular rav to appear at a *simchah*. "The greatest way to show respect for people is respecting their time," he said, "because there is nothing more precious."

"My rebbi, Rav Moshe would say that 'You don't hold up an *oilam*," Reb Meir would say. "Respecting a crowd means ensuring that their time isn't wasted."

When the children of his friends got engaged, Reb Meir would share his list with the new *mechutanim*, the precise schedule of how to run a wedding without creating an unnecessary waste of time. He used times such as 6:03 on the schedule, not rounding if off to the nearest ten, a way to drive home the point that each and every minute counts. ArtScroll employees noted that the morning after making a *chasunah*, Reb Meir would arrive at work as early as he did every other day, his way of making the point that a person could host a *simchah* and still maintain his regular schedule.

One Shabbos morning, Reb Meir's son came into the kitchen at 8:35; he was surprised to see his father sitting there five minutes after the designated time for Shacharis at their usual shul.

"We're five minutes late," Reb Meir said, "and so we'll go to another shul which starts at 9:00 — but we won't come in late to shul."

Not just time, but words as well.

Each word that issued from his mouth was viewed as a tool with potential to build or destroy, and given the appropriate respect.

Reb Meir would retell the story of his encounter with Reb Moshe Yair Weinstock, one of the *tzaddikim* and *mekubalim* of Yerushalayim. Reb Moshe Yair, a descendant of the Rebbes of Lelov, was a prolific author, writing various works on Kabbalah, on *tefillah,* and on Jewish history.

Reb Meir had noticed a *peirush* on *Seder Olam*[7] written by

---

7. A Baraisa, based on Midrashic accounts of creation and history.

Reb Moshe Yair and wanted to own it, but it wasn't available in stores. On his next trip to Eretz Yisrael, Reb Meir called the number printed in the flyleaf, and spoke directly with the *mechaber*, asking to purchase the *sefarim*.

"Fine," said Reb Moshe Yair, "meet me tomorrow morning in front of my home, at Meah Shearim 4, at 11 o'clock sharp."

Reb Meir confirmed the meeting, and the next day, he left the Merkaz Hotel a full half hour before the scheduled appointment. Because walking was painful, he took a taxi. When the car came down Strauss Street toward Kikar Shabbos, it encountered a massive traffic jam. Kikar Shabbos was filled with people, and after minutes of waiting in a complete standstill, the driver suggested Reb Meir get out and walk.

It wasn't easy to walk, but Reb Meir wouldn't come late to a meeting. He paid the driver and made his way down the street and through the dense human traffic at Kikar Shabbos, where it appeared some sort of gathering was taking place. Focused on reaching Meah Shearim 4, Reb Meir made his way through the crowd — which he soon realized was a *levayah*. He wondered how he would even find Reb Moshe Yair on the teeming sidewalk.

Reb Meir approached the building and was stunned to see them carrying the *mittah*, the body of the deceased, out of that very building, Meah Shearim 4. He stood back out of respect and waited silently as a great wailing went up from the mourners. It was clear that this was the funeral of a *tzaddik*, and Reb Meir asked someone whose *levayah* it was.

"Reb Moshe Yair Weinstock," was the reply.

It was precisely eleven o'clock.

Reb Meir, unable to speak, accompanied the *levayah* of this *tzaddik*.

Though traditionally, the first day of a *shivah* is reserved for close friends and family, Reb Meir was scheduled to return to New York that night, so he visited the mourners that first evening. He felt compelled to share the extraordinary story with them.

He came into the *shivah* house and introduced himself. He told the children of his conversation with their father the day before — and suddenly, one of the sons interrupted. "Ah, you're the American who wanted the *sefarim*?" He stood up and returned with a package of *sefarim*. "My father left this for you; he said you would be coming by."

Reb Meir would tell the story, but typically, his focus wasn't on the supernatural elements. He was taken by the precision of Reb Moshe Yair's words, how a person who respects his own words receives help from Heaven.

Reb Meir made a comment while on the phone with a grand-daughter and she laughed. A few moments later, she said something that made it obvious that she hadn't really heard what he had said earlier and she had been laughing out of politeness.

"Listen, I want to teach you an important lesson," he said. "If I said something, it was because I wanted you to *hear* it, the words meant something. If you didn't hear what I said, then you should have said, 'Zaidy, I didn't hear that, can you please repeat it.' But don't pretend you heard me when you didn't. There will be situations in life where people speak and you may not hear them; ask them to repeat themselves, because it's the proper thing to do."

Reb Meir once had a disagreement with a senior editor, who, he felt, had wronged him. Reb Meir didn't speak to this man for an extended period of time. (During that time, the editor notes, the flow of work never stopped — Reb Meir kept his disagreements respectful, and was never spiteful or mean.) One day, they were in a meeting together with another person, and Reb Meir excused himself to get something from a side room. The third man immediately offered to go, since walking was difficult for Reb Meir. It was obvious to this editor that Reb Meir had been hoping for just that — he clearly wanted a private moment with his colleague.

The two men sat there alone and Reb Meir looked the other man in the eye. "I just want to say that I'm sorry. I was wrong."

That was the end of the conversation; a moment later the third man returned and they got back to business.

"I saw greatness in the way he said, 'I'm sorry,' " reflects this *talmid chacham*. "Most people offer explanations and excuses along with an apology, but not him. His 'I'm sorry' was so strong because *every* word and term he used was thought out, it had the force of his personality behind it. If he said something, he meant it."

An acquaintance was trying to reach Reb Meir, but the secretary made it clear that he was in a meeting and unavailable. The fellow called again and, in what he considered a cute prank, told the secretary that it was Jay Schottenstein on the phone. Reb Meir immediately stepped out of his meeting and took the call.

"It's just me and it was the only way I could get you," laughed the caller after introducing himself.

Reb Meir was shocked. "You lied. You used someone else's name. You violated my trust. I can't speak with you." He ended the call and returned to his meeting.

He understood people, often better than they understood themselves. Reb Meir would say that when someone calls and says, "I called you for two reasons," then the first reason for the call is generally unimportant: the second topic they raise is the actual reason for the call and the first is the "small talk."

Rabbi Meyer May, a close

With Rabbi Meyer May

friend of Reb Meir, would often help with soliciting West Coast donors for ArtScroll. "Inevitably, they would try to negotiate on the price for whatever project was on the table," recalls Rabbi May, "and Reb Meir would calmly explain that the price wasn't open to discussion, because it was based on his projected costs. His respect for his own price list really impressed the donors, because it showed them he took the project seriously."

Reb Meir would articulate this. To a would-be vendor negotiating about the price for a particular item, Reb Meir wrote: *To help you in moving forward and potentially working with ArtScroll, which we would very much like, it's important for you to know the following. We have a virtually iron-clad rule here for the past nearly forty years. We don't negotiate. When we are offered a service or product, or we solicit a price, we ask the provider to quote the lowest price he can while maintaining his appropriate profit level.*

If we subsequently contact another vendor and find we can get the same product for less, we never go back to the first vendor to ask him to match the lower price. Nor do we respond positively when the vendor offers to lower the price to match a competitor. It's simply not the way we do business. We need to develop a relationship so that we KNOW he's giving us the best price he can without our always having to compare.

It was a respect for the task at hand. His grandchildren knew that when they came to visit, his face would light up and he would greet them with excitement — but then he would excuse himself and go back to finish whatever task he was in the middle of.

"I just need to finish writing this email," or "I'll just finish reviewing this draft" — only then would he sit down with them and completely give himself over to the conversation with them.

"If you push off a task," he would explain, "it might never get done and even if it does get done, it won't be done with the same focus. A person who has self-respect finishes what he or she started before turning to another task."

And finally, the respect showed itself in his attitude toward possessions, the respect he had for inanimate objects as well.

He appreciated quality pens, and had a collection of fountain pens he had assembled over the years. He would proudly show his grandchildren the pen he had received as a gift for his own bar mitzvah. "And it still works," he would say, "because I take good care of it."

"And people aren't that different than pens," he would laugh, "If you show respect and take good care of them, then they will give you respect too."

Reb Meir was a frequent flyer to Eretz Yisrael, and he accumulated many reward points over the course of the year. As he and his wife checked in for one such flight to Eretz Yisrael, the desk agent informed him that there was a vacant seat in first class and he was eligible for the free upgrade.

"Perfect, my wife will use it," he said.

Mrs. Rachel Zlotowitz wouldn't consider taking it, feeling that her husband — with his leg pain and exhaustive work schedule — should enjoy the spacious seat.

But he was adamant: he would sooner forfeit the upgrade rather than take a better seat than his wife. It looked like the agent might give the seat to another passenger, since neither Reb Meir nor Rachel would take it.

When they boarded the aircraft, the stewardess informed them that the staff had been too impressed to give the seat away to another passenger. Instead, they had managed to locate a second seat in first class for this couple to whom respect was more important than personal comfort and convenience.

Only then did Reb Meir and his wife accept the spacious seats, together.

11

TO SEE DEEPER

SOME PEOPLE ARE KINDHEARTED," SAYS REB SHMUEL
Blitz, "but Meir was different. It wasn't just compassion
that motivated him in dealing with others, but a clear
sense of what the person standing before him really needed."

Reb Meir had an ability to see deeper. He was a *"maskil
el dal,"*[1] blessed with both the perception to see what others
lacked and the generosity of spirit to fill that need for them.

A respected *talmid chacham* was establishing a new yeshivah
high school and Reb Meir had registered one of his sons for the
coming year. Opening the new institution proved more difficult
than expected, and the *talmid chacham* spent months pulling
together funding, students, and a qualified staff. In midsummer,
just weeks before the new year was to start, it became clear that
the yeshivah wasn't meant to be.

---

1. "Fortunate is the one who considers the poor" (*Tehillim* 41:1). *Maskil*, the
commentators explain, means more than to merely see the needs of the poor; it
denotes perceiving and contemplating their needs.

The *mechanech* had the unpleasant task of calling the parents who had registered their sons and informing them that they would have to find other *mosdos* willing to take the boys on the eve of a new school year.

He phoned Reb Meir and said, "I'm so sorry, the yeshivah isn't working out. I hope you're able to find a good yeshivah for Baruch."

Reb Meir didn't hesitate. "I'm not worried about Baruch, he'll find the right yeshivah — I'm worried about *you*. What will you do this Elul? You have a wife and children."

The *talmid chacham* admitted that he hadn't been able to come up with a plan yet.

"Great, then you'll come work for us until things settle down," Reb Meir said firmly.

"But who says I can write?" the *mechanech* asked.

"I saw the letters you sent out for the yeshivah and it's clear that you have literary abilities; I'm confident that you can do this."

This talented young man started to work at ArtScroll, writing and editing, for several months, drawing a respectable salary.

At the end of the first month, Reb Meir handed him a check with a broad smile. "You're not in *chinuch* anymore, so you don't have to check the date on the check," he quipped.

The few months at ArtScroll afforded the capable *talmid chacham* exposure to new opportunities. He learned about his own abilities and, in time, he rejoined the *chinuch* world as a dynamic and effective *maggid shiur* — but he continued writing as well. Until today, he learns, teaches — and writes, a welcome source of additional income.

Reb Meir would often point to an incident from his youth that had taught him about perceiving the needs of another.

While in yeshivah, Meir Zlotowitz earned a side income by making artistic plaques for organizations, which they would present to honorees at dinners or events. He once received an order from the Bobover *mosdos* and when the plaque was ready, he went to deliver it to the Rebbe's home.

Reb Meir would talk with admiration about the *"Erev Shabbosdik'e"* atmosphere in the Rebbe's home that Thursday evening. After Reb Meir knocked, the Rebbe, Rav Shlomo Halberstam, called out that he should come in — but the house was empty. Reb Meir wandered through the empty rooms, wondering where the Rebbe was, when he finally located his host.

The Rebbe sat near the large dining-room table, shining his shoes in honor of Shabbos, performing the task with obvious joy.

The Rebbe came out to greet him, and, after accepting the plaque, the Rebbe took another look at Reb Meir's face. "You haven't really eaten anything all day, right?"

Reb Meir conceded that it was so, and the Rebbe insisted he come to the kitchen, where the Bobover Rebbe himself prepared a tuna fish sandwich for the young yeshivah *bachur*.

"Most people would see a young man waiting to get paid, but the Rebbe, with one glance, saw something much deeper," Reb Meir would say.

Tzvi Zlotowitz and Rav Porush

Reb Meir was often in Eretz Yisrael, and was a regular participant in the *vasikin minyan* at the Kosel. He davened at what's referred to as "Porush's *minyan*," a traditional yeshivah-style, *nusach Ashkenaz minyan* generally held right in the middle of the davening area. Such luminaries as Rav Beinish Finkel and Rav Moshe Shapira would daven at that *minyan*, and even though the pace was

At the Kosel with (L to R): Efraim Perlowitz, Chaim Zlotowitz,
Reb Meyer Birnbaum, Rav Chaim Smutni, and Duvie Morgenstern

slower than that of the other *minyanim*, Reb Meir felt at home there.

(He would often return from Eretz Yisrael with stories about the colorful, vibrant people he encountered at the Kosel. The kaleidoscope of *minyanim* and individuals gathered before the Wall at the start of each day were, to him, a microcosm of Klal Yisrael. He recalled with enjoyment the time he'd been davening Shacharis, and he noticed that an older, distinguished looking Sephardic gentleman seated directly in front of the Kosel seemed agitated. The older man stood up and began to scurry around in front of the Kosel, peering at each and *every mispallel*. It seemed strange, and Reb Meir looked on with curiosity. Eventually, the Sephardic *chacham* stopped in front of Reb Meir and lifted Reb Meir's *tallis*. The elderly man gave a little cry and pointed to the fact that Reb Meir's right and left hands were woven together, his fingers clasped as he davened.

"That's the problem, your *yad yemin* [right hand] and *yad semol* [left hand] shouldn't be together, it's preventing the *rachamim* from flowing."

With that, the *chacham* turned and returned to his station in front of the Kosel.)

Reb Meir formed many close friendships at that *minyan*. One of the distinguished members of that *minyan* announced that his daughter was engaged. After wishing him mazel tov, Reb Meir asked, "Perhaps you need a loan in order to meet the wedding expenses?"

The *ba'al simchah* nodded: he could certainly use a loan. There was no other way he could deal with the commitments he had made.

Reb Meir immediately took out his checkbook and they wrote a *shtar*,[2] concluding the transaction. A few months later, Reb Meir was in Yerushalayim again and the borrower came to bring Reb Meir a check, repayment for the loan. Reb Meir thanked him warmly and then, without saying another word, he tore up the check and dropped the pieces of paper into the wastebasket. He never mentioned it again.

On his next visit, Reb Meir davened with his regular *minyan,* then asked this friend if they might meet later in the day. The two men sat down in the lobby of the Plaza Hotel and Reb Meir handed him a stack of documents. "These are the galleys of the upcoming *lashon kodesh* Siddur, our first such work. It's meant for the people here, and it needs a real *Eretz Yisrael'dik'e Yid* to review it. I know that you have the mesorah and the knowledge to do it right. Could I ask you to look it over and share your *he'aros*, your observations, as a personal favor to me?"

"Now I know," this friend reflects, "that Reb Meir didn't need my input, he had a qualified staff capable of doing a better job than me — but he saw an opportunity to create the sense that I was giving him something, and he seized it!"

---

2. A halachically binding document, with witnesses and a time for repayment.

With Rav Chaim Smutni

When Reb Meir would daven at that *minyan*, *tzedakah* collectors would swarm around the generous American visitor, waiting for their donations. At one point, Reb Meir felt unable to meet the demand presented by the stream of collectors and he davened elsewhere, forfeiting his regular *minyan*.

"Why can't you just do what most tourists do, and prepare a stack of American $1 bills?" asked Reb Meir's friend, Rav Chaim Smutni. "Then you can have something ready for each one and it doesn't have to cost you an unreasonable amount."

Reb Meir looked at him in surprise. "Reb Chaim, these people really need help!" he exclaimed, "I can't give someone who needs money $1."

Another close friend from that *minyan* was Rav Shalom Gold, the rosh yeshivah of Yeshivas Rabbi Akiva, a yeshivah established specifically to teach Torah to those who were first tasting the sweetness of Torah after the age of forty.

Rav Shalom would come to visit his family in America, and he would often visit Reb Meir at the office. "Always, Reb Meir would say, 'Go take books, whatever you need, fill up boxes and we'll ship them to your yeshivah. Don't show me what you're taking, you know what you need,'" Reb Shalom recalls.

"Aside from the books, he would give me a donation for the yeshivah and invite me for dinner. I remember one evening, Rachel made this beautiful meal for us, and I was sitting there feeling completely overwhelmed by the kindness of this couple. I had taken more than I deserved. And then, suddenly, Reb Meir looked at me with this very serious expression and said, 'Reb Shalom, I'm so lucky you're my friend. You inspire me!' He made me feel as if I were doing him a favor by being there."

When Rav Shalom's father passed away, he flew home for the funeral, which was held in Long Island, New York. A committed *ba'al teshuvah* for many years, he felt very uncomfortable at the secular event.

"But when I was leaving the funeral home, mourning my father and mourning the general state of Jews cut off from their heritage, I saw three familiar faces, three men standing on the curb — Rabbi Meir Zlotowitz, Rabbi Nosson Scherman, and Rabbi Sheah Brander. I felt embraced, and so honored that my father could have these great men there at his funeral."

Another *ba'al teshuvah* friend had a similar experience. "I was sitting *shivah* for my father and was depressed by the atmosphere; my irreligious family was sitting there enduring the long week by making jokes. I was doubly broken, by the loss of my father and by the sense of profound loneliness. And then in walked Reb Meir with a gift: four freshly printed volumes of *Maseches Bava Metzia*.

"I know you're not allowed to learn yet," Reb Meir told his mourning friend, "but I wanted you to see them, they just came off the press. You'll take them back to Eretz Yisrael and find people to share them with, I'm sure."

"It was the ultimate *nechamah*," recalls this friend, "because he reconnected me with my real world that way, gave me the sense of being home when I was feeling so out of place."

Reb Yaakov Munk, the father of Reb Meir's son-in-law Reb Yehuda, was unwell for several years, suffering from Alzheimer's disease. One day, Rabbi Munk asked his son to come into his room so they could discuss something private. Reb Yaakov began to speak with a clarity he hadn't displayed in years, and his son immediately sensed that it was an *eis ratzon,* an auspicious moment.

Reb Yaakov handed Yehuda a notebook filled with handwritten *chiddushei Torah*. "In our family, we believe that Torah should be shared, that's what my father believed as well. I'm giving this to you to share with your siblings."

The next day, Reb Yaakov had a stroke.

The moving story, the clear final message from a father bound up with Torah and words of Torah, was passed around the family.

Reb Meir didn't just react, though.

He asked his son-in-law for the notebook, then called in his graphics team. He had an idea.

"For your daughter Estie's *sheva berachos*," Reb Meir told his son-in-law, "we'll have the *sefer* ready."

Reb Meir immersed himself in the project, creating a beautiful cover for "his *mechutan's sefer*" and by the time the *sheva berachos* arrived, a few weeks later, the *sefer, Divrei Yaakov,* was ready. Several hundred copies were distributed to grateful guests and relatives; and the *mechaber* himself, Reb Yaakov, spent his final days in

Sefer Divrei Yaakov

this world with the *sefer* at his side, visitors sharing his own *divrei Torah* and lifting his spirits.

Rabbi Shimon Finkelman's classic work, *Shlomie!*, on the life of the legendary *ba'al chessed* Reb Shloime Gross *z"l*, was scheduled for a post-Pesach release. Without being asked, Reb Meir arranged for a small batch of books to be printed earlier, so that the book could give the Gross family pleasure over Yom Tov.

A young couple, close friends of his children, gave birth to a baby with severe medical issues. Reb Meir called the new father. "I imagine that you're going to be facing many difficult decisions over the next few days," he said, "some of them very weighty. You might need to consult with Rav Dovid Feinstein and it can be hard to reach him, but I can usually get through; please call me any time of day or night and I'll help you."

When his nephew, Chaim Kiffel, was heading to the airport

With Chaim Kiffel

to pick up his *kallah*, Reb Meir — not much older than the new *chassan* — insisted that the young man use his new car. "It's a nice car and you'll feel so much better," Reb Meir said with a smile, "and there's nothing wrong with impressing her a little bit!"

For several years after his move to Flatbush, Reb Meir davened at a shul called Congregation Sfard, along with his father. On Yom Kippur of 1977, he purchased the *aliyah* of *shelishi* during Minchah. The *aliyah* — known as *Maftir Yonah* — has a tradition of being associated with blessing, and is considered a *segulah,* an auspicious omen for the one who receives it.

Reb Meir honored a 19-year-old boy named Saul Lieberman with the coveted *aliyah.* The recipient was surprised, as he didn't have any sort of meaningful relationship with Rabbi Zlotowitz and wasn't expecting to receive such a prominent *aliyah.* "You had a rough year," Rabbi Zlotowitz told the young man, who had lost his father several months earlier. "May the *berachos* accompany you from now on."

A *talmid chacham* caught what he felt was a halachic error in an ArtScroll book and he faxed a letter to ArtScroll headquarters, saying that he had first noticed the mistake while perusing the *sefer* in shul, and then borrowed the book from a neighbor to confirm what he had seen. Reb Meir himself sent back a response — not a letter, but a package. "Thank you for sharing the observation. We reviewed it and agreed that the layout of the page might have led others to reach the same halachic conclusion, which is indeed an error, and we will adjust it in future editions. As an aside," Reb Meir wrote, "I noticed that you borrowed the *sefer*: enclosed is a copy of your own, so you will no longer have to borrow it."

He once noticed that the shoe-repair shop near his home seemed empty of customers. He chatted with the shoemaker who admitted that business was slow.

A few days later, a visitor to the office saw that Reb Meir was sitting at his desk, shoeless. This was most out of character and the visitor inquired about the anomaly. He learned that Reb Meir had sent his shoes to the Flatbush shoemaker via the office delivery man. Reb Meir was sitting and working — shoeless, but content in the knowledge that the craftsman repairing the shoes had a bit of work, something to allow him to feel pride.

While on the phone with an off-site technician helping with a computer issue — a man Reb Meir did not know — he commented that the gentleman sounded tired. "Is everything okay?" he asked.

The technician admitted that he wasn't having the easiest day. His son was in the hospital, he said, and after working long days at the office, he would go to relieve his wife at the hospital and spend the night there. He hadn't slept normally in several days and the fatigue and worry for his son's health were getting to him.

Reb Meir offered his heartfelt wishes for a *refuah sheleimah* and then, when the call was complete, Reb Meir phoned Chaim Kahn, the president of the IT company. "Chaim, I just want to make sure you realize what your employee is going through," Reb Meir said. "You're his boss and it's up to you to do whatever you can to help him through this."

Reb Meir never forgot his own difficult moments, and used those memories as a means of helping others. Reb Meir was sitting in a restaurant when a young man, the grandson of a close friend, approached and introduced himself. His stutter was so pronounced that he could barely articulate his own name. It took him a full minute to say who he was, and Reb Meir sat there patiently, smiling broadly all the while.

Reb Meir responded with effusiveness and warmth, and after the young man had walked away, Reb Meir looked at the grandson who was dining with him. "I know exactly what it feels like, I also stuttered badly. I worked very hard to conquer it, but sometimes, I still have moments when it's hard to get a word out. The worst thing you can do to a person who stutters is rush them; just be patient and let them say what they're trying to say."

A young friend of his went through a difficult divorce. The day he gave the *get*, he arrived home to a message on his answering machine. It was Reb Meir, who had never forgotten his own times of challenge. When Reb Meir had gotten divorced, his rebbi, Rav Moshe, had told him that there would be "dark nights ahead," but he would pull through and persevere: he wanted to share that message. "I know that this period won't be easy, and I want to let you know that I'll be there for you, so please call me anytime and tell me what I can do to help. I'm thinking of you and I know life will get better, with Hashem's help!"

He would share memories of that period of his life with those involved with divorce situations, especially when there were children involved. He took pride in the fact that he and his children's mother had succeeded in maintaining a polite relationship with each other. He had raised the children, and at Reb Gedaliah's wedding, Reb Yosef Mayer — Reb Meir's former father-in-law — approached and whispered, "Meir, you did a good job with them." It was more than a compliment on Reb Meir's *chinuch* skills, and he appreciated that. He would tell young people facing divorce that if a person is committed to the good of the children, to following the advice of *talmidei chachamim* and always taking the high road, it could be done right — and he would use himself as an example.

Reb Meir would often be called upon to use his network of contacts and diplomatic skills and get involved in sensitive situations. His experience, insight, and ability to keep secrets made him a sought-after consultant in various unpleasant or politically explosive situations. Even when both sides could agree on nothing, they both felt reassured that Reb Meir wanted what was best for each of them. In such cases, Reb Meir would generally work to get them to agree to sit down with his friend, Ronnie Greenwald, a seasoned arbitrator. If he could achieve a meeting between the two sides and Ronnie, he was satisfied, confident in Ronnie's abilities to steer them to a resolution. In an email to an *askan* working hand-in-hand with him on one

With Rav Dovid Cohen and Ronnie Greenwald in Camp Munk

such divorce case, Reb Meir urged patience, explaining that in a sensitive situation, there would be hurdles along the way that might dissuade him from seeing the only real goal: *There will be many bridges, and we'll cross all of them with EZ pass! We'll wink to one another as the ink dries on the 12th line,*[3] Reb Meir emailed him.

One of his acquaintances was involved in helping an *agunah* obtain her divorce. After investing large amounts of time, energy, and money, he was successful and the young woman was finally free to rebuild her life.

Reb Meir called to wish the *askan* a sincere mazel tov. "I know how hard you worked, and you have every right to feel good, but think about it: the real challenge for this woman starts now. The *askanim* often feel that once they've gotten the *get*, they've been successful and they move on to the next case, so she's left alone with no one to turn to. She's still a single mother who needs help. Please don't forget about her, and please let me know how I can help."

---

3. A Jewish divorce, a *get*, traditionally has twelve lines.

A gifted *mechanech* made an introduction for ArtScroll, putting the editors of a project in touch with the owner of a massive collection of ancient artifacts, vessels, and coins — items that could provide clarity and insight in explaining various halachos and *dinim* included in the book.

In the introduction to the volume, the editors thanked the owner of the collection profusely, but neglected to mention the name of the *mechanech* who had made the connection.

This gentleman received a phone call from Reb Meir himself. "I am so, so sorry, I'm embarrassed at the oversight and I assure you that we will correct it in future volumes."

"Please, Reb Meir, you're embarrassing me," the *mechanech* replied. "It's no big deal; I don't need my name to be there."

"Yes, I know that *you* don't," Reb Meir replied, "but remember this: you have a mother and you have a wife. They might feel good to see your name!"

When his nephew, Rav Meir Platnick, entered the *shidduchim* period with his eldest child, Reb Meir called him over. "Listen Meir, you're new at this. Let me tell you what's expected of you, what you can expect from the other side, and how you have to treat married children. If you know the rules, then you can play the game."

With Rabbi Meir Platnick

Reb Meir walked him through what was to come — engagement, wedding, and support for the young couple — apprising him as to what was appropriate to offer at each juncture and what he could reasonably anticipate from his future *mechutanim*.

Reb Meir and Rachel owned a summer home in Camp Morris, in Woodridge, New York. In earlier years, the Camp Morris shul was near the house, but when the camp shul was relocated, it became too difficult for him to walk there. The Perlowitz family would also spend summers there, and Reb Meir's son-in-law, Reb Efraim Perlowitz, arranged for a *leil Shabbos minyan* in the house to accommodate Reb Meir. After a few weeks, Reb Meir cancelled the private *minyan*.

"Men work hard all week, and they also need to socialize," he explained. "Friday night after davening, they enjoy seeing their friends and schmoozing for a few minutes, it's *oneg Shabbos*. When we daven here, in the house, they are deprived of that experience, because they don't get to see too many people. I don't have a right to take that away."

There was an ArtScroll employee who wasn't performing as expected. Along with subpar work, he had a very difficult personality, and the editors felt that there was no justification for keeping him. They discussed it with Reb Meir, who agreed.

Reb Meir saw it as his personal duty to do the unpleasant task of letting people go, and he was planning to share the bad news with the employee at the end of the week, but Reb Nosson felt differently. "Even if you have to let him go, how can you give him such news on a Thursday? You'll destroy his *oneg Shabbos* and that of his family."

Reb Meir agreed to wait until Monday.

But that Monday, Reb Meir was traveling and he wasn't there Tuesday either. On Wednesday, this very employee came to his superior to request a raise. "I'm simply not able to make it on the salary I'm getting and I'm falling into debt," he said.

The editor came to tell Reb Meir of the conversation, and Reb Meir made an immediate decision. "Of course we can't fire him anymore. Give him more work and give him the raise."

The editor was intrigued. "But we agreed that he's not qualified and he's difficult to work with, and that hasn't changed," he said.

"That may be true, but it's no longer relevant," Reb Meir explained. "The only way we can let someone go is because we assume that he has a safety net until he finds another job, or savings or investments he can access to tide him over; this man clearly has none of that and is already in debt. We'll have to make it work. Please find time to train him better or shift his responsibilities, whatever it takes — but please make sure that he has work. He's staying right here."

A friend of Reb Meir had a difficult employee whose contract he had decided to terminate. He wanted Reb Meir's advice on how to go about it. They spoke for a few minutes, and the next time they met, this friend nonchalantly remarked, "By the way, I finally dumped him."

Reb Meir grimaced. "Firing someone is *dinei nefashos,* a matter of life and death. I understand that you felt you had no choice, but don't speak so cavalierly about a subject that is so weighty!"

Reb Meir himself once had to lay off an employee; after a long, honest conversation with the man, Reb Meir sent him off with warm blessings. The next day, a check for $5,000 arrived in the fellow's mailbox, a gift from Reb Meir in acknowledgment of his devoted service and insurance that the family would be able to meet its expenses until the father found another job.

"Even as a *bachur,* he never did just what was expected, he always went the extra step," recalls Rabbi Avie Gold. "When he went to learn in MTJ, under Rav Moshe, I asked him to buy me a copy of *Igros Moshe,* which was available at the yeshivah. But Meir did more: he bought the *sefer,* and then asked Rav Moshe to please inscribe it to me with a *berachah*! That was typical Meir."

A painting hangs on the wall of the home of Rav Dovid and

Rebbetzin Malka Feinstein, a depiction of a ship in a tempestuous blue sea, the words of Yonah HaNavi's *tefillah* written on top of it. The rosh yeshivah had simply complimented Reb Meir on the cover image of ArtScroll's *Sefer Yonah*, which Reb Meir had designed.

Two days later the beautifully framed picture arrived at the rosh yeshivah's home.

Reb Meir's generosity was matched by the speed with which it was dispensed. He met his old friend Rav Meir Stern at a

With Rav Meir Stern

chasunah. The two old friends caught up and Reb Meir asked the Passaic rosh yeshivah how fund-raising for the yeshivah was going. The rosh yeshivah sighed.

A week later, an envelope arrived at the yeshivah: a donation from Reb Meir Zlotowitz — not one check, but twelve head checks, post-dated over the upcoming year, his part in easing the burden of an esteemed friend.

In his later years, Reb Meir felt an obligation to teach others how to give. If he heard that a rav of a shul was making a *simchah*, he would call one of his acquaintances in that shul. "I assume you know that if a rav makes a wedding, the *baalebatim* are expected to help out: I'd like to be a part of whatever you're doing."

"Giving *tzedakah* as if you are rich," he would often quip, "is the greatest *segulah* to actually get there."

Occasionally, when he received a wedding invitation in the

mail, he would respond with a phone call. "I see you're making a wedding, and money might be tight. I'd like to know if you need help and if yes, can I arrange for a loan, at any terms that work for you?"

A Flatbush woman came to the shivah for Reb Meir and shared a single memory. She wasn't a friend or acquaintance of his, but his name was on a list of names she was meant to call on behalf of a tzedakah organization. She phoned the Zlotowitz home and Reb Meir answered. She started her pitch and he politely apologized, explaining that he was on his way out to a meeting. He asked her a few questions about the cause, and then requested her address. He assured her that he would send something, but she didn't really expect him to follow through on the vague promise.

The next morning, there was an envelope at her door with a generous check.

"Meir grew up very poor," reflects Reb Shmuel Blitz, "and he couldn't bear to see poverty. His parents had lost a child, an infant, because they didn't have enough money to pay the doctor, and he never forgot that. It tore him up when people couldn't afford basic necessities."

And Reb Shmuel shares a memory. At the end of one week, as Reb Meir was leaving the office for Shabbos, Phil Martino, who managed the bindery, stopped him. "Rabbi, we need your help. Juan here," Phil indicated one of the bindery workers, "has got nothing for the weekend, he spent his whole paycheck."

Reb Meir reached into his wallet and removed a $100 bill. "No, Meir," Phil whispered, "I mean just five or ten bucks, enough for some beans and vegetables so he doesn't starve. A hundred bucks is way too much."

Reb Meir ignored him and handed the bill to Juan.

"In truth," says Reb Shmuel, who watched the story unfold, "it was too much money, but I remember thinking that Meir simply couldn't tolerate another person feeling hungry or anxious about being able to buy food."

When Reb Meir heard of an *almanah*, he would call her directly and offer help. He didn't simply say, "Please call if you need me," but "please tell me specifically what you would like me to take care of, what task I can take off your head. Give me a job!"

He was even generous with the one item most organizational heads don't part with: the names of his donors.

He once offered to set up a meeting for Rav Shalom Gold with ArtScroll's own patron, Jay Schottenstein. Rabbi Gold was

With Jay Schottenstein

surprised at the selflessness inherent in the offer, but Reb Meir was very casual about it. "What Jay is giving, what we'll get, what you'll get, it's all written in Heaven: why should I get possessive?"

Another friend of his had a business meeting with one of ArtScroll's most generous donors. Reb Meir spent time coaching his friend on how to approach the donor. "It was like my success was his success," remembers this friend. "His desire to benefit other people made it personal."

Reb Meir and Rachel were once getting a ride up to a weekend bar mitzvah in the Catskills with their friends, Mr. and Mrs. Nochum Silberman. Reb Nochum was involved with a *gemach* in Yerushalayim, and he asked Reb Meir if it would be okay to request some of the donor addresses from the ArtScroll mailing list.

Reb Meir immediately took out his phone and started to compile a list of names of donors who might respond positively. "And then," Nochum recalls, "I pulled over at a gas station to

With Rachel, and Nochum and Malky Silberman

buy some snacks and a check slid over my right shoulder from the back seat: Meir's own donation, because he wanted to be part of it. It was for a substantial amount, and I asked if he wanted it given in memory of a loved one. 'No,' he replied, 'I want it to be used, that's all I want!' "

A Flatbush resident who had a passing acquaintance with Reb Meir lost his job. For the first few days of his unemployment, there were many offers of help and advice, different suggestions from well-meaning friends, but in time, the general concern seemed to fade. Not for Rabbi Zlotowitz, however. Reb Meir called this person several times a week for months, listening, advising, encouraging, and letting him know he had a friend, until the man ultimately found a new job.

Mrs. Rachel Zlotowitz remembers that period. Her husband adopted this cause as his own, working the phones day after day. If he had a quiet moment, he used it to send yet another email or make another phone call on behalf of his unemployed friend, trying to help him find a job.

With Rachel

Reb Meir would explain the great challenge of joblessness to his children, urging them to help as well. "It's not even about the money," he would say, "but about the inherent respect a person has for himself, his sense of self-worth, the way his family sees him. A person needs to be productive to be happy; helping someone find a job is a means of giving him life."

Reb Meir wrote an email to his son on behalf of a job-seeker, his passion showing through in each line:

> *Dear Baruch—*
> *As we discussed, I am sending you David's resume. You know that I give "haskamos" on people very conservatively (I have enough to klap "al cheit" about); I don't need to add meaning to "ya'atznu ra," but in David's case I am enamored by his whole being and I will do anything to help. Without reservation.*
>
> *He's exemplary in his efficiency, warm social skills, loyalty. He's a hard worker who "gets it done." On top of that, his outreaches for tzedakah and chessed know no bounds. (I couldn't be more enthusiastic!)*

If you have someone who can benefit from his talents, and needs a truly "ehrlich" employee, he should meet David and grab the opportunity.

So please network and forward the attached resume (with this entire email if you think it's appropriate) and follow up on each one. Let's have the zechus of helping make a lasting and mutually rewarding employment shidduch. The person who has the vision to hire him will thank you!

Regards,

Dad

A few days later, a follow-up email came.

Good voch!

Were you able to make any calls yet and send David's resume and background to some well-placed people? I'm obsessed with this, and he needs a proper job. It's nearing hatzalas nefashos… no more savings…

Let's try our best. Even if chas v'shalom we draw a zero, let's know we made a real hishtadlus. It'll be a real zechus.

Reb Meir wasn't a *"maskil el dal"* only when it came to money, but also with his words. He instinctively knew what other people needed to hear. There was a young man in shul who was struggling with *Yiddishkeit*: he appeared a typical angry teenager. One Shabbos, he said something to Reb Meir and Reb Meir replied. It was an insignificant conversation, but they exchanged a few sentences and Reb Meir stopped and looked at the boy, as if seeing him for the first time. "Wow!" he exclaimed, "that's a great line, you're going to go far in life, you know that?"

The boy's face lit up at the comment — and in the following weeks, its effects became apparent, as he recommitted himself to succeeding in school and life.

Sometimes, Reb Meir would allow other people to drive him to the office or *simchos* so that he could work on the way, or on days when he felt unwell; inevitably, even if the driver was someone he didn't know, they would be close friends at the end of the ride. Reb Meir was a fountain of compliments, praise, and enjoyable conversation, leaving more than one driver with a restored sense of hope.

He had a special connection with struggling teenagers, an ability to get through their hardened exteriors. Reb Meir's friend, Rabbi Zecharia Wallerstein, asked Reb Meir and Rachel to join him at an Ohr Naava Shabbaton: they accepted. Late on *leil Shabbos*, Rabbi Wallerstein finished delivering an intense speech to a large group of girls, and the participants broke up into informal little groups, discussing and debating the ideas they had just heard. As Rabbi Wallerstein made his way down the hallway, he was stunned to see Reb Meir listening to one of these conversations. "Reb Meir!" he exclaimed, "It's 2:30 a.m. Aren't you usually very careful to get to sleep on time?"

Reb Meir conceded that in fact, he didn't like being up late at night. "It's past my bedtime, you're right. But Zecharia, I want to help these girls, I really do, and to help someone, you have to understand them. I'm just walking around and listening, so that I can be effective too."

His schedule in Eretz Yisrael was carefully arranged, but if ever he had a few extra minutes, he would use it to visit acquaintances who had moved to Eretz Yisrael. He understood that they would get pleasure from being able to show visitors their apartment or neighborhood and he wanted to give them that satisfaction.

One of Reb Meir's grandchildren got married during a snowstorm. It was difficult to reach the hall, and a young man was sent to drive and assist Reb Meir and Rachel in getting there. When they reached the hall, Reb Meir turned to his driver, a young man whose father suffers from a debilitating condition. "You should know," Reb Meir told him, "that you are my

With Rabbi Chaim Nosson Segal at a Torah Umesorah Presidents Conference

inspiration; the way you help your father is amazing to me. You're always a happy boy, with a big smile on your face. You inspire me." Reb Meir kissed the boy on both cheeks and said, "You're going to go far in life."

On Erev Shabbos at the Torah Umesorah Presidents Conference in Florida, Rabbi Chaim Nosson Segal of Torah Umesorah met Reb Meir. Rabbi Segal, whose speeches are highly anticipated, was preparing his *derashah* for that evening and he solicited Reb Meir's opinion regarding whether he should include a particular story. Reb Meir assured him that it was a good story and would be well received.

A few hours later, they met as they both entered the hotel ballroom for *Kabbalas Shabbos.* "I thought about what you asked me again," Reb Meir said, "and I don't think you should use that story after all."

"What's incredible to me," Rabbi Segal reflects, "isn't the advice itself but how seriously he took the responsibility of giving advice. Most people get this sort of question and they give an answer, but that's where it ends; they think about it for a moment and then they move on. Reb Meir genuinely cared enough to consider what was best for me and even rethink it, and then tell me what he thought was right. People asked him for advice and trusted him not just because he was a *pike'ach*, a wise man, but because he took their questions seriously."

A friend of his, a prominent, successful businessman, called Reb Meir to solicit help in getting a child accepted into school. Reb Meir got involved, calling the *menahel* of the school, whom he knew well, and asking him a personal favor — to accept this child.

The *menahel* said no.

Reb Meir tried again, but the *menahel* was adamant that he simply didn't have any space for another student. Reb Meir had to call his friend back and admit failure — and along with the news, he offered a surprising piece of advice. "We tried. He said no. I'm hurt, you're hurt, now we move on. Don't spend the rest of your life being angry at him, he did what he had to do for his *mossad*, and now it's over."

His advice was appreciated because it came along with practical assistance too. In the early days of ArtScroll, Reb Meir was in his Manhattan office when an old friend came in to say hello. He had a shidduch date that evening, and was already dressed. Reb Meir looked him up and down.

"You can't go out with a girl wearing bell-bottom pants," he said, "you need to look more elegant."

The young man shrugged, and explained that there wasn't much time before he was supposed to be at the girl's home.

"There's enough time," said Reb Meir as he left work, took his friend to a tailor across the street, paid for a new suit then persuaded a nearby tailor to alter it on the spot.

"Now," Reb Meir said with satisfaction, "you're ready to go."

With Rabbi Simcha Bunim Cohen, at the celebration for the *Sefer Torah*
Reb Meir dedicated to Rabbi Herzberg's shul

It wasn't only advice to family, influential people, or friends. Reb Meir would often field phone calls from young fund-raisers eager for direction, and he made it clear to them that his time was theirs, and that he felt it a privilege to be able to help.

Reb Meir had undergone a particular medical procedure and he became an expert on the topic. He would often get "referrals," unfamiliar people calling him for insight into different doctors and approaches.

Two of his children davened in the Lakewood shul led by Rabbi Herzberg. On a visit, Reb Meir noticed that the step leading from the street into the shul was just a bit high, making it difficult for less agile people to enter. Rather than simply point it out and complain, Reb Meir had a new step put in at his own expense, an enduring favor for the members and their own aging parents.

And along with donations of money, time, and heart, there were the secret contributions, the sort of gifts that leave no records, check numbers, or receipts as evidence.

A couple he knew had been married for several years, but had not yet been blessed with children. Reb Meir speculated that perhaps their parents hadn't been generous when paying their *shadchan* and the matchmaker still had a bad feeling about it. He investigated, and learned that it was so.

He arranged for a third party to drop off an envelope filled with cash at the *shadchan's* home, as a belated gift from the family. A year later, they had their first child, and no one —other than the secret messenger — knew of Reb Meir's involvement.

"My husband was aware of the fact that he had many *zechusim*," says Mrs. Rachel Zlotowitz. "When Meir heard about a sick person, or someone in distress, he would look to Heaven and say, 'I am giving up my *zechusim* as a merit for this person.' He wanted to help others so much, and this was one of his ways."

In fact, his desire to give was strong enough to overpower long-held habits. One of his daughters once tried to articulate her thanks to him; he meant so much to his children, he was such a generous, kind, wise, loving father, and she simply wanted to tell him so.

But he wouldn't allow her to, and he kept stopping her in mid-sentence.

Finally, she said the one thing she knew would make him listen. "Daddy, I need to say this. It's not for you, it's for me."

He was silent.

"Thank you," she said, and expressed the thought — her father sitting silently, listening to words of gratitude not with pride, but with benevolence and love — not taking, but giving.

12

BE'AHAVAH, MEIR

PEOPLE WHO KNEW REB MEIR'S WORK SCHEDULE WOULD marvel at his approach to *simchos*. This busy man was invariably early for special events, and he would be completely "present," engaged and emotionally invested in rejoicing with others.

To Reb Meir, relationships were important, and like any valuable item, they needed constant maintenance and attention. Loyalty, he believed, was the truest measure of a man — and a *simchah* was the chance to show that devotion to family and friends. A *simchah* is a major moment in a person's life, Reb Meir would say, and if you consider a relationship significant, you should be with those you care about at their biggest moments.

Attending a *levayah*, he once told Rabbi Yechiel Spero, was an obligation, a *chiyuv*, and so it wasn't a true measure of *yedidus;* joining wholeheartedly in a *simchah* was a sign of real friendship.

Those *ba'alei simchah* who hosted events in snowstorms or torrential downpours remember the sight of Reb Meir's beaming face as he would come in, Rachel at his side, as an obvious declaration that, no matter what, they were there.

A younger business associate received an invitation to the *chasunah* of Reb Meir's daughter, but he didn't go, reasoning that Reb Meir Zlotowitz didn't really care if he attended or not.

The next day, Reb Meir phoned him. "I invited you. How come you didn't come?"

Embarrassed, the acquaintance apologized and said nothing else.

A few weeks later, this same acquaintance was blessed with a newborn son. When the *avi haben*, the new father, entered his own shul at 6 a.m. for davening on the day of the *bris*, Reb Meir — whom the *ba'al simchah* hadn't even notified — was already in his *tallis* and tefillin, ready for Shacharis: his way of making a point about how much every individual adds to a *simchah* simply by being there.

"It was routine for him to remain at work until 9 or 10 o'clock at night," recalls a veteran ArtScroll editor, "but if he had a *chasunah* — not only in his own family, but even his friends' family — he could leave as early as 5 o'clock so that he could really participate in the *simchah*."

That was for happy occasions.

In times of difficulty, he was even more steadfast.

Nochum Silberman was sitting *shivah* for his father; on the first day, when only family was present, his friend Meir was there. Reb Meir came on the second day as well, and when he showed up on the third day, it became clear just how seriously he took his obligation as a *menachem*, a comforter. He came every day of *shivah*, simply to sit there and let Nochum know he cared.

Charlie Grandovsky lost his mother: she had passed away on Shabbos in Eretz Yisrael and Charlie was in New York. That Sunday, New York was struck by the Northeastern United

States Blizzard of 1978. Not only had her son missed the *levayah*, but even the *shivah* was a lonely affair, with few people able to venture out to be *menachem avel*.

In the meantime, his friend Meir was in Eretz Yisrael. Reb Meir had gone to the *levayah* in Eretz Yisrael, but was prevented from returning home since flights were cancelled due to the blizzard, and he remained there until the end of the week.

With Charlie Grandovsky

On Thursday, at the close of a painful week for Charlie, the door opened in his home to admit Reb Meir, who had just arrived.

"You know," he told Charlie, "I went over to your father at the *levayah*, and he said to me, 'Meir, we're burying her here in Eretz Yisrael while our son Yechezkel is singing *zemiros* for *seudah shelishis* in America.'"

Charlie reflects on that moment. "It's hard to explain what happened then, but I hadn't really been able to experience the *aveilus* properly all week; I had felt cut off from Eretz Yisrael and there hadn't been many *menachamim* because of the harsh weather. With that one line, Meir connected me to my mother and father, to the *kevurah*, he made the whole thing real. I finally burst into bitter tears, allowed the mourning to wash over me — and when that happened, there was no one I wanted in front of me more than Meir. It was typical that he would be the one to help me mourn — and then be the one to comfort me."

Meir's longtime lawyer and close friend, Judah Septimus, had a similar experience after his father passed away. The family was sitting *shivah* in Manhattan; but Reb Meir, along with Reb Nosson, came *every* single day of the *shivah*, a way to convey that they felt not like friends, but family.

He offered comfort with well-chosen words as well. Reb Yaakov Kiffel, husband of Reb Meir's sister Shirley, was a key figure in Reb Meir's life. Born in Poland, he had survived World War II and arrived in America, where he became a *talmid* of Rav Yitzchok Hutner. A brilliant *talmid chacham*, he introduced his younger brother-in-law to the depth of Polish chassidus. He worked as an engineer, and to Reb Meir, Reb Yankel was the embodiment of the old-time chassid who prefers to support himself by the toil of his hands even as his heart and mind are planted in the *beis medrash*. When Reb Yankel passed away, Reb Meir turned to the *niftar's* son, Chaim, and said, "He was like a father to me: now I will be like a father to you."

And sometimes he conveyed his loyalty with humor.

A close friend was being honored at a yeshivah dinner. Reb Meir and Rachel showed up on time and stayed for the entire evening. The honoree, who knew well that, along with Reb Meir's intense work schedule, he was also in physical pain, was overcome with gratitude.

"I can't believe you sat here all night in my honor," he said.

"Look," Reb Meir grinned, "if I got a call in the middle of work that it was a *levayah*, *lo aleinu*, of someone I liked as much as I like you, I would drop everything and go sit there for as long as it took, so how can I complain about this? I got to show you honor and not only are you still alive, I also got a full meal while doing it!"

The same way he was able to connect with the most elevated Jews in the world, he was able to create a bond of friendship with those far from Torah.

He once stopped to admire the work of an Israeli artist. The artist was very taken by the American rabbi with the black hat and white beard, amazed at his grasp and insight into art. Reb

Meir showed him pictures of his own paintings, creations that lined the walls of the Zlotowitz home.

The artist felt he was speaking with an equal and they became friendly. On subsequent visits to Eretz Yisrael, Reb Meir would visit him. They discussed everything — except religion.

Until one day, when Reb Meir was home, in Flatbush, and he received a telephone call from his friend across the ocean. The artist had a family member who wasn't well, and he wanted someone to daven — and so he reached out to the religious person in his life that he felt could help him.

Reb Meir agreed to daven, but also patiently explained to his friend the power of each Jewish prayer and just how welcome those prayers would be in Heaven.

Reb Meir didn't have too many casual acquaintances; a single encounter was enough to form a genuine, lasting friendship.

He once spent Shabbos in Cleveland for the *simchah* of his close friends, the Klein and Jaffa families. A severe snowstorm closed Cleveland airport that Motza'ei Shabbos, forcing the guests to remain overnight — but Reb Meir had a flight to Eretz Yisrael scheduled for Sunday morning.

The *ba'alei simchah* worked feverishly to find someone willing to drive their distinguished guest back to New York. A young chassidishe fellow, a member of the choir that had performed at the *simchah*, had experience in long-distance driving and offered to drive through the snow.

Before Reb Meir agreed to accept the ride, he first

With Amir Jaffa

ensured that the offer was genuine and that the driver wasn't frightened or anxious. For the next eleven hours, Reb Meir and Rachel and their kind driver chatted: light banter, serious discussion, personal stories and struggles — all of it. At one point, Reb Meir insisted on taking the wheel so that the driver could rest, refusing to play the part of "VIP passenger."

The driver had faced health challenges, as did several of his children, and Reb Meir offered compassion, support, and encouragement.

When they finally reached Flatbush, Reb Meir asked the driver to wait for a few minutes while he washed up and changed, and then they continued on to John F. Kennedy Airport. When they reached the end of their trip, Reb Meir handed the driver a check.

No, the young man protested, the *ba'alei simchah* had already compensated him nicely for the job. Reb Meir insisted that *hakaras hatov* obligated him to add a little bit, a tip.

It was a check for $3,000.

A few weeks later, a huge box arrived at the driver's home: a shipment of various ArtScroll books with yet another thank-you note from his new friend, Reb Meir.

> *Shalom Uvracha*
>
> *I have been traveling extensively in the weeks since we drove together on that memorable trip from Cleveland to New York. It is a trip I won't forget for a while. Baruch Hashem, everything worked out fine.*
>
> *Having just returned, I realized that my machshavah was never taken care of, and I apologize.*
>
> *May I take this opportunity, erev Purim, of thanking you for your kind efforts on my behalf, in your being so special to me and my wife on that trip home. It was also very special to meet (and be mesamei'ach) with you and your chaverim over Shabbos. Please accept the enclosed sefarim as a token of my appreciation and hakaras hatov.*

Over the next few months, Reb Meir and his new friend kept in touch. The driver experienced a health setback and Reb Meir came to visit him several times.

One day, Reb Meir came bearing a gift. It was a single volume of the ArtScroll *Shas*, but Reb Meir explained that he was sharing something much greater. "You told me that when it's hard to get out of the house, our *Shas* is your *chavrusa*. I know that you're not feeling that great these days, so I want to make sure you always have your *chavrusa* nearby. I made a deal with the local Judaica store; here's the first volume, and when you're ready for the next one, they'll send it over. They will give you the entire *Shas* as you need it."

The last time they saw each other was just a few months before Reb Meir passed away. He was a guest at a *simchah* where his young chassidishe friend was performing as part of the choir. Reb Meir approached and called him aside. "I want to share something personal with you, because we're so close. I've often davened for you, and now I need you to daven for me. I'm quite sick and in need of *rachamei Shamayim*, but I haven't told anyone outside of my immediate family — and you. Have me in mind, please."

And with that, two friends — an alliance forged on a stormy winter night along a deserted highway — parted for the last time.

A friend was honored by an institution, and Reb Meir and Rachel placed an ad in the dinner journal in his honor. The friend emailed a personal thank-you message to Reb Meir, who responded with an outpouring of warmth — and humor:

> *It is truly my honor to be your friend. In addition to the ahavas nefesh I have for you, my sense of hakaras hatov overshadows everything. You were there for me — at potentially great jeopardy to yourself and your various dynamic interrelationships — at a time that was most challenging for me, and I can and will never forget it.*

May our friendship continue to deepen and flourish ad me'ah v'esrim shanah, amidst good health, nachas, and simchah.

And a lot of money.

Even small-talk had a point. One Chol HaMoed day in the Bronx Zoo, the son of an acquaintance saw Reb Meir and went over to say hello.

Reb Meir warmly greeted him, then asked the young man how business was going.

"You know, it's a new business...," the man answered, and then his voice trailed off.

Reb Meir turned to look at him. "No, I *don't* know!" he said emphatically. "Tell me what you mean."

For the next few minutes, Reb Meir listened intently as the younger man shared the challenges and struggles of establishing a new business. Reb Meir offered pointed advice, direction — and most of all, a sense that the young man had a good friend he could always call on.

The eye for detail that could catch an irregularity in a cover design was equally adept when it came to spotting anxiety or fear in a person. One Erev Yom Kippur, a Flatbush business-man received word that a major customer would be terminating their relationship with him; it was the sort of development that could seriously cripple his business.

He headed to Minchah that afternoon weighed down by the news. He entered the shul along with the usual flow of people, each *mispallel* focused on his own thoughts at that serious time. Only one of them stopped him.

Reb Meir Zlotowitz wasn't even a regular *mispallel* in that shul, and had, at most, a passing acquaintance with this gen-tleman — but he noticed. "I see something is bothering you. What's wrong?" Reb Meir asked.

The businessman told Rabbi Zlotowitz about the phone call he had received. "Please, don't leave after Minchah, let's talk for a few minutes," Reb Meir told him.

Following Minchah, Reb Meir told this acquaintance about the early days of ArtScroll, the challenges and hurdles he had faced. Then he told him about the work that had gone into lining up a dedication for the *Shas* project, and how triumphant they had been when it appeared that they would have an agreement with a particular donor. And then, Reb Meir continued, it all fell apart when the would-be donor backed out. Reb Meir told of his acute disappointment, how discouraged he had been. He recalled Rav Dovid Feinstein's *chizuk*, and how things had worked out so much better with the Schottensteins: how the last-minute decision that had caused him such distress had been a blessing to ArtScroll.

On Erev Yom Kippur, two men sat at a table in a Brooklyn shul, one reassuring the other and enabling him to welcome the holiest day of the year with his spirits restored. Until today, the businessman draws on that conversation — the *chizuk* and encouragement and spirit of true empathy — to carry him through various struggles.

One Shabbos, a fellow *mispallel* unexpectedly started to berate Reb Meir, publicly humiliating him over a perceived injustice. Reb Meir was quiet: after davening, he went to apologize to the gentleman for whatever aggravation he may have caused him. It was obvious to onlookers, and the man himself, that Reb Meir had done nothing wrong, but Reb Meir did more than apologize.

From then on, he made it a point to be friendly to that man, showing him tremendous affection and respect. "If someone could act that way for no reason," Reb Meir told his children, "it means he's in pain, and we have a responsibility to lessen that pain."

Reb Meir once told a grandson, "When you speak with people, look them in the eye. It sends the message that a conversation is more than just words: it makes it personal."

He took that approach with donors as well: it was never just business. Phil Rosen's father's eyesight had suffered as he had aged: when he passed away, his son dedicated the Siddur Yitzchak Yair in his memory. Along with the beautiful binding and layout, Reb Meir excitedly pointed out that the letters were larger and clearer than they had been in previous Siddurim, so that those with vision issues would be able to see them easily.

"And that was classic Rabbi Zlotowitz," says Phil. "He found a way of conveying a sign of respect that made the whole transaction into an act of friendship, instead of business. He made it personal."

Reb Meir found a way to connect with the younger generation as well. He would often tell children of his friends, "You know that I love you — and not just because of your father."

After his children hosted a Shabbos bar mitzvah, Reb Meir emailed his son's friend. "I just want to tell you how happy I am that Gedaliah has friends like you."

At the *shivah* for Reb Meir, Beryl Septimus — a son of Reb Meir's attorney and dear friend — came to be *menachem avel*

Inscription to 5-year-old Beryl Septimus

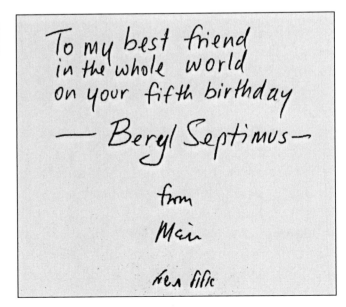

To my best friend in the whole world on your fifth birthday

— Beryl Septimus —

from

Meir

Reb Meir

bearing a copy of the ArtScroll *Zemiros*. He had received it when he turned five years old, inscribed: *To my best friend in the whole world on your fifth birthday — Beryl Septimus*. It was signed *Meir*.

Aaron Orlofsky, a close friend of one of the Zlotowitz children, happened to be flying home from Eretz Yisrael on the same flight as Reb Meir. Aaron had come to the airport dressed in comfortable attire for the long flight — and he immediately regretted it.

"I arrived in my tee-shirt, shorts and flip-flops, feeling relaxed and loose and, because of my status and points, they decided to upgrade me to first class," he recalls. "I walked into the lounge and felt the disdain of the other passengers — and then heard someone calling my name. It was Rabbi Zlotowitz, immaculate in his suit and tie, exuding dignity and class, and he sat with me schmoozing for close to an hour."

When it came time to board, Reb Meir smiled. "I wish I knew you better," he said. "If I were thirty years younger, I bet we

With Aaron Orlofsky

would be such good friends" — a single comment that made it clear that the difference in approach to proper airport attire wasn't that significant against the backdrop of the bigger picture of shared values.

Over time, Reb Meir would become close friends with Aaron, and after one of their conversations, Reb Meir emailed, *I truly enjoyed schmoozing with you. Oh, to be young again!* — conveying appreciation for the energy and vitality of his young friend.

When his friend and donor, Geoffrey Rochwarger, made a bar mitzvah, Reb Meir flew to Eretz Yisrael to join in the *simchah* — but he didn't come as a VIP, refusing to sit at the dais or give a speech. "What he did do," recalls Geoff, "is arrive early and sit down alone with my son, the bar mitzvah, as if he wanted to get to know him. They spent about 15 minutes together and my son was smiling the entire time. When my son stood up, his face was shining."

Then Reb Meir headed back to the airport for the flight home.

After Reb Meir's *levayah*, Rav Yisroel Reisman, a rosh yeshivah in Torah Vodaath and a rav of Agudas Yisroel of Madison, remarked that the word he had heard repeated most was "*ahavah*," the true legacy of Reb Meir: love for his Creator, love for his People, love for the Torah, love for the ArtScroll family, and love for his own family.

It was not uncommon for him to call friends and say, "I'm calling just to hear your voice. I miss you."

He was unabashed in expressing affection, as a

With Rav Yisroel Reisman

longtime employee recalls: "He signed every single email *'love Meir'* and it made me uncomfortable. In time, I got used to it and ultimately, I would sign off the same way to him. He changed me."

A senior editor opted to work mostly from home. One afternoon, a call came in from the office. "Please try to come in at least once a week because I enjoy discussing matters with you and seeing things from your point of view." It was his way of conveying respect and letting his employees know they were valued not just for their skills, but for themselves.

Emails and letters often began with the Yiddish expression, *Tiyere,* rather than its more formal English-language "dear" and were signed "Uncle Meir."

A Flatbush rav asked for permission to copy some text from an ArtScroll book: Reb Meir responded to the request himself. *Permission granted with love from Mesorah Publications,* he wrote.

He remembered small details about his friends — birthdays and anniversaries, the accomplishments of their children, their challenges and worries.

Six months after Reb Meir's passing, his son and successor got a phone call from Joel Fleishman, chairman of the Board of Trustees. "Gedaliah," Mr. Fleishman said, "I guess you don't know that you have another new job. Your father would call me every year on this date, December 4, to let me know that we begin reciting *V'sein tal u'mattar livrachah* in *Shemoneh Esrei.*"

Elly Kleinman had once mentioned that as a young boy, he'd played the drums. A few months later, Reb Meir's son got married. During the dancing, the bandleader called out, "Elly Kleinman on the drums." Mr. Kleinman, a well-known businessman and ArtScroll donor, was caught off guard, but he saw that Reb Meir meant it seriously — He wanted Elly to play. "It was his way of including me in the *simchah*, of letting me know that the relationship was deeper than business."

A few months later, Reb Meir sent him an email: *Elly, we're watching Chaim and Shira's wedding video...boy, you can really play those drums...*

When Asher David Milstein was going out with his future wife, he told Reb Meir he had met a young woman in whom he was interested. Even before they were engaged, Reb Meir insisted on meeting her, and Reb Meir and Rachel joined Asher and Michal for dinner.

Once the wedding date was set, Reb Meir booked a ticket to Eretz Yisrael for the wedding of Asher and Michal Milstein — but it turned out that Reb Meir was then in the hospital.

On the Thursday night preceding Asher's *aufruf*, Reb Meir wrote what might well have been his last email.

Dear Asher—

As you might know I am unfortunately STILL in the hospital after 5 weeks and several major life-threatening surgeries, be'ezras Hashem.

I feel so close to you and your absolutely wonderful kallah. I could never have imagined that I would physically be unable to join you in this special simchah. I had already booked tickets the day you shared the date with me. You are a visionary marbitz Torah and wonderful human being! And I so enjoy the times we spend together.

So at this juncture of your aufruf, you have my and Klal Yisrael's every berachah for a mazel tov, a fruitful marriage that you both especially deserve — years of good health, simchah, nachas, prosperity, and shalom al Yisrael.

With great love —
Uncle Meir
   and the ArtScroll family.

Reb Meir passed away that Shabbos.

A few days later, Asher David Milstein and his *kallah* stood under the *chuppah;* and at that exalted moment, as they stood in the heart of Yerushalayim, the letter from Asher David's mentor and beloved friend was read, a final *berachah* from a heart overflowing with love.

Many salespeople form relationships with their clients, reflects an ArtScroll donor, but Reb Meir created real friendships, evident from the fact that, even when donors faced hard times and couldn't continue to give, the bond remained the same — and at times, it even grew stronger.

A donor admitted to having endured a difficult few seasons in business: he was no longer able to give. Reb Meir sighed deeply. "I feel bad about the loss we're taking," he said, "but I'm much more disturbed by the fact that you were going through a rough time and didn't tell me about it."

ArtScroll's IT needs are handled by a company called Intellicomp. Its president, Chaim Kahn of Baltimore, occasionally comes to the office to talk business. "Reb Meir was known as a tough negotiator and the first time I sat down in Reb Meir's office, I expected a tense meeting about pricing and service," he later recalled. "But Reb Meir's first question was whether I had eaten, and then he wanted to know about my children and grandchildren. I found myself getting more and more comfortable. We eventually got down to business, but after that, every time I would come into the office, we would first just schmooze.

Celebrating his 60th birthday with rabbanim, family, and friends

Above (L to R): Rabbi Burton Jaffa, Rabbi Ronnie Greenwald, Elliot Schwartz, Charlie Grandovsky, Asher Dicker, Rabbi Yehudah Levi, Rabbi Michoel Levi, Shmuel Blitz, Nachum Silverman

Left: Rav Dovid Cohen

Below (L to R): Chana Scherman, Leah Berliner, Rebbetzin Malka Feinstein, Judy Schwartz, Miriam Greenwald, Raizy Levi, Esther Levi

I had lost my father fifteen years before I first met Reb Meir and from that moment until I met Reb Meir, I'd been missing that feeling so much: the sense of speaking with someone who genuinely cares about you, and during those moments, only you. I cherished every second in his presence."

Reb Meir, usually so busy, had no problem simply sitting and chatting with friends. "He taught me," says a hard-working friend, "the value of conversation, even without an agenda or specific goals; just to be together and share ideas or stories is itself a productive use of time. He was right. I would always get up after schmoozing with him feeling refreshed."

Reb Meir could converse on many subjects. Along with Torah knowledge and a mastery of Jewish history and thought, he had an executive's understanding of business and a psychologist's insight into people. He could discuss current events or politics — but found himself unable to talk about sports.

"It was interesting, because sports discussions are a natural ice-breaker, and as a relationship builder, it would have been helpful to him," reflects an ArtScroll employee, "but he was simply incapable of talking about something so utterly inconsequential. It was beneath him, and he couldn't devote his mind to something that didn't have some sort of depth to it."

There was another sort of conversation that would cause Reb Meir to go completely silent: if he felt that someone's confidence was being betrayed.

Reb Meir was a keeper of secrets, the confidant of wealthy businessmen and community leaders. And all the information he absorbed each day was kept safe, in the privacy of his own mind and heart.

A gifted young *mechanech* was releasing a work that required a sponsorship. He suggested a potential donor whom he thought might appreciate his work and Reb Meir agreed to contact the gentleman in question. A few hours later, Reb Meir and the *mechanech* spoke again. "I think it's a good time to call the donor," the *mechanech* said, "I just spoke with him and he's in a good mood."

Reb Meir laughed. "I called him earlier today and he already agreed!"

The *mechanech* was astonished. "But he didn't even mention a word about it to me!"

Reb Meir was silent for a moment, and then said, "That's incredible. We can all learn from him."

Reb Meir would say that although he had considered himself a keeper of secrets, he had learned a new "halachah" from his rebbi, Rav Dovid Feinstein.

Reb Meir was once on the phone with Rav Dovid when the rosh yeshivah put him on hold to take another phone call. Reb Meir waited patiently for several minutes until Rav Dovid returned to the call. The rosh yeshivah didn't explain what

In front of MTJ with Rav Dovid Feinstein and (L to R) Eli, Ahron, and Chaim Zlotowitz

had occupied him, and simply resumed the conversation from where they had left off.

That Shabbos, one of Reb Meir's children mentioned that they had encountered an urgent halachic *shailah* during the week and they had called Rav Dovid, who had given them several minutes of his time on the phone to help them arrive at a conclusion. "One second," Reb Meir exclaimed, "what day was it?"

"Tuesday morning," was the reply.

Reb Meir laughed out loud. "I was the person that the rosh yeshivah put on hold for you," he said.

The next time that Reb Meir spoke to the rosh yeshivah, he mentioned the story. "The rosh yeshivah put me on hold for my own children and didn't even mention it to me," he said.

Rav Dovid was quiet. He didn't even chuckle. He simply did not react to Reb Meir's comment.

"I thought I knew what it meant to be a *ba'al sod*. I had learned from the rosh yeshivah, Rav Moshe, and experience had taught me a thing or two, but in that story, I saw a whole new dimension," Reb Meir said, "of what it means to be a secret-keeper. Even once the secret is out, you have to continue to safeguard it. The rosh yeshivah understood that I already knew that my children had called him, but he still wouldn't acknowledge it, because to him, it was a secret!"

One of Reb Meir's married grandchildren called to share the good news that she was expecting a child. She wasn't really telling people yet, she admitted, but she knew he had been very concerned and had been davening a lot. "I assure you of two things," he told her after reacting to the happy news. "One is that I won't share your secret and two is, no one will ever know that I knew it first."

Another of the traits that made Reb Meir such a loyal friend was his focus on *hakaras hatov*. Family members and friends looked forward to Reb Meir's visits and prepared foods he

enjoyed just because of the way he said "thank you." When he felt that someone had helped him or his family, he felt indebted to them and would not forget it.

Rabbi Avrohom Biderman authored ArtScroll's classic Mishkan Book. When the book was released in Hebrew, Reb Meir brought a copy to Rav Elyashiv. Along with the grandchildren Reb Meir brought with him to the *gadol hador*, he invited Reb Avrohom's son, who was learning in Eretz Yisrael at the time, to come as well.

As Rav Aryeh Elyashiv was leading them out of his grandfather's room after the audience, Yaakov Biderman peered back

Showing Rav Elyashiv the Mishkan Book

in and saw how Rav Elyashiv was perusing the book: he quickly snapped a few pictures.

It would end up being the last time Reb Meir would see Rav Elyashiv, and from then on, Reb Meir would profusely thank the young man for those memorable pictures whenever they met.

Each year, when the *parshiyos* discussing the Mishkan arrived, Reb Meir would commend Reb Avrohom on the book he had authored — and the great pictures taken by his son!

The yeshivos and schools attended by his children saw just how deeply his *hakaras hatov* ran. "His *middah* of *hakaras hatov* was extreme," says the rosh yeshivah of Riverdale, Rav Avrohom Ausband. "It's common to see fathers of current *talmidim* responding generously to our appeals — but for Reb Meir, it never ended. His son learned by us more than thirty years ago, but Reb Meir's friendship and loyalty never waned; he would come to each yeshivah dinner as if he were a new parent, and he made sure to keep a vibrant connection with us."

With Rav Avrohom Ausband and Reb Gedaliah

When Rabbi Michoel Levi, principal of Bais Yaakov d'Rav Meir, would attend *chasunos* of *talmidos*, he and his wife would generally offer Rebbetzin Privalsky, one of the respected *mechanchos*, a ride as well. One evening, an alumnus was getting married, and the Levis assumed that the rebbetzin would join them, as usual.

But then the rebbetzin called to say that she wouldn't need a ride after all. "Are you not coming to the *chasunah*? Is something wrong?" Rabbi Levi asked in concern.

The rebbetzin explained that she was planning to attend, but earlier that day, the father of the *kallah* had phoned her. "You had such a *hashpa'ah*, such an influence on my daughter," he said, "and I feel like she chose to marry a real *ben Torah* because of your lessons. If she were a boy and you were her rebbi, I would give you a *berachah* under the *chuppah*, but that's not the case; allow me to at least bestow the honor of sending a car for you, a small way to acknowledge your role in this *simchah*!"

"Of course," Rabbi Levi concludes the story, "that father was Meir. It was so typical."

The sense of duty wasn't only to those institutions where his children learned, but to his own yeshivah as well. He would

At an MTJ Dinner with sons-in-law, Efraim (left) and Asher

often tell *ba'alei simchah*, "I won't miss your *simchah* for the world, unless it's the same evening as the Mesivtha Tifereth Jerusalem dinner. That's the only thing that comes first."

Each year, Reb Meir would ask his children to attend the MTJ dinner out of respect to Rav Dovid.

In an email with the subject line *My Annual Outreach*, he wrote to his children:

> *Dearest —*
>
> *This is my annual outreach to ask whoever of you can possibly make it, to please join me at the MTJ Dinner, a week from this Sunday night, November 15th, at the Brooklyn Marriott downtown. It means a lot to Rav Dovid.*
>
> *It'll also give you an opportunity to wish me a good trip, as I'm be'ezras Hashem leaving to Israel that night right after the dinner... Please let me know so I can make appropriate reservations.*
>
> *With love,*
>
> *Dad*

One year, MTJ asked Reb Meir to serve as guest of honor at their annual dinner. "It was extremely difficult for him to accept

Reb Meir as Guest of Honor at the MTJ Dinner, with
(L to R) Reb Yisroel Eidelman, Rav Dovid Feinstein, and Rav Reuven Feinstein

With Rav Dovid Feinstein and Reb Nosson Scherman

it," recalls Reb Nosson Scherman. "It meant accepting public honor, which was anathema to him, but even harder was the fact that it meant reaching out to his own donors for another cause. It was difficult, but of course he did it — he would never consider saying no to his yeshivah or to Rav Dovid, it was unthinkable! He made personal requests of his steady donors, asking that they help the yeshivah even if it meant cutting back for ArtScroll!"

Reb Meir felt that someone had wronged ArtScroll by using copyrighted materials for commercial use without having asked permission. He mentioned it to Rav Dovid Cohen, who phoned the other party and passed on the grievance. Hearing what he had done incorrectly from a leading rav and *posek*, the gentleman regretted it and sent a check to ArtScroll.

Reb Meir came to Rav Dovid's home to thank him. He walked into the rav's study and asked if perhaps Rav Dovid, a prolific writer, had any notebooks of *chiddushei Torah* that were ready for printing. Rav Dovid indicated several and Reb Meir took one.

Within weeks, the new *sefer* was printed and in stores, Reb Meir's expression of *hakaras hatov* to the rav.

A successful rav was releasing a book with ArtScroll; the project needed a sponsor and the author suggested one of his wealthy *baalebatim*, a member of his shul.

"But didn't you tell me that you're considering an offer from a larger shul, and you may be moving to a different community?" Reb Meir asked.

"Yes, I'm thinking about it," the rav said.

"Imagine what will happen if we ask this person for a sponsorship: he will happily give the money out of respect to you. Then, in another six months he'll learn that you're leaving the shul — that's the ultimate act of ungratefulness. Better not to take his money than to be a *kafui tov*!"

Reb Meir had twice sponsored the writing of *Sifrei Torah*, and he became very involved in the actual process. He carefully selected an expert *sofer* in Eretz Yisrael, and spent hours

At the *Hachnasas Sefer Torah*

At the celebration for a *Sefer Torah* dedicated by Reb Meir to Rabbi Weinfeld's shul

(L to R) Reb Nosson Scherman, Yossi Stern, Rav Dovid Feinstein, Rabbi Yosef Weinbaum, Reb Meir

(L to R) Rav Dovid Cohen, Reb Meir, Rabbi Meir Platnick, Yisroel Zlotowitz

With the *sofer*, Rabbi Avrohom Maybloom

Dancing with the Novominsker Rebbe

(L to R) Rav Dovid Feinstein, Rabbi Yosef Weinbaum, Reb Meir

in discussion with the *sofer* regarding the size of the letters, the choice of ink, and the overall look of the *Sefer Torah*. He picked out the pieces of *klaf* himself, looking for a perfect, clean parchment upon which to write the holy letters.

The *sofer* appreciated the American customer with the artistic eye and they became quite close.

The *sofer* was in America for the completion of a *Sefer Torah* he had written for another client and he called to invite Reb Meir to the *siyum*. Unbeknownst to the *sofer*, Reb Meir was in Eretz Yisrael when he answered the *sofer's* call and heard about the *siyum* in Lakewood the following day.

Reb Meir promised that he would try to attend — then cut his trip short and booked a flight back to America for that evening, returning home in time to join in the *simchah* of a *sofer* to whom he had so much *hakaras hatov*.

Rabbi Michoel Levi made the acquaintance of a brilliant young chassidishe *talmid chacham*; the *avreich* from Monsey seemed to have instant recall not just of the classic Torah sources, but of lesser-known *sefarim* and Torah personalities as well. Rabbi Levi called Reb Meir and said, "Meir, this is someone you'd love to have around your office."

Reb Meir met the young scholar and was very taken by him: he hired Rabbi Menachem Silber on the spot. From then on, Reb Meir would often call his friend Rabbi Levi in the middle of the day just to thank him. "We just asked Reb Menachem where a certain *teshuvah* appears and he brought us the *sefer* two minutes later; I have to thank you. It was a great *shidduch* for us."

Reb Meir moved into the Flatbush apartment upstairs from Rabbi and Rebbetzin Gornish before he married Rachel. During that difficult period, Reb Meir was working full-time while also caring for his young family, and the rebbetzin's active involvement made it easier. When Reb Meir and Rachel married, Rebbetzin Gornish coached Rachel in caring for the young children and stood at her side in the kitchen, teaching her how to cook for a family.

In 2015, the Gornishes were in Lakewood for the wedding of a grandchild when Reb Meir and Rachel walked into the hall. "You came from Brooklyn just for our *simchah*?" Rebbetzin Gornish asked in surprise.

Reb Meir smiled. "We will never, ever, forget the help you gave us when we needed it most."

To those who helped ArtScroll, his gratitude was eternal. Reb Meir was in Yerushalayim's Plaza Hotel for Succos and a prominent donor invited him to a Kiddush in nearby Rechavia. Reb Meir was experiencing intense pain in his leg and getting there meant being pushed in a wheelchair, the ultimate indignity for this dignified man — but *hakaras hatov* took precedence over personal comfort.

Rabbi Meyer May's *shiur* at Los Angeles's YULA high school would learn using the ArtScroll Gemaros. One semester, they were learning *Maseches Arachin*, but the ArtScroll edition of that *masechta* was not yet ready.

Reb Meir would zealously guard the materials being used in projects while they were in the process of being completed. He didn't want any materials to be released until they were perfect — but there was something more important to him: the chance to show appreciation to Rabbi May, a dear friend.

Reb Meir overcame his usual fastidiousness and sent unfinished *Arachin* galleys, with no binding, to the *talmidim* in Los Angeles, a sign of esteem and love for their rebbi.

When Reb Meir and Reb Nosson had originally met with Mr. Irving Stone, patron of the Stone Chumash, Reb Meir asked Reb Reuven Dessler to join them for the meeting. Mr. Dessler, who was close with the Stone family and a dear friend of Reb

Meir, had been helpful in making the connection, and he agreed to Reb Meir's request.

Reb Meir never forgot it, and wouldn't miss an opportunity to refer to Reb Reuven as a partner in the Chumash, which would become standard in shuls and homes across the world.

Reb Meir would often quote good advice he had received from Rabbi Nochum Stilerman, who told him that though it seems counter-intuitive, a donor who has already given money once has formed a connection with the cause and is more likely to give again. He would credit Reb Nochum with contributing to ArtScroll's success with this insight.

The Mesorah Heritage Foundation was experiencing financial pressure and Reb Meir reached out to several friends for emergency help. One of them came through for Reb Meir and was able to arrange for a donation that relieved the stress. In return, he earned a classic Reb Meir email:

> *Dear —*
>
> *There are not enough words in the 30-volume Oxford Unabridged Dictionary to thank you for your graciousness to me in helping keep us alive.*
>
> *I won't even try. Hashem keeps score, not us. And He is the Hakol Yachol.*
>
> *With boundless love and awe,*
> *Meir*

Reb Meir's friend Nochum Silberman, an expert architect, had overseen the planning of ArtScroll headquarters — a major undertaking — and refused to accept payment.

The first Pesach after Nochum's mother passed away, a brand new ArtScroll Haggadah arrived at his home: the first copy in the newly released Silberman Edition, dedicated to the memory of Nochum's beloved mother.

It was Reb Meir's way of saying thanks.

One of Reb Meir's grandsons was filling out the standard thank-you cards after his bar mitzvah. The boy thanked this one for *sefarim* and the next one for the camera, when suddenly, on a whim, he filled out a thank-you card to his beloved grandparents, Zaidy and Bubby Zlotowitz. He thanked his grandfather for the tefillin, Reb Meir's gift to *every* grandson for their bar mitzvah, and for the gift of the close relationship they shared, the Shabbos *seudos* and long conversations. Once he started writing, the boy opened his heart, expressing how much that connection meant to him.

Reb Meir was very touched by the card, and told the bar mitzvah boy that he would always treasure it. The years passed; the boy's relationship to his grandparents deepened.

Then, Reb Meir passed away, leaving a void that can never be filled.

About a month after Reb Meir's passing, this young man was visiting his grandmother and happened to look through his grandfather's orphaned *sefarim*. Reb Meir's copy of *Nachalas Ahron*, written by his revered father, was especially precious to him and he kept several valuable papers inside its covers. On that day, a card fluttered out. It was that very card, the thank you of a 13-year-old boy to his loving grandparents that meant enough to Reb Meir that he kept it in that cherished *sefer*.

Reb Meir had many close friends — several of them since childhood, others whom he'd met along the journey. The week of the ArtScroll dinner, he excused himself from a meeting. "I have my hands full because I'm getting together with two thousand of my closest friends this week," he wrote — and he meant it.

The Graff family of California ordered *bentchers* for a family *simchah*. When Mrs. Pnina Graff called the sales department, Reb Meir insisted on handling the order himself, busying himself with the small details of the order — not because he didn't have a staff capable of dealing with it, and not because he didn't trust them.

It was because he saw an opportunity to show *hakaras hatov* to close friends, and that became more important than anything else on his calendar.

In a written tribute to Reb Meir, his close friend Chanoch Weisz — who spoke to him almost daily for a period of twenty-five years — recalled: *Another aspect in which Reb Meir excelled was his middah of hakaras hatov. I can say from first-hand knowledge that he never forgot a favor someone did for him — meaning for ArtScroll/Mesorah (he didn't need personal favors from anyone). He would remember and do whatever he could for that person. I personally know many beneficiaries of his undying loyalty...*

In the early 1990's, Rabbi Pinchos Lipschutz, publisher of the *Yated Ne'eman*, did a personal favor for Reb Meir. More than twenty-five years later, Mesorah Publications was going through a difficult financial period and it looked like they would have to cut the advertising budget. "No matter how rough things are," Reb Meir told his son, Reb Gedaliah, "we remember what Pinny did for us back then: tight as we are, we keep advertising in the *Yated*."

The ultimate sense of gratitude was to the Master of the World. One year Reb Meir had endured a medical scare before Pesach; on the anniversary of that occurrence, he would send an email to his children expressing his thanks to the Ribbono Shel Olam. When reciting the *berachah* of *Shehecheyanu* on Yom Tov, he would be visibly emotional, charging his gathered children to share the experience of acknowledging Hashem's blessings and feeling the moment.

In the organizational world, people looked to Reb Meir not just for advice and encouragement, but also as a role model; they

With Reb Nosson

observed the relationship between Reb Meir and Reb Nosson and saw that it was possible to work hand-in-hand with another person for over forty years and enjoy complete harmony.

It appeared to be the perfect partnership, and in a rare interview printed about a year before his passing, Reb Meir candidly discussed the reasons it worked so well.

"Most *shalom bayis* fights are about money; we make a living, *baruch Hashem*. If we go out for lunch, if I order kishke and Reb Nosson doesn't, he looks away and doesn't mention it. You know what I mean?" Reb Meir told the interviewer.

"But joking aside, we get along because we both believe in what we're doing, and we appreciate each other's talents."

Reb Nosson looked on in awe as Reb Meir cultivated donors, raised funds, gave graphic direction, organized deadlines, and motivated the hand-picked staff. Reb Meir would marvel at Reb Nosson's literary flair, his depth and nuance and ability to convey abstract ideas with a few well-chosen words. Both of them respected Reb Sheah's graphic brilliance and ability to visualize a page and how it would look before it was a reality.

It worked.

In that same interview, Reb Meir looked at the young, talented feature writer and said, "Reb Nosson was the best writer in the *frum* world and he is still the best writer in the *frum* world. Period. It's okay if you're insulted. It's the truth, deal with it."

Blunt, straightforward, and pulsing with admiration for his partner, Reb Meir never stopped believing it, from the day he first invited Reb Nosson to work with him until his final day on earth. They had been charged with a shared mission and there was no one he would rather have at his side.

A prominent ArtScroll donor was being honored at a public event, and he emailed that he had reserved seating in the VIP section for Reb Meir.

That's very gracious of you, Reb Meir wrote back. *Please be aware that Reb Nosson is accompanying me in your honor as well, and he should be accommodated more than me...he's the true VIP...*

At an event, a respected person insulted Reb Nosson, and then approached Reb Meir with a wide smile. "If you hurt *him,*" Reb Meir pointed to his friend, "then you've hurt *me.* I'm sorry."

Jay and Jeanie Schottenstein would often host their friends, Reb Meir and Reb Nosson, who would come join in Schottenstein family events. Each year, Reb Meir and Reb Nosson would travel to Columbus in the depths of winter to mark the *yahrzeit* of Jerome Schottenstein, sitting around the table with children, grandchildren, and close friends while sharing memories. What inspired their hosts, recalls Mrs. Jeanie Schottenstein, wasn't just the dignity and graciousness of the guests.

"It was the relationship between them, the way Meir and Nosson interacted; we would look on and marvel."

It was clear that each one knew his role and was amazed at the talents of the other, but there was something deeper. "We saw the shared sense of mission. It was about something much bigger than either of them," Mrs. Schottenstein reflects.

At family *simchos*, Reb Meir would give in to emotion and publically say that Reb Nosson had changed his life. At one gathering, Reb Meir introduced Reb Nosson by saying, "If I accomplished anything in this world, then this man is responsible."

The room was completely silent when Reb Nosson took the microphone. "No, no," he cried out, "I am *not* responsible for him," he joked, sending ripples of laughter throughout the room. "Other people are responsible!" he continued, as the laughter intensified. Reb Meir loved Reb Nosson's quick wit and would often repeat the story.

In an email to a donor, Reb Meir wrote: *May I respectfully and confidentially make a suggestion. Rabbi Scherman is a venerated talmid chacham. He has no airs about him and is very modest. Nevertheless, when you refer to him in your emails as "Nosson" it makes it difficult for me to simply forward your emails to him. I do hope you don't mind my bringing this to your attention.*

Reb Meir didn't just want to be called Uncle Meir by the Scherman children; he acted like an uncle too. He came into a restaurant one evening and saw that Reb Nosson's son-in-law, Rav Mordechai Yehuda Groner, was dining there along with his family.

Reb Meir approached with a serious expression and advised them against ordering the kishke sticks, a dish he enjoyed. It seemed a strange suggestion — until a few minutes later, when the waiter brought over a large serving of kishke sticks, courtesy of "Uncle Meir." When it came time to pay the bill, Rabbi Groner was told that the bill had already been covered.

One of Reb Nosson's grandchildren got married out of town and Reb Meir and Rachel couldn't make it to the wedding. Reb Meir sent a very generous check, well more than is customary, as a gift for the new couple, and explained his calculation. He should have come, he explained, and because of his leg pains, he would have flown business class. The amount of the gift was the cost of the two tickets he didn't get to buy, a reflection of respect, exactitude, and deep friendship.

After hosting a Scherman grandson for a Yom Tov meal in Eretz Yisrael, Reb Meir emailed the parents of the young man.

Dear Dovid and Chaya —

Your son spent the 2nd day (for us) of Yom Tov together. Wow, is he delicious! A chip off the old blocks. He's a pleasure to be with, very eidel yet insightful and "with it" in a very modest ben Torah way.

Have continued nachas from your entire family.
Good Shabbos!

Uncle Meir

The bond between the two partners transcended speech: they were simply there for each other.

Reb Nosson had a health scare and underwent a heart valve replacement at the Mayo Clinic in Rochester, Minnesota. When he woke up twenty-four hours after the surgery, Reb Nosson saw his family sitting there — and Meir. It was freezing cold and icy and it was hard for him to walk, but Reb Meir needed to be there, to see firsthand that Reb Nosson was on the road to recovery.

Reb Nosson remembers the painful period after his own life's partner, Mrs. Chana Scherman, passed away. When it came time to mark the *hakamas matzeivah* for Mrs. Scherman, Reb Nosson and his family stood around the newly erected tombstone in Beit Shemesh when they saw someone walking slowly up the hill: Reb Meir had flown in especially to be there.

The two men looked at each other. "That moment," recalls Reb Nosson, "epitomized Meir to me: there are those who are there to rejoice and others who show up to mourn, but he was there always."

13

THERE IS NOTHING SWEETER

BEFORE HIS SONS WENT OFF TO LEARN IN YESHIVAH, Reb Meir would offer a piece of advice that he considered essential. "If a person has any hope of growing, he must have a rebbi; along with the practical benefits of having a guide for life, he will become a *talmid*, and there is nothing sweeter."

Reb Meir would credit his own father with conveying this message to him at an early age. Reb Ahron Zlotowitz knew the entirety of *Shas* and *poskim*, but when he saw Rav Moshe Feinstein, he would be overcome with reverence. "If my father felt such respect for Rav Moshe, you can imagine the awe that I felt," Reb Meir would say.

From the moment Meir Zlotowitz first walked through the portals of Mesivtha Tifereth Jerusalem, he was determined to become close with the rosh yeshivah, Rav Moshe.

When Rabbi Shimon Finkelman's classic biography of Rav Moshe was being prepared for print, Reb Meir was personally involved with each decision, no matter how insignificant it seemed. Rabbi Finkelman remembers how Reb Meir agonized over the appropriate text for the book's subtitle. The few biographies on *gedolim* published by ArtScroll up to that point were about *gedolim* from earlier generations. The book on Rav Moshe would be

At the *kever* of Rav Moshe

the first about a contemporary *gadol*.[1] Rabbi Zlotowitz felt that *"The Life and Ideals of Rabbi Moshe Feinstein"* was not sufficient. It would have to say *"HaGaon Rabbi Moshe Feinstein,"* to indicate how Rav Moshe's Torah knowledge towered over that of the rest of the generation.

After the book was released, Reb Meir was visiting Eretz Yisrael. He asked Reb Shmuel Blitz to drive him to Har HaMenuchos, where he made his way to the rosh yeshivah's *kever*. Reb Meir stood on the quiet ridge and spoke to his rebbi, saying, "I hope the Rosh Yeshivah is happy with the work we did, and that we drew the appropriate lessons with which to inspire others."

---

1. Reb Meir charged the same author, Rabbi Finkelman, with re-releasing the biography in honor of Rav Moshe's twenty-fifth *yahrzeit*, since there were many new stories and rulings that had only emerged with the passage of time. Reb Meir felt that his rebbi was still teaching Klal Yisrael, and he wanted to be sure he was doing his part in sharing those lessons. Eventually, Reb Meir also oversaw the release of a biographical volume on Rav Moshe Feinstein for younger readers.

Rav Moshe Feinstein with Meir and Rachel

"I write as a talmid who had a personal closeness to him as to no one else. My picture of the Rosh Yeshivah is in many ways personal but it is also the reflection of the way countless others saw him...," Reb Meir wrote in his very moving, personal preface to the biography.

"We approached him with reverence, and that feeling of awe was still upon us as we left him. We knew we were standing before the gadol hador and we felt that his throat was our conduit from Mount Sinai."

As a *bachur*, he was already a frequent visitor to the rosh yeshivah's home and office, speaking in learning and soliciting advice on behalf of others. He would share different episodes with his children, some involving open *ruach hakodesh* on the part of Rav Moshe. There were many hopeful messages for which Reb Meir was the intermediary, *berachos* from the rosh yeshivah that were realized, and some painful stories as well. Reb Meir would recall requesting a *berachah* for a childless couple and Rav Moshe telling him, with evident distress, that it wasn't meant to be.

In his foreword to the re-release of the expanded Rav Moshe biography, Reb Meir wrote: *His extreme simplicity was misunderstood by some as naiveté, but he had a full grasp of every facet of a situation. The most intractable disputes came to him and he had to sift the truth and apply the halachah in disputes at which both sides were presented by forceful, learned, influential people. Once, during a recess in a heated din Torah, he remarked to me as he passed my seat, "They think they are fooling me."*

Reb Meir was present in the rosh yeshivah's room when a woman from South America entered. She had traveled to the United States with an urgent halachic question, she said, since only Rav Moshe Feinstein could help. Her son was about to be married when her first husband, thought to have been killed in the Holocaust, unexpectedly appeared. The shocking re-emergence of the husband cast doubts about the lineage of the *chassan*. In desperate search of a lenient ruling, the mother took a flight to New York City and went straight to the apartment on the Lower East Side.

Rav Moshe spent hours reviewing the details and relevant halachic sources, but he couldn't find a path to a lenient *psak*. Perplexed, he asked the woman which rav had given her the original *heter*, permission to remarry, after the war. She named a respected *posek* and claimed she had lost the written ruling.

"Really?" Rav Moshe asked her, "are you sure it was him?"

The woman assured the rosh yeshivah that this was the rav who had ruled her free to remarry.

Rav Moshe looked skeptical and asked her a second time, "Are you sure?" When she maintained that she was, he asked the question a third time. Onlookers wondered why the rosh yeshivah was being so tough with the poor, shattered woman.

Rav Moshe stood up abruptly, leaned across the table, and spoke firmly to the woman.

"It cannot be, the story can't be true," he said. "I've ruled leniently in nearly 2,000 such cases, permitting *agunos* to remarry; with Hashem's help, no husband has ever reappeared. Now, the rav that you claim allowed this was a *gaon* and *tzaddik*, far greater than I am. I don't even reach his ankles in Torah. Now, if my *psakim* merit this sort of *siyata d'Shmaya* then his *psakim* certainly do! I don't believe your story!"

The woman broke down crying and admitted that she was lying and she had used the rav's name on her own once he had passed away.

Reb Meir was a close *talmid* of Rav Moshe before his marriage; during the period following his divorce, he would say that Rav Moshe "carried him." That relationship sustained him.

In later years, when he assumed more of a public role, Reb Meir — counselor and adviser to so many institutions and individuals — was known as a keeper of secrets. He would tell his grandchildren that he had learned that art of protecting a confidence from his rebbi, Rav Moshe.

Reb Meir had once shown the rosh yeshivah a very private document and Rav Moshe assured him that no one else would see it. A while later, Reb Meir was visiting the rosh yeshivah and Rav Moshe asked him to wait a moment.

The rosh yeshivah, diminutive in stature, pulled his chair over to the bookcase, and then stood up, stretching his arm to the top shelf. He took down that document, which had been taped shut. "See?" Rav Moshe told his *talmid*, "I keep it private."

Rav Moshe gave the document back to Reb Meir and instructed him to destroy it, to make sure that it would never be seen.

During the difficult period following his divorce, the *berachah* from his rebbi, Rav Moshe — that Reb Meir's children would become *bnei Torah* and marry *bnei Torah* — heartened him and allowed him to dream of happier times.

Reb Meir once asked Rav Moshe about the permissibility of using dishwashing soap on Shabbos. "In our family we don't use it,"[2] Rav Moshe said. "And you," the rosh yeshivah continued, "are family."

In virtually every public address, Reb Meir would quote a *dvar Torah* from his rebbi. Reb Meir's son-in-law once asked why the ArtScroll Siddur included the custom of standing up for the recitation of *Mizmor LeSodah* as halachah, when in fact, it's a *machlokes*.

"I davened in the *minyan* in Rav Moshe's home at the end of his life," Reb Meir replied, "and I saw how, even when the rosh yeshivah no longer had the strength to stand for other parts of davening, he stood up for *Mizmor LeSodah*."

In the next edition, another opinion — that some do not stand — also appears, but Reb Meir's devotion was such that he saw only the reality of his rebbi's practice.

A *talmid chacham* once came to ArtScroll with a manuscript, a comprehensive halachic treatise with the potential to be a well-received book. In it, the author was dismissive of Rav Moshe's *psakim;* Reb Meir didn't need to see any more than that.

"Thank you for considering us," he said politely and returned the manuscript to its author.

One cold, snowy, winter Motza'ei Shabbos, Reb Meir called Rav Yisroel Gornish. He asked the rav to please come out to a particular hall in the neighborhood, and Rabbi Gornish could detect that his old friend was agitated. He assured Reb Meir that he was on the way.

When Rabbi Gornish came to the hall, he realized that it was a benefit Melavah Malkah for Mesivtha Tifereth Jerusalem, but

---

2. See *Igros Moshe, Orach Chaim* 113, where Rav Moshe writes: "Therefore, in my home we do not use this *heter*, and people should be stringent."

because of the harsh weather, very few people were there: the rosh yeshivah, Rav Moshe, was sitting alone at the head table.

Reb Meir hurried over and greeted Rabbi Gornish. "Thank you for coming out. The rosh yeshivah is sitting all by himself and it's not *kavod* — so I needed a *talmid chacham* to come and sit at his side!"

Reb Shmuel Blitz came to work at ArtScroll and knew Reb Meir as dynamic and self-assured. "And then I got to see Meir in the presence of *gedolei Torah*, and I couldn't believe it was the same person; suddenly he was overcome with a new level of humility and deference. He would speak to Rav Moshe on the telephone and remain standing throughout, frozen in place. It was incredible to see."

Reb Meir paid a visit to his close friend Rabbi Burton Jaffa one Shabbos; he noticed a new picture on the wall, a framed portrait of their shared rebbi, Rav Moshe. Reb Meir frowned.

"The picture is beautiful," he told his friend, "but the frame doesn't do it justice."

On Motza'ei Shabbos, he showed up at the Jaffa home and removed the picture from the wall. A few days later, he brought it back with an attractive new frame.

"Now," Reb Meir said, "the picture is a *kavod* for the rosh yeshivah."

Reb Meir's friend Gary Torgow was once scheduled to speak to a group of Jewish activists and leaders. In preparing his remarks, he reached out to Reb Meir. "I'd like to share an idea from the *gadol hador*, Rav Moshe Feinstein," Gary said, "and I figured that you would have something appropriate."

"Yes," Reb Meir replied, "I will share something I've never said in public."

He recalled how Rav Moshe had once told him that in each generation, there are a few select people charged with a Divine mission: to take responsibility for the growth of Torah and *Yiddishkeit*. A *bas kol*, a voice from Heaven, comes forth and those who merit hearing it are, in the words of Rav Moshe, the ones who are "tuned in to the frequency." Those who hear the call and heed the call are fortunate, for they have been given the *zechus*, the task of bringing glory to Heaven.

That was the thought Reb Meir shared, one he had heard directly from his rebbi. "I am certain," Gary told Reb Meir, "that Rav Moshe told this to you because the rosh yeshivah was telegraphing you your own destiny, because the rosh yeshivah was confident that you were going to take responsibility for the growth of Torah and *Yiddishkeit*."

"No, Gary, of course not," Reb Meir replied, "the rosh yeshivah was talking about himself. He heard the *bas kol*!"

When Rav Moshe grew older and less accessible, Reb Meir showed that same reverence to the rosh yeshivah's son and successor, Rav Dovid. When Reb Meir had first brought the *Megillas Esther* to Rav Moshe for approval, the rosh yeshivah had given the manuscript to his English-speaking son to review.

In the introduction to the *sefer*, Reb Meir writes:

> *Perhaps the single greatest yasher koach is due Harav Dovid Feinstein, whom I am privileged to call Rebbi, Alufi Umeyuda'i. He has read and commented on nearly every selection. He graciously took time from his busy schedule to read the manuscript on a daily basis and allowed me to benefit from the abundant storehouse of*

his learning. He removed stumbling blocks and guided me to interpretations I might otherwise have misunderstood. Most of all, he graciously gave me the gift of time, which cannot be repaid.

In the early years of ArtScroll, the company faced daunting financial problems and Reb Meir needed a loan; Rav Dovid Feinstein was able to provide that loan, giving over his life's savings — but Reb Meir saw it as so much more. To him, it was a personal message that his rebbi believed in what he was doing, the greatest possible sort of *chizuk*.

In time, Rav Dovid's role in ArtScroll would increase.

Rav Dovid would often share *divrei Torah* in his conversations with Reb Meir, and he once shared an interpretation of a *pasuk* in *Koheles*,[3] "*VehaElokim yevakesh es hanirdaf*, G-d seeks the pursued." Rav Dovid suggested that often, people see a situation and draw their own conclusions as to who is the "*rodef*," the pursuer, and who is the "*nirdaf*," the pursued. Only Hashem, the rosh yeshivah explained, He Who can search the hearts of men, knows the real intentions of the parties involved, and can decide who the true *nirdaf* is.

Reb Meir liked this *peshat*, and sometime later, he showed Rav Dovid that he had been quoted in the commentary. "And just like that," the rosh yeshivah recalls, "I was part of the family."

Over the years, Reb Meir noticed that Rav Dovid had a unique approach to explaining the *simanim*, the words used by Chazal as mnemonic devices to remember the number of *pesukim* in each *parashah*, showing how the word contained a reference to the essence of the *parashah*. Reb Meir kept the notes and eventually, these explanations were included in the ArtScroll Stone edition Chumash.

The relationship deepened to the point that Reb Meir spoke to the rosh yeshivah daily, and would try to visit him every few

---

3. 3:15.

weeks. Whenever Reb Meir traveled overseas, he would call Rav Dovid to receive a *berachah* before leaving, and then again upon landing.

On their Erev Shabbos phone calls, Rav Dovid would often share the ideas he had discussed in his Chumash *shiur* that morning. Reb Meir would find himself a quiet place to stand when Rav Dovid spoke words of Torah so that he could concentrate on the rosh yeshivah's words.

A colleague had an argument with Reb Meir about whether to include particular information in a book. Reb Meir was adamant in his position, and eventually, with no resolution in sight, Reb Meir said, "Let's call Rav Dovid."

With both men on the line, the *shailah* was posed to the rosh yeshivah — who ruled against Reb Meir. All Reb Meir's firmness and conviction faded in a moment, replaced by a serene, tranquil acceptance. He had asked, and the rosh yeshivah had answered. Everything was clear.

Reb Meir's daughter and son-in-law were blessed with a baby boy, and they excitedly offered the proud grandfather, Reb Meir, the coveted honor of *sandaka'us*. Reb Meir thanked them, but instead of accepting it, he had a suggestion. "If you'd like to honor me," he said, "and I appreciate that you do — then please give the *kibbud* to my rebbi, Rav Dovid, instead."

Reb Meir, who was able to access Rav Dovid "off-hours," took on the role of unofficial *gabbai* to the rosh yeshivah. He was able to balance the rosh yeshivah's right to privacy and the desperation of people who felt their questions could not wait. Reb Meir respected both sides, and so Rav Dovid trusted him implicitly.

A business associate had a complicated halachic *shailah*, and Reb Meir arranged a meeting with the rosh yeshivah.

"But I have one condition," Reb Meir told his friend. "Before you meet with a potential mega-investor, you prepare, right? You're ready for any question he may have, because you respect him, his time, and you want him to be impressed with you! I urge you to prepare for this meeting the same way; the rosh yeshivah's time is precious and he's going to grasp the whole situation much quicker than you anticipate. Be ready!"

The ArtScroll receptionists all knew that even though Reb Meir was to be interrupted when any of his family called, there was one exception: if he was speaking with Rav Dovid, then everyone else would have to wait. Meetings at ArtScroll were often interrupted if Rav Dovid was on the phone. It meant that whatever Reb Meir had been busy with was suddenly less important, as he would give himself over to his conversation with the rosh yeshivah.

There was a period of time that the telephone system in the Zlotowitz home played music for callers waiting on hold. During the year in which Rav Dovid was in *aveilus* for his mother, Reb Meir disabled the music in case the rosh yeshivah would call.

ArtScroll Printing, a totally separate business, is located in Manhattan, and Reb Meir was not involved with its day-to-day operations; his interactions with the staff there were invariably pleasant and warm. Except for once. They had printed the invitation for an upcoming Mesivtha Tifereth Jerusalem dinner and someone in the yeshivah office had neglected to show the final draft to the rosh yeshivah, Rav Dovid. There were some errors in the final text and the rosh yeshivah must have shared his frustration with Reb Meir, who called ArtScroll Printing immediately.

"I will not allow Rav Dovid to have *agmas nefesh*," he said. "We will get this fixed and mailed out again."

Over the next several hours, Reb Meir called the MTJ office and ArtScroll Printing several times, making sure every single error was corrected and that the rosh yeshivah had approved the final draft. Only once he felt comfortable that the rosh yeshivah would experience no further distress did Reb Meir get back to his regular work.

One year, the MTJ dinner was scheduled for the very same night as the dinner of Brooklyn's Mirrer Yeshivah — and Reb Meir's son, Chaim, was slated to serve as chairman at the Mir dinner. Reb Meir wasn't one to look for excuses; he called the Mir office and found out exactly when his son would be speaking. In the middle of the MTJ dinner, Reb Meir, along with his wife and children, left and headed to Brooklyn to hear Chaim deliver his remarks; then they turned around and went back to the MTJ dinner.

The Shabbos-table conversation in Reb Meir's home invariably consisted of both a *vort* from Rav Moshe and a *shailah* Reb Meir had heard from Rav Dovid.

In time, a Zlotowitz family *minhag* developed: Reb Meir, and whichever children and grandchildren were available, would go daven with Rav Dovid on Erev Yom Kippur and receive his *berachah*.

They would drive to the Lower East Side for Shacharis,

With Yisroel, receiving a *berachah* from Rav Dovid Feinstein on Erev Yom Kippur

At Rav Dovid Feinstein's Mishnayos *shiur* on Erev Yom Kippur

usually in several cars. Reb Meir would encourage his grand-children to watch as Rav Dovid donned his *tefillin*, telling them that through observing *gedolim*, one develops in his own fear of Heaven.

After Shacharis, they would join Rav Dovid's daily Mishnayos *shiur*, after which the rosh yeshivah would distribute pieces of honey cake.[4] Reb Meir would insist that the men wrap up pieces of cake to share with their wives and daughters as well, so that the women could also access the rosh yeshivah's *berachah* for a sweet year.

Ultimately, Reb Meir fused two of his unique traits — noticing the needs of others, and reverence for his rebbeim — and created a unique tradition, the annual summertime vacation.

---

4. Following a *minhag* practiced by Rav Moshe as well, the rosh yeshivah delivers the cake along with a *berachah*. "If there is a *gezeirah* on you that you will have to resort to accepting help from others in this new year, may it be fulfilled with this piece of cake," the rosh yeshivah says.

Reb Meir himself didn't take vacations, seeing his job as a mission that didn't allow for any sort of respite, but in the year following the passing of Rebbetzin Sima Feinstein — Rav Moshe's rebbetzin — Reb Meir noticed that Rav Dovid appeared weary.

He decided that the rosh yeshivah and rebbetzin needed a change of scenery; rather than share the idea with others and offer suggestions, Reb Meir set out to make it happen.

He got Rav Dovid to agree, then assured the rebbetzin that he and Rachel would make all the arrangements. Rav Dovid, of course, would only agree to go when the yeshivah was not in session, and one summer day, after davening Minchah in yeshivah, they set out on a trip.

That first year they went to Washington DC and visited the Holocaust Museum; the rosh yeshivah benefited from the change of scenery and break. The following summer, Reb Meir got to work on the next trip. Although he had never been a vacationer, Reb Meir would immerse himself in the task of creating an itinerary, coordinating *minyanim*, travel times, and destinations.

Reb Meir and Rachel with Rav Dovid and Rebbetzin Malka Feinstein
while on vacation

When he would come back, recalls a secretary, Reb Meir was excited as a little child, sharing the details and stories he had witnessed.

One summer, they visited the Boeing Plant in Seattle, Washington, where the two couples took the tour together. Reb Meir enjoyed describing how Rav Dovid had grasped the basics of the jet propulsion engine within minutes, able to conduct his own learned discussion on the subject with the astonished guide.

One summer, they drove through scenic mountains featuring different rare species of trees, and Rav Dovid identified each one on sight. Another summer, on a tour of the New York State Capitol in Albany, the tour guide mentioned the year in which the building had been constructed. Rav Dovid quietly informed the guide that he was off by a year. The guide insisted that he was right, and in his determination to prove the tourist wrong, he led Rav Dovid to the archives, where they checked the information.

The rosh yeshivah was proven correct, and the flabbergasted guide wondered how the rabbi knew precisely in which year the New York State Capitol building had gone up. Rav Dovid shrugged and explained that he had read a history book in elementary school that contained the information.

On these trips, they would occasionally daven at a local Chabad House; after the *minyan*, the rosh yeshivah would invariably leave a check with the local *shaliach*, a sign of *hakaras hatov*.

Rebbetzin Malka Feinstein reflects on those trips. "It wasn't Meir's dedication for the rosh yeshivah that amazed me, but the way he managed to walk that fine line between *talmid*, companion, and attendant. He would keep the rosh yeshivah company, they would go for walks and on tours, and Meir was simply a good friend — and then he would go back to taking care of my husband like a *talmid*, and always, he would apologize at the end of the trip if he had been disrespectful in any way."

The rosh yeshivah — who never went on vacation before Reb Meir made it a personal mission and wouldn't do so with anyone else — has his own insight into those annual trips. "It wasn't just Meir's devotion to us. It was his unique ability to see what no one else saw, to see what people need, and then, being an *'ish hama'aseh'* to make sure that need was met. He was special."

A successful young businessman had the ability to do for the *klal*, but he felt unmotivated; an admirer of Reb Meir, he asked if he might come to ArtScroll headquarters for lunch. He explained that he was seeking *chizuk*, inspiration, and he felt that being exposed to the work — the breadth, reach, and impact — of ArtScroll would stimulate him to do more. Reb Meir agreed to meet him the next day, and gave him the address.

The young man set out for ArtScroll headquarters, only realizing while en route that the address given to him was in Manhattan, rather than Brooklyn. He was perplexed — even more so when he arrived at the destination, a bustling street on the Lower East Side in what appeared to be a Chinese neighborhood.

But Reb Meir stood on the sidewalk, to welcome him and lead him into the Mesivtha Tifereth Jerusalem building. Reb Meir showed the visitor to the office of the rosh yeshivah, Rav Dovid, who graciously sat and spoke with them for several minutes.

Only then did they head to Brooklyn, to ArtScroll headquarters, for lunch. "You wanted *chizuk*," Reb Meir explained, "so I took you to the place where I get *chizuk*!"

Reb Meir considered himself a *talmid* of Rav Yosef Sholom Elyashiv as well, and that too became a relationship he cherished. The connection started when Rav Elyashiv had encouraged the publication of the ArtScroll *Shas*, but in time, it became about the relationship itself.

Rav Elyashiv learning from a Schottenstein Gemara

"Reb Meir revered the '*demus*,' the image, of a classic litvishe Yid, like his father had been, like Rav Moshe had been," observed a close friend. "Rav Elyashiv was made from that mold and Reb Meir appreciated that."

Rav Elyashiv would give more than *berachos*; he would become a vocal and public supporter of ArtScroll's work.

When Reb Meir and Reb Nosson traveled to Eretz Yisrael before embarking on the Hebrew-language Schottenstein Edition of *Shas*, they brought a prototype to show Rav Elyashiv. This was long after he had stopped giving letters to any organizations or individuals, and Reb Meir had been cautioned not to request a letter.

Rav Elyashiv sat there analyzing the text for a while, and Reb Meir, reading the situation, went ahead and asked anyhow; the others in the room held their breath.

Yes, Rav Elyashiv replied, he would give a letter. He instructed Rav Yosef Efrati to take care of it the following day.

The next morning, Rav Yosef arrived at his rebbi's home, ready to work on the letter, then bring it to his rebbi to sign — as was the usual custom.

He was astonished to find that the letter had already been written — not by one of the other *gabbaim* or family members, but by the rav himself!

Rav Elyashiv had woken up even earlier than usual, cutting into his precious few hours of sleep so as not to waste time from learning, and he had written the letter in his own hand.

"I wanted to make sure that no one says that the letter is *mezuyaf*, a forgery," Rav Elyashiv said.

"If people asked him to sign a letter, he would sometimes agree," Rav Aryeh Elyashiv reflects, "but I never saw my zaide write a letter of his own volition to any other cause or organization, nothing even close to that kind of personal support. Clearly, it meant a lot to the Zaide."

In that letter, Rav Elyashiv writes:

> As I said when they proposed to elucidate tractates in English — I see in this "a time to act for the sake of Hashem" ... It is necessary to compose an elucidation by those who fear Hashem and who know that it is holy work that they perform.

Eventually, Rav Elyashiv would develop a personal appreciation for the Hebrew-language Gemaros.

Rav Aryeh Elyashiv, the rav's devoted grandson, remembers how that started. Rav Elyashiv would sleep very little, and each day, after he ate his dinner, he would feel tired and weak; those were the only moments in the day when he allowed himself to relax. The way he did so was by reaching across the table to the *sefarim* shelf and removing whichever *sefer* met his fingers first; he would peruse that *sefer* while he gathered his strength.

One day, the *sefer* he happened to pull off the shelf was the Hebrew Schottenstein Gemara, and he opened it. "The Zaide looked for two minutes, five minutes, ten minutes," recalls Rav

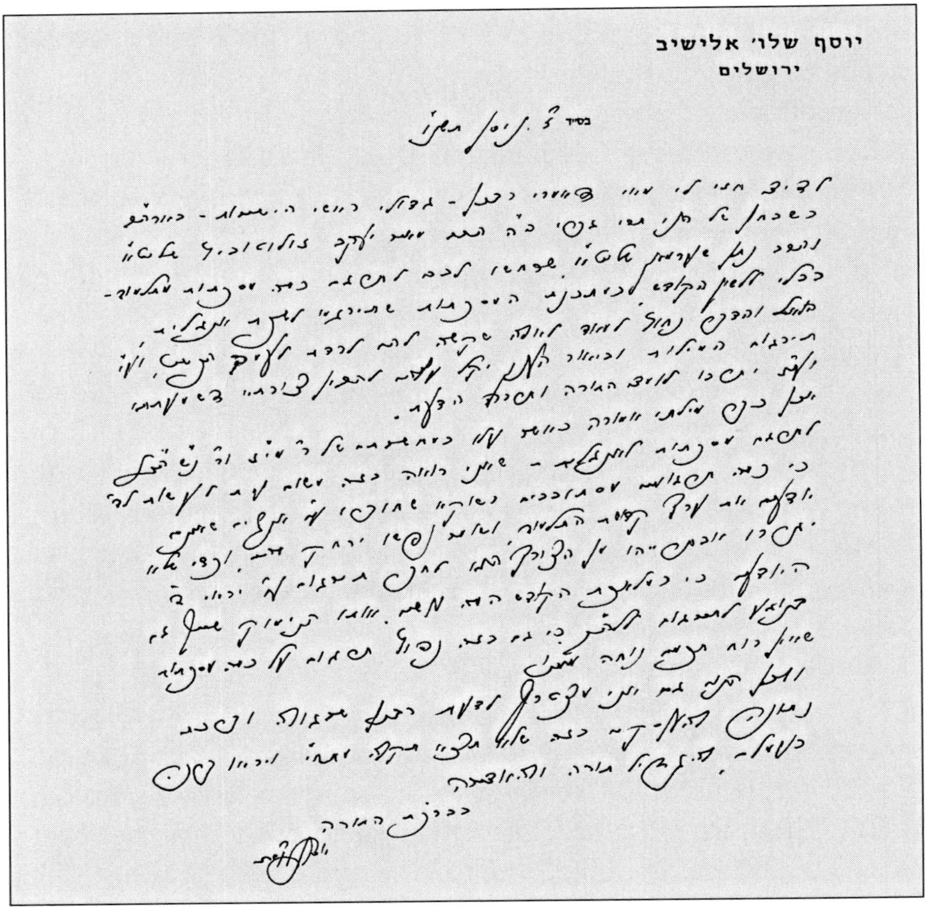

The handwritten *haskamah* from Rav Elyashiv

בס״ד ז׳ ניסן תשנ״ז

לדידי חזי לי מאי דאמרי רבנן – גדולי ראש הישיבות – בארה״ב בשבחן של הני תרי גברי ה״ה הרב מאיר יעקב זלוטוביץ שליט״א והרב נתן שערמאן שליט״א שרחש לבם לתרגם כמה מסכתות מתלמוד בבלי ללשון הקודש במתכונת המסכתות שתירגמו לשפת אנגלית הואיל והדבר נחוץ למאוד לאלה שקשה להם לרדת לעומק הפשט, וע״י תרגום המילות וביאור הענין יקל עליהם להבין צורתא דשמעתתא וע״י יתרבו לומדי התורה ותרבה הדעת.

אכן כבר מילתי אמורה כאשר עלה במחשבתם של ר׳ מי״ז ור׳ נ״ש הנ״ל לתרגם מסכתות לאנגלית – שאני רואה בזה משום עת לעשות לד׳ כי כמה תרגומים מסתובבים בשוקא שחוברו ע״י אנשים שאינם יודעים את ערך קדושת התלמוד, ושומר נפשו ירחק מהם. וכדי שלא יגררו אבתרייהו מן הצורך הוא לחבר תרגום ע״י יראי ד׳ היודעים כי במלאכת הקודש המה עושים. אותו הנימוק שייך גם בנוגע לתרגום ללה״ק כי גם בזה נפוץ תרגום על כמה מסכתות שאין רוח חכמים נוחה ממנו.

ולכן הנני גם אני מצטרף לדעת רבנן שבגולה וברכתי נתונה להעוסקים בזה שלא תצא תקלה מתח״י ויראו ברכה בעמלם להגדיל תורה ולהאדירה

יוסף שלו׳ אלישיב

340 / RABBI MEIR ZLOTOWITZ

Aryeh, "sitting like that for close to an hour, turning pages and never looking up. It was astounding."

The ultimate *haskamah*, approval for the work, came when those very Gemaros became part of the preparation for the famed nightly *shiur*.

Rav Elyashiv's father, Rav Avrohom Elyashiv, had been rav of the Tiferes Bachurim shul, initially established as a group for young men who worked by day and wanted a framework for growth in Torah in their free time. He delivered a *shiur* each evening, a standard Gemara class that dealt primarily with actual *peshat*, along with some deeper analysis. After Rav Avrohom passed away, Rav Elyashiv inherited his father's *shiur*. While the *shiur* delivered by the *gadol hador* would draw large crowds of brilliant, accomplished *talmidei chachamim*, the simple laymen and neighborhood locals who had always attended still did so, along with tourists and people eager for a distinct glimpse of Rav Elyashiv.

As Rav Elyashiv aged, the *shiur* was moved to a specially constructed trailer near his home, but he maintained the format of the *shiur*; and that style, the mix of clarity and profundity, led Rav Elyashiv to quickly peruse the ArtScroll Gemara each day before delivering the *shiur*. He told his grandson that the *mareh mekomos*, the sources on the bottom of the page, were suitable for all sorts of learners, "From great *amei ha'aretz* to great *talmidei chachamim*."

One day, a volume of the Gemara happened to be on Rav Elyashiv's table during an important meeting. His devoted grandson wanted to remove it. "They will take a photograph with it," Rav Aryeh explained, "and everyone will think that the Zaide uses this Gemara." Rav Elyashiv shrugged. "Let them," he said.

Rav Elyashiv appreciated the American visitor as well, sharing stories, and even jokes with Reb Meir. Once, Rav Elyashiv began to look around his room when Reb Meir came in to speak to him.

As an *eid* under the *chuppah* of a great-grandson of Rav Elyashiv

"Wait," Rav Elyashiv looked on the shelves and found what he was looking for, "*ich hub a matanah fahr eich*, I have a present for you." With a broad smile he handed Reb Meir a picture from a recent *chasunah*: Rav Elyashiv standing under the *chuppah* as *mesader kiddushin*, Reb Meir standing at his side as an *eid*, a witness to the *kiddushin*.[5]

Rav Elyashiv accorded special respect to the fact that Reb Meir was a *talmid* of Rav Moshe. "Your rebbi, Rav Moshe," Rav Elyashiv remarked, "would have been a *gadol hador*, *afilu mit tzen doros tzurik,* even if he had lived ten generations earlier!"

Reb Meir once confided in Rav Elyashiv that the pressures were mounting: the responsibilities to the "*kollel*," the team of *talmidei chachamim* on the ArtScroll payroll, and the large

5. Reb Meir, who generally rejected public honors and was known to avoid *simchos* if he anticipated he might receive a *kibbud*, was deeply moved by the fact that he had been called up as an *eid*, a witness, under the *chuppah* of one of Rav Elyashiv's great-grandchildren.

"Rav Elyashiv would get personally involved in the choice, and this decision doesn't speak about me, but about ArtScroll," Reb Meir would explain, "and it's a tribute to what we do."

sums needed to keep various projects afloat, were weighing on him. It was during a difficult fund-raising period, and he was unusually glum.

"Imagine the *talmidim* are in the classroom and instead of teaching, the rebbi walks out on them," Rav Elyashiv said. "Reb Meir, you have tens of thousands of *talmidim* waiting to learn, you need to keep publishing *sefarim*!"

The personal relationship grew deeper, as Reb Meir would bring copies of the latest *sefarim* to Rav Elyashiv whenever he was in Eretz Yisrael. Before Rav Elyashiv started learning *Maseches Bechoros* in the *shiur*, his grandson Rav Aryeh called Reb Meir in his Brooklyn office. Rav Aryeh explained that while he knew that the Gemara was not yet printed, the Zaide had asked if the manuscript was ready, as he wanted to see it.[6]

Reb Meir brought two new volumes of the Hebrew Gemara to Rav Elyashiv just weeks before the rav was hospitalized for the last time. Rav Elyashiv smiled when he saw the *sefarim* and said, "You have only two more volumes before your *siyum*," indicating that he was clearly following the project's progress.

In 2005, when Reb Meir embarked on what would be his own final mission — the translation and elucidation of the Talmud Yerushalmi — he and Reb Nosson went to Rav Elyashiv for a *berachah* and *haskamah*. Rav Efrati, present at the meeting, commented on how difficult it would be to translate the Yerushalmi, which is intricate and complex. "Yes," Rav Elyashiv said with a broad smile, "but they have *siyata d'Shmaya* (the assistance of Heaven)."

After Rav Elyashiv's passing, Reb Meir developed a close relationship with Rav Chaim Kanievsky.

---

6. After receiving that phone call, Reb Meir remarked, "I wish that phones had never been invented. Imagine, a hundred years ago, I'd have received a postcard from Rav Elyashiv requesting the Gemaros...now, who's going to believe it?"

לכבוד חתני היקר...

[handwritten Hebrew inscription]

An inscribed copy of R' Chaim Kanievsky's *sefer* on Chanukah and Purim

Reb Meir would try to personally bring in new volumes of the Yerushalmi, and when Rabbi Naftali Weinberger worked on the ArtScroll biography of Rebbetzin Batsheva Kanievsky, Rav Chaim took a personal interest in the work and gave practical guidance.

Rav Chaim being shown the *Haggadah Shel Pesach* with his own commentary

Copy of Rav Gifter's check

Reb Meir's relationship with Rav Mordechai Gifter meant a lot to him. When Rabbi Yechiel Spero wrote the biography of the Telshe rosh yeshivah, Reb Meir undertook the role not just of editor, but of *talmid* as well. He cherished the memory of those occasions when Rav Gifter had come to visit ArtScroll headquarters to share in the *nachas*. On one occasion, the rosh yeshivah wanted to purchase several *sefarim* and books. Reb Meir wrapped them up and refused to accept payment. The rosh yeshivah insisted on paying, however, so Reb Meir quoted him a price of one dollar and seventy-five cents. Rav Gifter wrote out the check: Reb Meir accepted it, and gave it to his daughter, Estie Dicker — who keeps it in her wallet, until today.

Another one of the roshei yeshivah whom Reb Meir considered a rebbi was Rav Zelik Epstein, rosh yeshivah of Sha'ar HaTorah Grodna in Queens. Reb Nosson had learned under Rav Zelik in Torah Vodaath and he and Reb Meir would visit the rosh yeshivah's home when they needed to discuss sensitive issues.

In later years, Reb Meir would play the role of *ba'al eitzah*, called upon to counsel others. The main qualification for one who dispenses advice, he would say, is to be able to make a suggestion that has no traces of *negius*, personal interest. He would often retell a story he had heard from Rav Zelik's son and successor as rosh yeshivah, Rav Kalman Epstein.

One Motza'ei Shabbos, Rav Kalman came home to see an unfamiliar person talking to his father. The visitor, clearly burdened by problems, sat there for quite some time. When the conversation ended, Rav Zelik asked his son to drive the man back home.

It took a while, and Rav Kalman only returned home about a half-hour later. "Kalman, I need you to go back and pick up that man, please," Rav Zelik told his son. "I need to speak with him again."

And the rosh yeshivah explained. "He is in such pain, that I worry that the compassion I felt clouded my judgment. I wanted to comfort him, so I gave him advice to put him at ease, but it wasn't what he needed to hear. Please bring him back so I can give him the advice that's best for him, not the advice it's easiest for me to give and for him to hear."

Reb Meir would say that someone who has that sort of clarity, who is that free of "*negius*," can give advice to others.

Every summer, Reb Meir and Reb Nosson, along with their wives, would be invited to a festive *seudah* at the Deal, New Jersey summer home of their friend Ellis Safdeye. The event was open only to rabbanim and their wives, Mr. Safdeye's way of expressing respect for those men and women who allowed him to partner with them for the benefit of Klal Yisrael.

What most impressed Reb Meir wasn't the food, the décor, or even the prestige of the guest list: it was the fact that the host, Mr. Safdeye, insisted on acting as waiter, serving the guests himself, the ultimate act of *kavod* for *talmidei chachamim*.

Reb Meir considered himself a "chassid" of the Belzer Rebbe, whom he often consulted and looked to for advice. In the last year of Reb Meir's life, the Belzer Mosdos were hosting a benefit dinner in Los Angeles. A representative of the Belzer Rebbe came to ask Reb Meir to serve as guest speaker at the event.

Reb Meir explained that he didn't speak publicly, and couldn't accommodate them. "But even though I am a *litvak* through and through," he continued, "out of respect for the Belzer Rebbe, you can use my name however you feel it can be helpful and I will go to Los Angeles to be *mechazek* the dinner."

He was listed as dinner chairman and, true to his word, Reb Meir juggled different meetings and prior commitments to fly to California, simply in order to show his respect and appreciation to the Rebbe.

Reb Meir once confided in a close friend that it was an *avodah,* an internal process, to develop reverence for the younger generation of *talmidei chachamim.* "Not because they don't deserve our respect," Reb Meir explained, "but because we knew our own rebbeim once they were already older, we saw the greatness the first time we met them. Those younger rabbanim with whom we grew up don't have that same mystique, because we observed them in the process of becoming great. We have to believe that Torah elevates a person and that Hakadosh Baruch Hu provides leaders to each generation, and look at them with similar respect."

As Reb Meir himself wrote in his preface to the ArtScroll biography of his rebbi, Rav Moshe. *"The Rosh Yeshivah is gone. His beauty is gone. His wisdom is gone. Who will replace him? Well may we weep. At the same time, we are reassured by our faith and our history. Klal Yisrael survives and new gedolei Yisrael have always arisen. The Rosh Yeshivah's heroic work for Torah will not be in vain..."*

Before embarking on the elucidation of a particular *sefer,* Reb Meir accompanied the writer to seek a *haskamah* from a very influential rav, who was an expert in this *sefer.* The rav laughed and joked that clearly, they were coming to him because this *sefer* wasn't something with which Rav Moshe was familiar.

Reb Meir and Rachel with Rav Reuven and Rebbetzin Sheila Feinstein

There was a tense moment as Reb Meir sat up straight in his chair, clearly unwilling to tolerate a slight to his rebbi's honor.

Even as others in the room hoped he'd let the comment pass, Reb Meir — well aware of the ramifications of what he was about to do — spoke firmly. "Rav Moshe is my rebbi. He knows *kol haTorah kulah*, and I'm making a *mecha'ah*[7] for his *kavod*."

In the last year of Reb Meir's life, he was sitting at a *chasunah* in Lakewood. A young rav seated at the same table asked Reb Meir to what *zechus* he attributed the success of ArtScroll.

Reb Meir thought for a moment, then said, "I think it might be because I stood up for my rebbi's *kavod* at a time when it was difficult for me. Perhaps that's the *zechus* that carries us..."

---

7. Protest.

14

THE SPIRIT
OF THE BEIS MEDRASH

I F THERE WAS A TIME IN THE WEEK THAT BELONGED TO REB
Meir, it was Shabbos morning before Shacharis; always an
early riser, on this day the hours were his. There were no
emails awaiting his response, no one in Eretz Yisrael desperate
to speak with him — just he and his *sefarim*.

It was, a child observed, Reb Meir enjoying the serenity to
return to his first love. As a *bachur*, he had earned *semichah*
from Rav Moshe, and when his eldest son, Reb Gedaliah,
earned his own *semichah* from Rav Avrohom Pam, Reb Meir
was overjoyed. To his mind, it was a prerequisite to serving Klal
Yisrael.

There was nothing more important than learning Torah.

Rabbi Shimon Finkelman was present when a children's book
about a great *talmid chacham* was being discussed. Someone
suggested that the book cover feature an image depicting an

exciting scene in the life of that great man, but Reb Meir disagreed. He felt that the cover had to show the *gadol* learning Torah, because it's that, more than anything else, that defines an *adam gadol*.

When one of his sons-in-law announced that he was leaving *kollel* for a career in *chinuch*, Reb Meir greeted the news with happiness — and a touch of concern. He called his children aside and said, "If you are leaving the *beis medrash* because it's your dream to teach Torah, then I couldn't be prouder; but if you are leaving the *beis medrash* because of financial stress, I beg you to tell me that, and I will do more to help you."

While learning at MTJ, friends recall, Meir Zlotowitz would spend all day in the *beis medrash*. Rav Moshe thought that the young man had the potential to be an effective *dayan*. Eventually, his mission to Klal Yisrael laid claim to most of Reb Meir's waking hours, but his deep love for learning never waned.

In his *haskamah* to Reb Meir's first published work, the ArtScroll *Megillas Esther*, Rav Moshe Feinstein wrote that the author was, "*Ben Torah veyerei Shamayim be'emes uve'samim… behanhagah yesharah u'nechonah kera'ui l'ben Torah veyerei Hashem* — A true ben Torah and one who fears Heaven…with proper and upright conduct, as befits a true *ben Torah* who fears Heaven."

In his final years, Reb Meir returned to halachah, using that time to delve into the *Choshen Mishpat* section of *Shulchan Aruch*, the intricacies and complexities of business halachah; he enjoyed the *limud* immensely, and at the Shabbos table, he would repeat different interesting *shailos* he had encountered.

He would speak of the years during which he wrote the comprehensive translation and commentary on *Sefer Bereishis* as the best ones of his life. "I got to be *to'eim*, to taste, the '*kol hayom hi sichasi*,'[1] learning Torah all day, dreaming in learning, being consumed by learning."

---

1. *Tehillim* 119:97: "How I love Your Torah! All day it is my conversation."

"I believe that Reb Meir's translation and commentary on *Sefer Bereishis* is the very best anthology on *Sefer Bereishis* in existence until today," Rav Dovid Cohen remarked to *Yated Ne'eman* columnist Rabbi Avrohom Birnbaum.

When writing on the topic of *"nevuah l'tov"* for that *sefer*, Reb Meir often went to speak with Rav Dovid Cohen. Those conversations regarding prophecy were so wide-ranging and profound that Rav Dovid ultimately wrote his own *sefer* on the subject.

"I knew Meir as a *bachur*, knew that his heart was bursting with *ahavas Torah*. It was what he had absorbed at home so it was part of him, and I continued to see it throughout the years," says Nochum Silberman. "Even if he couldn't learn as much as he had in yeshivah, there were other ways it was obvious."

A business associate once called Nochum to inquire about ArtScroll. "I can see that they do nice work," he told Reb Nochum, "but I want to know if they're for real before I commit to sponsoring a project."

Reb Nochum suggested that they pay a surprise visit to ArtScroll and come unannounced, so that the other man could get a clear sense of what it was all about.

The two men drove to Second Avenue and parked the car. Rather than come in through the lobby, Reb Nochum led his friend through the bindery and they went up in the freight elevator, then walked down the hall to where various writers, editors, and translators worked.

"It felt like any authentic yeshivah *beis medrash*: there were raised voices, open *sefarim*, *talmidei chachamim* arguing over the correct *peshat* in a *Tosafos*. We stood there, mesmerized by the beautiful sight."

"That was Reb Meir's real essence, the spirit and fire of that *beis medrash*; the *sefarim* that came out of ArtScroll were just a result."

Reb Meir's pride in his *"kollel"* was unmistakable. "In

discussing opportunities with him," reflects Reb Avrum Weinfeld of Chicago, "I had the sense that he was as proud of the people working on the project as the project itself. It wasn't academia that thrilled him: it was Torah."

A donor received a box of the *sefarim* he had sponsored, and sent a very warm email praising the excellence of the product. Reb Meir wrote back:

> Thank you for your very complimentary remarks. In all modesty, and on behalf of our wonderful, elevated team of scholars whom we support and who perform so selflessly their spiritual and scholarly role, I must say that the "mazel" you so correctly attributed to our sefarim is due to the ehrlichkeit of every one of the talmidei chachamim participating.
>
> They are role models, and I suppose that this is how the Ribbono Shel Olam rewards their efforts, as well as the visionary people like you who make their harbatzas Torah efforts possible in such an unprecedented way.

A close friend who was on his way to an appointment with Rav Chaim Kanievsky asked what *berachah* he could request on Reb Meir's behalf. Reb Meir emailed back:

> In addition to the berachah v'hatzlachah for us personally, I would like a strong berachah for the ArtScroll mif'al of harbatzas haTorah. Our kollel has a budget of $140,000 A WEEK for the talmidei chachamim, avreichim, who learn and write our sefarim. There are over 100 avreichim, many of whom live in Eretz Yisrael, and this is their full parnassah — b'revach.

Reb Meir's dear friend Reb Chaim Smutni would often speak with him about different needy people in Yerushalayim. "Meir would hear about an impoverished *talmid chacham* and immediately start thinking of ways in which ArtScroll could use his talents and provide a source of income. It meant a lot to him that he could allow *talmidei chachamim* to help support their families in a way that wasn't beneath their dignity."

The night *kollel* Reb Meir founded and carried in Lakewood, Nachalas Ahron, was unique. Along with gifting each *avreich* with a box of books for Chanukah and a cash bonus before Yamim Tovim, he insisted that they be paid for the months of Nissan and Tishrei, when the *kollel* was closed (and other *kollelim* don't pay). "When a *talmid chacham* takes a break, it's also part of his growth," he said.

Close friends noticed something poetic in Reb Meir's *ahavas Torah*. "His love for *talmidei chachamim* was very emotional, straight from his heart," says his close friend Rav Eliyahu Meir Klugman. "To him, there was no place more glorious than a *beis medrash*; nothing impressed him more than the sight of authentic *talmidei chachamim* sitting and learning."

In a tribute published in *Mishpacha* magazine following Reb Meir's passing, Rabbi Yehuda Heimowitz writes: *I will always recall his enthusiasm as he handed me a still-warm copy of the Yerushalmi Gemara Maasros, which had come off the printing press a few hours earlier. At that point, ArtScroll had completed the Bavli project in English and Hebrew, spanning nearly 150 volumes in all, and was well into elucidating Yerushalmi — aside from its classic Siddur, Chumash, Tanach, Mishnah series, and an endless list of other works. I would have expected the release of a new volume to be a humdrum experience for Rabbi Zlotowitz, but he was so proud of the Yerushalmi*

With Rav Eliyahu Meir Klugman

Maasros that an unenlightened observer could easily have mistaken it for his first published work...

Grandchildren who joined him for the weekly Shabbos Kiddush heard it directly from him. They would often ask him what was new at work, which titles were being released — but toward the end of his life, he would shrug at the familiar question. "I'm not completely up to date on each and every title, but," Reb Meir's face brightened, "if you want to know which line they're up to in the Yerushalmi, I can tell you!"

A young man came to pick up one of the Zlotowitz girls for a *shidduch* date on the Motza'ei Shabbos of *Parashas Lech Lecha*. While chatting, Reb Meir half-jokingly asked the young man if he had had a chance to look at the ArtScroll *Bereishis* on the *parashah*, Appendix B. The *bachur* replied that he hadn't, and Reb Meir started to explain that in the *sefer*, the calculation of Avraham Avinu's age when he left Charan appears.

The *bachur* was astonished. Just two days earlier, he and his *chavrusa* had been learning *Maseches Yevamos*, and they had looked up the commentary of the *Rosh*. The *bachur* noticed a *Rosh* on the same page they were learning that mentioned the names of Avraham and Sarah, and intrigued, he and his *chavrusa* learned it as well. In that piece, the *Rosh* concludes that Avraham and Sarah left Charan twice, when Avraham was seventy years old and again when he was seventy-five.

This was the very idea that Rabbi Zlotowitz was quoting, and the *bachur* responded, "Oh yes, the *Rosh* in *Yevamos*, of course. He says Avraham left Charan twice."

Now it was Reb Meir's turn to be flabbergasted at the breadth of knowledge of the young man.

Once on the date, the young man told the girl the true story and asked her to please tell her father what had really happened; he didn't want her father to get an inaccurate picture of him and how much he really knew.

Before the next date, Rabbi Zlotowitz informed the young man, Asher Dicker — who would marry his oldest daughter Estie — that he was still impressed, because not all *bachurim* would have been curious, intrigued, and determined enough to be drawn in by a *Rosh* that wasn't directly relevant to the *sugya*.

Rav Dovid Feinstein recalls how even after Meir left yeshivah and went to work, he maintained a special practice: The talented artist would design stickers for the yeshivah's *sefarim* and write them in a perfect *ksav Ashuris*, adding to the beauty of the *sefarim*.

Reb Meir would joke that even though he was a *"kalte Litvak,"* and his heritage was that of the more austere, less expressive Lithuanian yeshivah world, he loved a chassidishe davening. He appreciated *chazzanus* and *neginah*, and would always enjoy the davening of his close friend, Reb Abish Brodt. "You've warmed my cold Lithuanian heart," he would say.

The nuances and depth of old-world *chazzanus* appealed to him, and he would often grow visibly emotional while sitting in

Dancing with Reb Abish Brodt at an ArtScroll retreat
Also seen (R to L) Malcolm Hoenlein and Ahron Moshe Hoberman

With Malcolm Hoenlein

place, enraptured by its sound. He would try to teach his grandchildren to appreciate the profundity of *chazzanus*, and on those occasions when he succeeded, he was very pleased.

The success of ArtScroll in reaching all sorts of Jews, speculates a friend of Reb Meir, was connected to the fact that its founder had a genuine appreciation in his heart for every stream of *Yiddishkeit*, with its particular holy Mesorah.

"I saved the pre-Yom Tov emails that Meir would send out," recalls his friend Malcolm Hoenlein. "They were different than the usual organizational updates. They always gave me such encouragement, because he managed to convey his wide view, his focus on all Jews, not just the ones he saw in shul. Those emails were his mission statement, and they showed a little bit of the *ahavas Yisrael* in Meir's heart; he was writing from Brooklyn, but in his mind's eye, he saw every Jew on earth."

The words of *tefillah* meant a lot to Reb Meir: He would translate the words of the more obscure *tefillos* for his sons, going through the words of *Brich Shmei* for them, explaining the concept and structure of the *piyut* of *Ki Hinei Kachomer* recited on the night of Yom Kippur; then, he would ask the child to repeat it back to him.

He took his own children, and eventually tried to take every bar mitzvah or bas mitzvah-age grandchild, to Eretz Yisrael.

Reb Meir and Rachel with bas mitzvah-aged granddaughters in Eretz Yisrael

The first time he traveled with his family was when his son Yisroel became bar mitzvah; before they disembarked from the airplane, he gave them a short speech. With tears in his eyes, he spoke of Moshe Rabbeinu's desperate longing to enter the Land, how the Vilna Gaon yearned to breathe its air. "And we, little people that we are, are about to walk on the holy ground... realize how blessed we are, what an opportunity we have."

When he traveled to Eretz Yisrael for the respective *yahrzeits* of his parents, he liked to daven from the *amud* at Yerushalayim's Zichron Moshe shul. He appreciated the authenticity of the people and their prayers, and felt it added honor to his parents to daven in that sort of *minyan*.

Those who knew Reb Meir best — witnesses to his perpetual motion, one-meeting-after-the-next schedule while in Eretz Yisrael — would look on in wonder at his practice after davening Shacharis at the Kosel. "When the *vasikin minyanim* were over, Reb Meir would walk up toward the Wall, and then simply remain in place, frozen," recalls Judah Septimus. "He wouldn't hold a Siddur or *Tehillim*, but would simply stand

The Spirit of the Beis Medrash / 357

Enjoying a family dinner in a restaurant

there motionless for several minutes. In a way, that image is the one I hold onto now, the picture of Reb Meir as himself: not listening, not speaking, not moving, just one with his Creator."

"Reb Meir wouldn't just hear *divrei Torah*, he would internalize them," says Rav Dovid Feinstein. "He would listen eagerly, and then make the lesson part of him. He loved a good vort, that's what shaped his inner world."

The Zlotowitz children and grandchildren could anticipate which *divrei Torah* he would inevitably share on each *parashah*: when they called Erev Shabbos *Parashas Kedoshim*, they expected to hear the Ramban's words about a *"naval birshus haTorah."*[2]

"We understood that zaidy wasn't looking to impress us with a *chiddush*, but rather, the *parashah* was a means to convey essential truths, so he had no problem repeating the same *dvar Torah*, year after year," explains a grandson.

---

2. *Vayikra* 19:2. The Ramban on the first *pasuk* in the *parashah*, *Kedoshim Tihyu* — the mandate to be holy — sees it not as a reference to specific prohibitions, but rather to living a life of holiness as opposed to indulging excessively in worldly pleasures. One can be a *"naval birshus haTorah* — repulsive, without actually violating any specific commandment."

At Chaim and Shira's wedding

Reb Meir didn't only preach it, he taught them by example. He enjoyed teaching them to appreciate genuine Jewish foods: he would tease them if they didn't like *kishke* or *grivven*.

"The most important person to be friendly with is the cook," he would often quip, and he would joke with his *eineklach* that "parve ice cream tastes like melted Havdalah candles." He didn't see these comments as beneath him, because he was confident that his grandchildren understood that his appreciation for real dairy ice cream wasn't because he was a "foodie" — though he certainly enjoyed the treat — but part of his larger joy in spending time with family and sharing pleasant experiences with others.

He always connected them with the person who had worked to prepare the food. The Shabbos meal inevitably ended with his instructions to "go tell Bubby how delicious the cholent was"; and when he spent Shabbos at the home of one of his children, he made sure that the entire family knew that no one else could prepare a main dish, or set a table, or spice a salad, like their mother.

One Motza'ei Pesach, Reb Meir stood in the hotel parking lot watching various family members as they packed up to leave after having spent Yom Tov together. He pulled a granddaughter aside and indicated the commotion and activity — cars being loaded, luggage carts being wheeled back and forth, the happy noise of a family that enjoyed each other's company filling the early spring night — and he waved his hand. "You see all this, Chaya? Look what we have here now. This entire family is just from one person — me. I'm one person. Bubby is one person. Think of the six million Jews that were killed in the Holocaust. Each and every one of them could have had a family like this. We didn't lose just six million people. We lost six million families."

Reb Meir appreciated quality, but never at the expense of his value system. He once expressed his confusion at the fact that young couples who can barely make it through the month would purchase $700 brand-name strollers for their babies.

"Oh, come on, Zaidy," one of the granddaughters teased, "you don't get luxury? You drive a Lexus!"

He immediately turned serious. "There's luxury and there's functionality. In a car, I'm not paying for the brand-name but for the increased safety, quality, and comfort; in a stroller, it's just the name and the ego boost, and that's a very silly thing to spend money on."

"What struck me about his explanation," recalls the granddaughter, "was how seriously he took our light banter. It went from being a cute joke to a *chinuch* conversation, and it was important to him that we understood the lesson he was trying to impart."

He took their comments seriously. One Erev Yom Tov, he gave some money to his granddaughter as a gift. She said thank you, and earnestly added that she would save the money because she hoped to marry a *ben Torah* one day. He looked at her seriously. "Really? That's great."

Then he reached into his pocket and handed her two additional $100 bills. "That's for your savings account."

Then he smiled warmly, a way of letting her know not just that he appreciated her dreams, but that he believed in them as well.

Reb Meir was a *ba'al yissurim*, in pain through most of his life. The act of putting on his socks in the morning and tying his shoes could be excruciating and take several minutes. Walking up a flight of stairs could sap him of his energy. Perhaps his greatest achievement, close friends reflect, was the way he concealed this from nearly everyone who knew him.

Reb Meir once joked to Rav Dovid Feinstein that if he woke one day and didn't feel pain, he would know he was already in the Next World. "But you only saw the smile and warmth," the rosh yeshivah remarks. "He didn't complain. He accepted *yissurim be'ahavah*."

That discipline and self-control served him well. Late one Friday night in 1984, Reb Meir was informed that his mother had passed away.

Rachel Zlotowitz remembers that moment. "My husband was devoted to his mother; they were extremely close. But once he processed the information, he looked at me and said, "Okay, it's Shabbos, we didn't just get this information. That's the halachah, we won't tell the children and we won't discuss it with anyone else and we certainly won't mourn."

Reb Meir conducted himself that Shabbos as on any other, pleasant and friendly in shul, leading the singing and *divrei Torah* at the Shabbos table. Only when the flame of the Havdalah candle was snuffed out did he allow his emotions to overtake him as he began to mourn his beloved mother.

When his children would ask how he was feeling, especially in his final months, he would respond, "Did I tell you how much I love you?"

His family got glimpses of the perpetual struggle. On a visit to Eretz Yisrael, Reb Meir invited his grandchildren to join him for dinner; the restaurant was at the top of a steep flight of stairs. As Reb Meir slowly, determinedly made his way up, he whispered something to himself. It sounded like, "I won't stop," and a grandson asked what he had said.

"I said," Reb Meir looked at him, "that throughout my life, the Satan has been trying to get me to stop, to make it hard for me to go forward, to keep climbing. But," continued Reb Meir, "he won't win. I won't stop."

15

RAV MOSHE'S BERACHAH

ZAIDY," CRIED OUT A GRANDSON AT THE *LEVAYAH*, "*YOU were so busy with us, when did you have time for ArtScroll?"*

Reb Meir was proud of what ArtScroll had accomplished, but his greatest joy came from being with his family and discussing their achievements.

Colleagues who knew him from work, familiar with the focused, efficient executive of office hours, would see him at family *simchos* and marvel. Reb Meir would sit with children and grandchildren enjoying every moment, exuding happiness and tranquility, clearly in his element.

Behind the titles and publicity and impact was the person that never disappeared, the man who never got swallowed up by the legend.

During the Succos season, many of Reb Meir's friends and supporters were in Yerushalayim; it was a busy time, heavy in

(L to R) Mendy Klein and Reuven Dessler

social obligations and events. Reb Meir's close friend Mendy Klein of Cleveland recalls walking into a quiet restaurant just after Succos.

"I saw Reb Meir and his wife at a corner table, deep in con-

Picture captured by Mendy Klein for posterity

versation," he recalls. "They sat there for hours, just talking to each other. And *that* was my Rabbi Zlotowitz — the person!"

"I knew Meir well, we worked hand in hand, and I was amazed at his professional accomplishments; but what most impressed Jeanie and me was the family he and Rachel built," reflects Jay Schottenstein.

He would inspire other business colleagues to invest in their families, to express love and make time for children and grandchildren. He taught them that successful as they were at the office, there was no shame in being expressive about their feelings with their families. A business associate was traveling to Eretz Yisrael and sent an email to Reb Meir, "If I meet your grandson, I'll give him a hug from you," he wrote.

"No," Reb Meir wrote back, "please give him two hugs."

The precision and mastery of details that made him so capable at work defined him as a father: he knew the likes and dislikes of his children, children-in-law, and grandchildren.

It wasn't just which foods or treats they appreciated; he was able to perceive who was experiencing a rough day and needed a kind word.

One Erev Yom Kippur, a grandson who was going through a stressful time in yeshivah walked into the house. Before he had said a word, Reb Meir met his gaze, then pulled him close in a tight embrace. "Everything will be okay, it's going to work out," he said.

Giving a *berachah* to a granddaughter

The wedding of one of his granddaughters took place during a fierce snowstorm. The day of the wedding, she got a text from zaidy, who anticipated that the forecast might have added tension: *Good morning, Kallah. Everyone is thinking about you. Can't wait! Love Z.*

Another granddaughter shared his artistic inclination; he took great pride in her work and would often discuss different paintings or images with her, as if they were equals. On a visit to Lakewood, he perused her personal sketch pad and saw her drawings. Rather than compliment her, he wrote on the back cover in permanent marker.

> *Zaidy Zlotowitz saw this beautiful sketch pad on Erev Shabbos Acharei-Kedoshim 5764. He shepped a lot of nachas and admires the exceptional talent of Chaya, shetichye. Don't ever throw this book out. Be'ahavah b'lev v'nefesh, HaSaba Meir Yaakov Zlotowitz.*

His married grandchildren joined him in Yerushalayim's Plaza Hotel for Shavuos. With the onset of Yom Tov, they noticed that their baby had a strange bump on his neck: it became Zaidy Zlotowitz's problem, and he circulated among the guests, determined to find a doctor. Eventually he did, and the doctor advised that the baby be hospitalized.

The couple headed to the hospital, and throughout the long night and first day, regular phone calls came from the non-Jewish concierge at the hotel, asking the non-Jewish nurse for updates. On the second day of Yom Tov, Reb Meir updated his nephew and niece — who live near the Plaza and keep only one day of Yom Tov — about the situation, and they were dispatched to the hospital, laden with food and concern.

And Motza'ei Yom Tov, when everyone was reunited at the hospital — loving grandparents, relieved parents, and a healthy baby — Reb Meir sat down with the doctor, eager to pay for his services. The doctor advised them how to go about avoiding the full fee, telling them how to get retroactive insurance coverage.

Reb Meir thanked him, but firmly reiterated his request to pay in full and deal with it honestly, in a manner with no trace of *chillul Hashem*.

His grandchildren spoke freely with him, sharing private struggles and dreams; he would simply listen, letting them know he understood. The one thing he wouldn't tolerate was complaints about their own parents. If a child expressed frustration with his or her parents, Reb Meir wouldn't encourage them to continue. Rather, he would say, "Your parents love you, they want what's best for you, and they know what's best for you."

The children and grandchildren called each Erev Shabbos, but it was important to Reb Meir that the final hour before Shabbos be a peaceful time; he didn't appreciate it when they left the phone calls until the last minute. One Friday, a granddaughter called too close to Shabbos, and after exchanging good wishes, he hung up without having the usual chat about the week that had passed.

A moment later, her phone rang. It was zaidy. "Even though I like when you call earlier in the day," he said, "I don't want you to go through a whole Shabbos thinking that I don't love you."

The first Erev Shabbos after one of his children or grandchildren would get engaged, he would call the new *chassan* or *kallah*. He advised his children to do the same with their own engaged couples. "At the beginning, it can be uncomfortable for a new *chassan* or *kallah* to make that phone call: don't stand on ceremony. You be the one to make the call for as many weeks as it takes for them to realize that it's part of Erev Shabbos to call parents, in-laws, and grandparents. Eventually, you won't have to do it!"

He was very involved in the lives of his children, but they didn't find it invasive, because they saw his concern as part of the generosity and giving. "When Dad made a suggestion," recalls one of the children, "he would always offer help as well. He told us he thought one of the boys could use supplementary

With grandchildren at a Chanukah party

help in school and immediately offered to pay. He pointed out that one of the children seemed to be walking awkwardly, and commented that if we agreed and wanted to get it checked out with a doctor, he thought he had the right doctor for us."

While leaving one of his children's houses after spending Shabbos, Reb Meir mentioned that he thought the living room needed a paint job, then casually placed an envelope with money on the table.

If they were hesitant to accept the money, he would say, "Don't be silly, when my father gave me money, I took it. If a parent gives money, you take it!"

When he would extend financial help to his children and grandchildren, whether it was assistance with a down payment for a home or something as small as a new hat for Yom Tov, his children knew that he would treat that information just as he did all the sensitive information that crossed his desk each day: with silence. He wouldn't speak of it, remind them of his largesse, or share it with others. As soon as he finished giving, it was as if he had already forgotten it.

When he dispensed *chinuch* advice, he would preface his comments by saying, "Of course I'm not a *mechanech*, I'm speaking only as a caring zaidy."

Before any of his grandchildren finalized an engagement, Reb Meir and his wife would meet the prospective match. The Barnes and Noble bookstore near Lakewood is a location of great significance in the Zlotowitz family, because it was the designated meeting point; between its book-filled aisles Reb Meir and Rachel would meet the grandchild in question along with his or her prospective spouse. These meetings were brief — but it didn't take Reb Meir long to form an assessment of someone. His married children appreciated the custom. "It wasn't because Dad wanted to weigh in on whether they should get engaged, because at that point, it was usually 'too late,'" speculates Rabbi Duvie Morgenstern. "The reason he wanted the meeting was in order to encourage his own children; he would always call after the meeting to say how impressed he was, because he knew that his approval would make it easier

On a family Chol HaMoed trip

for us. It was also a way to start building the relationship with a new member of the family."

(Although Reb Meir didn't involve himself in the *shidduchim* of his grandchildren, trusting his children to choose wisely, he did share a steady piece of advice. *Don't take yourselves too seriously.* Don't be too picky in *shidduchim*, he would say, a suggestion that reflected both his characteristic humility and his practical wisdom.)

When grandchildren got engaged, they could expect a private moment with zaidy after the *vort*. He would take them aside to tell them what kind of wonderful impression their *chassan* or *kallah* had made. "You know that I can read people," he would say, "and wow, did you do well!" He would then point out the particular traits of the new *chassan* or *kallah* that had impressed him.

One of the married children lived with Reb Meir and Rachel while their own house was undergoing renovations. When his son-in-law would come in after a long day at work, Reb Meir would leave the kitchen to give his daughter and her husband their privacy — in his own home!

(L to R) Baruch Zlotowitz, Yehuda Munk, Ahron Zlotowitz, Gedaliah Zlotowitz, Yisroel Zlotowitz, Reb Meir, Duvie Morgenstern, Chaim Zlotowitz, Rachel Zlotowitz

All the children together at Rachel's birthday party
(L to R) Bottom row: Chani and Baruch, Yehuda and Tzivi,
Rachel and Meir, Gedaliah and Daniella
Top row: Yisroel and Rochi, Shira and Chaim, Asher and Estie,
Faigie and Efraim, Duvie and Dvorah

When Reb Meir and Rachel joined their married children for the Shabbos meal, he not only insisted that the host sit at the head of the table — refusing to accept the honor — he would exclaim how happy it made him to see his son or son-in-law leading a Shabbos *seudah*.

He would leave his children messages after spending Shabbos at their homes, telling them how much he had enjoyed himself, how impressed he was with their friends, how fortunate they were to have such a rav or belong to such a shul.

A few weeks after his eldest daughter married, Reb Meir and his wife drove to Lakewood to join their children for supper; a beautiful thank-you card arrived in the mail a few days later, filled with compliments and appreciation for the meal.

He conveyed the value of family to them and taught by example just how important it was.

One of his grandchildren was staying at his home while his parents were on vacation. Before Shabbos, Reb Meir told the boy, "You're the oldest, and even though your brothers and

Reb Meir and Rachel at a family *simchah* with granddaughters

sisters are staying with friends, you should call them before Shabbos and make sure that they're okay. It's what siblings do for one another."

He would call his own siblings often, and made sure to be part of their lives, joining in their *simchos* and events and being helpful whenever possible.

He felt that grandchildren should call their grandparents — and would comment if they didn't. A grandson spent a month in summer camp and didn't call. Reb Meir greeted him warmly when he came home, then said, "Bubby and I were waiting for your phone call."

At *simchos*, he expected each grandchild to come say mazel tov to their grandparents — and he knew exactly who had come over and who had not. One granddaughter attended a *simchah* for a short time and didn't make it to the men's side of the *mechitzah* to wish mazel tov to her zaidy. The next time she called, he said, "Ah, I guess you're calling to wish mazel tov on the *chasunah*."

But at the same time, he made sure that phone calls with him were filled with real warmth and interest. He seemed to know exactly where they had left off the last conversation; was up to date on their progress in yeshivah, school, or work; and was updated on the family.

Grandchildren-in-law would find themselves unburdening themselves to him, sharing challenges at work or with family, confident in the fact that he would guide them wisely and keep their conversations a secret.

They could share jokes and stories, and he appreciated when his grandsons in yeshivah shared an idea they had heard from their own rebbeim; usually, he would counter with a *dvar Torah* from Rav Moshe.

There was a designated telephone line at work for his family, and his secretaries knew to interrupt any meeting if it was family on the line. Unless he was speaking to Rav Dovid Feinstein, he would answer — and if he couldn't speak, he would say so. "Is everything okay? I'm just in a meeting and will call you back later."

It wasn't only his relationship with them that was sacred, but also their relationships with one another. He tried to arrange the Pesach schedule so that even those families that would be joining him and Rachel for different parts of Yom Tov would overlap for one night of Chol HaMoed: he wanted everyone together.

Before reciting the *Shehecheyanu* on Yom Tov night, he would urge them all to look around the table and realize how much blessing each person there added to their lives, the gifts Hakadosh Baruch Hu had given them: only then would he start to say Kiddush.

At the *l'chaim* celebrating the engagement of his daughter, Reb Meir gave the new *chassan* a gift of an expensive camera. "Memories, moments spent with family, should be cherished like any other valuable item. You're starting a new life now, with Hashem's help, and there will be many such moments: take pictures and you'll appreciate them one day."

Celebrating
milestones
with grandsons

He lived these moments, trying to experience them personally whenever possible. If a child or grandchild was naming a new baby girl — even though he would make a separate trip for the Kiddush — he and Rachel would do their best to take part in that *simchah* as well.

He gave them the most precious gift of all: that of his time.

He loved retelling how one of the Zlotowitz boys, learning in the Mesivta of Long Beach, had asked his father for a ride back to yeshivah after being home for Shabbos.

Reb Meir wondered why he always seemed to be the only father available to drive the young man and his friends. "Why don't your friends' fathers ever drive?" he asked.

"Dad," the boy replied, "their fathers *work*!"

Humorous as the story was, it was rooted in a certain truth: Reb Meir himself found ways to show them that work was secondary. A young grandson came to visit him at work one day, and Reb Meir took him on a tour of the bindery. The child was fascinated — for a while — then grew bored, as children tend to do. He came back upstairs and sat down on the couch in his grandfather's office.

Reb Meir noticed that the boy was getting somewhat edgy. "I'll be leaving early today," the child suddenly heard his grandfather tell the secretary, "because I have Avrohom Yosef here and he really needs to get home already!"

He would arrive at their school events — Chumash parties, graduations and *siyumim* — precisely at the scheduled time, visibly enjoying himself throughout the program. In his later years, his children wouldn't tell him if there was an event, because they didn't want to bother him. Somehow, he found out and inevitably, when they arrived, he was there too.

A grandson learning in yeshivah in Far Rockaway called one day and mentioned that he would be delivering a *chaburah* that evening. Reb Meir was in Lakewood at the time, and he asked what time the *chaburah* was scheduled for.

Joining a *chaburah* given by his grandson, Ahron Morgenstern

The young man anticipated that his grandfather would consider coming to Far Rockaway to hear the *chaburah*, so he explained that it was an in-depth, complex analysis of the *sugya* they were learning in yeshivah and there was no reason to come.

But several hours later, when the grandson stood up in front of a group of friends in the *beis medrash* of Yeshivah Darchei Torah, there was a guest: While Mrs. Rachel Zlotowitz waited patiently in the car, Reb Meir — who had driven straight from Lakewood — sat there, glowing with pride as his grandson spoke in learning.

The man who had such difficulty accepting compliments reveled in the accomplishments of his children.

He didn't take credit, however. He would repeat, again and again, that it was a result of Rav Moshe's *berachah* on that lonely, cold winter night — that Reb Meir's sons would become *bnei Torah* and his daughters would marry *bnei Torah*.

At the engagement of his eldest daughter to a budding *talmid chacham*, Reb Meir looked at the *chassan* and repeated the rosh yeshivah's *berachah*. "*El hana'ar hazeh hispalalti,*"[1] Reb Meir said with great emotion. "This is the fulfillment of that blessing."

When he would receive glowing reports about his children or grandchildren from their rebbeim or teachers, he would murmur, "It's all Rav Moshe's *berachah*."

At the wedding of a grandchild, Reb Meir, seated on a chair with sons, sons-in-law, and grandchildren dancing around him, pulled a grandson close and whispered, "*Katonti m'kol hachassadim.*"[2]

As a young man, Reb Meir and his wife had gone to visit their friends, Mr. and Mrs. Avi Shulman, in Monsey. The Shulmans mentioned that they didn't own a television set — not a given at the time — because they felt it could negatively affect their children. On their way home, Reb Meir and Rachel discussed how impressed they had been with the Shulman children, and together, they decided to get rid of their own television set. They didn't push it off or find reasons to delay: that day, the TV was taken out of the house, an investment in the future of their beloved children.

Reb Meir would share the story, making the point that sometimes, a person can appreciate the wisdom of a decision only many years later.

Finally, in discussing the successes of his children, he would always attribute it to his wife. One of his oft-repeated maxims was that a wife sets the tone for the home. He enjoyed remembering how one of his yeshivah friends had become close to Reb Ahron and Fruma Zlotowitz. When this young man got engaged, he brought his *kallah* to meet the senior Zlotowitzes and the discussion turned to his rabbinic aspirations. Mrs. Zlotowitz turned to the *kallah* and said that it wasn't enough for

---

1. *I Shmuel* 1:27: "For this child did I pray."
2. *Bereishis* 32:11: "I have become small from all the kindnesses and from all the truth that You have rendered Your servant."

With Rachel at her birthday party

a man to have a position as rav. "I am not a rebbetzin because my husband is rav of a shul," she said. "He is a rav because I am a rebbetzin."

At a birthday party for Mrs. Rachel Zlotowitz, Reb Meir allowed himself to share something personal with the gathered children and grandchildren. "When the door closes behind you and you all leave the house, I'm still there. I see her *tefillos*, the way she stands and pleads with the Ribbono Shel Olam for you and your families."

He turned to where his wife was sitting and said, "I want to thank you for that. *Sheli v'shelachem*, what's mine and what's yours," he told his children, "*shelah hi*, is credit to her."

"It was true that my uncle had the potential to change the world, the energy and vision and drive; but it could have been Apple or some other business — what made his ultimate mission ArtScroll," says Reb Meir's nephew and confidant, Chaim Kiffel, "was Rachel. She elevated his vision, she made him

WIth sons and grandsons at the *Siyum HaShas*

believe that his life's work should inspire, rather than enrich them personally. He was always grateful to her for that, for giving him dreams that were spiritually sophisticated."

Rabbi Burton Jaffa shares an insight.

"Often, people of a certain age complain about their children; it's natural to look at the younger generation with some degree of skepticism. Reb Meir was the exact opposite; he would speak of his children — and children-in-law — and their achievements with obvious admiration and pride.

"Then, one day, I realized his secret. It wasn't that he thought his children were perfect, he well understood their struggles and that each of them had limitations; rather, he chose to identify them by their successes, that's how he saw them. That was reality."

In fact, Reb Meir's four sons all chose different career paths: Reb Meir saw each one of them as continuing his work.

The eldest, Reb Gedaliah, worked closely with Reb Meir at

Reb Meir with his sons

ArtScroll. He was Reb Meir's handpicked successor to carry on the mission. Yisroel went into business, and Reb Meir, with his financial acumen and sales skills, shepherded the company from its inception — actually housing it in his own office complex during its formative years. Baruch is a talented marketing professional and, like Reb Meir, gets a thrill from being visually creative. Reb Meir involved himself in each project Baruch undertook, down to the smallest details. The youngest son, Chaim, became an attorney. Reb Meir, who would often act as his own lawyer and draft his own documents, was immensely proud, and hung his youngest son's law degree on the wall of his home office.

"So even with his own constant achievement, he was living vicariously through all four sons," says Rabbi Jaffa, "seeing each one as an extension of his dreams and talents. Of course he was proud!"

Children-in-law and grandchildren-in-law were the same to him. It was common to find him on the phone giving advice and guidance, or simply chatting, with any one of them. "It's natural to be able to connect with children," remarked someone close to Reb Meir, "but it can be more difficult when it comes

On Purim with (L to R) Yitzy Gruen, Baruch Zlotowitz, Efraim Perlowitz, Duvie Morgenstern, Yisroel Zlotowitz, and Chaim Zlotowitz

to children-in-law. The way Reb Meir managed to do so was by immediately identifying the unique character traits of the new member of the family — this one had an eye for design, the other was a great cook, and the third was an expert in Jewish history. Then, Reb Meir would connect on their terms, calling to ask for decorating advice, or to share a story he knew would interest them. It was very important to him that each of them have a real connection with Rachel and him, so he made it happen. Then, in time, the bond became so natural that when he was *niftar*, they all felt like they had lost their own zaidy!"

In 2017, before the last Pesach of Reb Meir's life, ArtScroll released a children's book called "The Search Is On," written by Mrs. Rachel Zlotowitz in conjunction with her close friend, Mrs. Helene Ribowsky. Meir brought home the first copy of the book that rolled off the press and presented it to his wife. Chaim Zlotowitz had his mother pose holding the book, and snapped a picture — which he sent to his father.

The next day, Reb Meir came home with an enlarged, beautifully framed picture and placed it prominently in the living room for all to see, his way of expressing his approval of the book and his pride in his wife.

An ArtScroll secretary recalls that it was among the books Reb Meir was most proud of. "She's an incredible teacher," Reb Meir would say as he showed the book to visitors, "and this book is testimony to how well she understands children."

"Zaidy didn't just say 'I love you' a lot, he did things that showed us he loved us a lot," says a young grandson. The boy remembers when his ArtScroll Siddur began to tear, and he asked Reb Meir to take it to work and have it rebound. The loving grandfather returned the Siddur with a new binding — but because the original handwritten inscription had been lost with the old binding, Reb Meir made sure to replace that as well, a beautiful *berachah* to his grandson.

Once, he asked one of his married grandsons how things were going financially. Trying to be funny, the young man grimaced and said, "Don't ask, the landlord threw us out and we haven't eaten in days."

Reb Meir's face darkened. "Don't ever joke like that," he said sharply. "When I ask my children if they need money, I mean it, and I need them to understand that it's a real question and offer of help. Take it seriously."

One of his daughters-in-law was considering taking a year off from work to be home with her children. Reb Meir discussed it with her and listened as she deliberated about what was right. He told her that he didn't think she should give up her job, since along with the income, it gave her a sense of purpose and she was very good at it. He thought she would feel bored and unfulfilled at home. She disagreed, and reiterated why she thought it made sense.

A short while later, Reb Meir approached her. "I want you to take the year off," he said, "and I will personally give you the money you're losing by not working."

He hadn't changed his mind, he explained, nor did he agree with her — but he did respect her for thinking it through and arriving at a conclusion. It was her decision to make, and once she had made it, he was going to completely support her.

Reb Meir had a difficult time accepting gifts, even from his family. Soon after video cameras were available in stores, Reb Meir's son-in-law purchased one, certain that this was one gift his father-in-law would appreciate.

Reb Meir took the package and looked inside. "Oh wow, a video camera," he exclaimed. "Is this a good one? Is it a respected brand?" The son-in-law assured him that it came highly recommended.

"Great," Reb Meir smiled, "then here it is, enjoy it."

But there was one gift he accepted.

His granddaughter, Ahuva Koslowitz, was born on his birthday. From when she was a young child, he made it a point to take her out for ice cream on their day of shared celebration. When she was very small, he would strap her into a cart and feed her the ice cream, but as she got older, they sat side by side and chatted.

As a married woman, that granddaughter purchased a birthday present for her zaidy: a miniature ice cream cone and a tiny shopping cart, reminders of simpler times they had shared. He was deeply moved, and told her, "This gift is one I'll treasure."

A 12-year-old granddaughter wanted to interview her zaidy for the school newspaper. He

With his granddaughter, Ahuva Koslowitz

sat down with her at the kitchen table and answered each of her questions, complimenting her on her style and poise as the conversation progressed.

She typed it up and emailed it to him. He responded by praising her quality work, and then reformatted and redesigned the text to make it look even nicer, the extra touch one more way to show his love.

For Reb Meir's seventieth birthday, his children hosted a party. One of the sons-in-law came up with an innovative gift: He and his family compiled of all Reb Meir's favorite sayings into a small booklet — some profound, some humorous, some whimsical, and some reflective. Reb Meir greatly appreciated the gift, a true reflection of love, and the deeper message it conveyed.

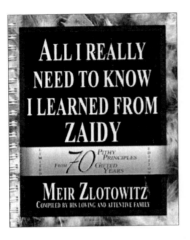

On Shabbos day, following davening, he enjoyed hosting for a Kiddush whichever grandchildren were local. Free of workplace responsibility, it was a cherished opportunity to catch up with them and chat.

When it was over, he would walk them to the porch, sending them off with the message that he loved them. Generally, when his married children were leaving after Shabbos, he would try to walk them out — even in later years, when his legs caused him near constant pain — and, clapping, he would sing, "*Ki v'simchah seitzei'u,*" parting in joy.

One of the newly married couples from Lakewood stopped by to visit one evening. Reb Meir saw that his grandson-in-law was dressed in a Shabbos suit and tie, and he asked why. The young man explained that he was en route to a *chasunah* in Boro Park, where he would be going in just to wish mazel tov.

"Okay, I'll take you," Reb Meir said.

"Are you going to the same *chasunah?*" asked the surprised grandson-in-law.

"No, I just want to take advantage of the opportunity to get to know you a bit better. When do we have time to just schmooze?"

When Reb Meir would arrive in Eretz Yisrael on one of his frequent visits, he would immediately reserve one evening to take the various grandchildren out to dinner; it was the highlight of his trip.

On one of these visits, he called a granddaughter and invited her to meet him for supper at a restaurant. "Sure," she said happily, "who else is coming?"

"This time," he said, "it's just you and me, and we're going to really talk!"

He saw his prime mission in life, he would often comment, to live the mandate Hakadosh Baruch Hu gave Avraham Avinu. *L'ma'an asher yetzaveh es banav ve'es beiso acharav...*[3]

Rav Elya Brudny recalls a request made of him by Reb Meir.

At Chaim's *Siyum HaShas*
(R to L): Reb Meir, Rav Elya Brudny, Chaim Zlotowitz, Nosson Tzvi Zlotowitz

---

3. *Bereishis* 18:19: "For I have loved him because he will instruct his sons and his household after him, that they should keep the way of Hashem to perform righteousness and justice, in order that Hashem will bring upon Avraham that which He spoke concerning him."

"We were friends for thirty years, and he never asked me to help ArtScroll, never urged me to show up at an event or *simchah* — but one day Reb Meir called me and said he really needed a favor. His son, Chaim, who had learned in my *shiur*, was making a *Siyum HaShas* and Reb Meir wanted me to come to the *seudah*. To him, that was a favor worth asking!"

In general, Reb Meir viewed a *Siyum HaShas* as the most monumental celebration possible. His daughter, Faigie Perlowitz, informed him that her husband, Reb Efraim, was being *mesayem Shas* and she was planning on doing "something" in honor of the milestone.

Booklet prepared by Reb Meir in honor of Efraim's *Siyum HaShas*

"Just *something*?" Reb Meir asked in surprise. "This calls for more than just something." He immediately swept into action, booking a hall and printing invitations, planning a lavish *seudah* in honor of his son-in-law's *siyum*.

With typical creativity, he marked the tables not with numbers, but with the names of the *sedarim* in *Shas*: guests were seated at *Zeraim, Moed, Nashim, Nezikin, Kodashim,* or *Taharos* — and with a twinkle in his eye, Reb Meir informed the younger children that they were to be seated at *Nezikin*.[4]

When his grandson, Ahron Zlotowitz, made a *Siyum HaShas*, Rabbi Nosson Muller was among the speakers. In his *derashah*, Rabbi Muller quoted the words recited at the *siyum*, "*Hadran alach*," which literally mean, "We will return to you." Rabbi Muller shared another understanding of the words. *Hadar*, he explained, means beauty. Turning to the proud grandfather, Reb Meir, the speaker said, "Reb Meir, you made the *Shas*

---

4. The section of *Shas* that deals with damages.

At the *Siyum HaShas* made by Ahron Zlotowitz
Speaking: Ahron and Rabbi Nosson Muller

beautiful — accessible and attractive and clear — for so many
thousands of Jews. Now, that *'hadar,'* that beauty, is *'alach,'*
being given to your own family. *Hadran alach!"*

Reb Meir was deeply moved by the thought and called Rabbi
Muller the next day, just to thank him for the beautiful and
meaningful interpretation.

At a private *seudah* with his children, Reb Meir shared a *dvar
Torah* from his rebbi, Rav Moshe. Rashi brings from Chazal
that Yaakov Avinu wished to sit in tranquility: *Bikesh Yaakov
leishev b'shalvah.*[5] Rav Moshe explains why this was considered
an improper request.

A person is liable to think that after all his children are grown
and settled, his *chinuch* responsibilities are complete: his work
is done. Chazal are teaching us otherwise; the job is never done,
because once the children are married, there is a new generation to worry about, to pray for, to guide and inspire.

Another *dvar Torah* he would share at family *simchos* cen-
tered on Yaakov Avinu's words when beholding Yosef's children. "*Re'o fanecha lo filalti, v'hinei her'ah osi Elokim gam es*

---

5. *Bereishis* 37:1.

zarecha, I had not expected to see your face, and behold, Hashem has shown me your children as well."[6]

Reb Meir asked why the *pasuk* says, *"her'ah osi Elokim"* rather than *"her'ah 'li' Elokim,"* which would seem more correct. He would share the answer he had heard from his father: *her'ah osi* means that Yaakov wasn't grateful only that he had merited seeing Yosef's children. He was thankful that he saw himself — *her'ah osi* — his values and ideals; he recognized his dreams in them as well.

Two of his sons came to spend Shabbos at his home, along with their families. On Motza'ei Shabbos, he walked into the living room and saw the two couples, Yisroel and Rochi and Baruch and Chani, simply sitting and chatting pleasantly.

The next day, he wrote to his sons:

> *Dearest—*
>
> *You can't imagine how much nachas — and true simchah — I had last night seeing the four of you sitting together so wonderfully and enjoying one another's company. I won't even belabor it with words other than to vintch you that your kids should continue to have harmony with one another always ... and you should derive even more nachas watching them, the love that flows, and the hatzlachah that you'll all have.*
>
> *And I should walk in on the great-grandchildren seeing such a scene also!*
>
> *Good Chodesh!*
>
> *With love,*
> *Dad*

---

6. *Bereishis* 48:11.

On his anniversary, rather than be the object of celebration, he and his wife would celebrate their children — those who had given the home its focus and meaning.

A year before his passing, he wrote to them:

> *Just a reminder that tomorrow, Wednesday, is our 44th anniversary.*
>
> *As we reflect, we must take this occasion to thank you for giving us so much nachas over the years, and for your raising such beautiful future generations.*
>
> *The tree blossoms and grows, baruch Hashem! And bli ayin hara.*
>
> *With much love as we move year by year toward our 50th, 60th, and beyond...*
>
> *Dad and Ima*

He would tell his grandchildren that they couldn't possibly understand how much he loved them. "But one day, you will become grandparents, *im yirtzeh Hashem*, and then you'll understand."

Fifteen months before his passing, Reb Meir was even more emotional than usual in the annual pre-Pesach email marking the date of his operation. He spoke openly to his beloved family.

> *My dearest children shlita —*
>
> *I wanted to share with you that today, Shabbos Ha-Gadol, was 16 years since I had the heart event in 2000 that resulted in an angioplasty with the insertion of 7 stents. That year it was April 15th.*
>
> *The technique of stents was very new then, and two of the patients who had the identical procedure in the same hospital, by the same surgeon, on the same day as I did (literally an hour or two apart) regretfully did not survive it beyond a few years. And others that did, needed subsequent surgery to replace the stents and often to do bypasses.*

I have to truly look around and be so thankful to the Ribbono Shel Olam for His chessed — שהחייינו וקיימנו והגיענו לזמן הזה. I feel blessed beyond description.

So much has happened in the last 16 years that I have been zocheh to see and appreciate:

- Many chasunos in the family to very special "tzugeku-miner" spouses from extremely chashuveh families, who are all building a bayis ne'eman on the highest plane that my parents never could have imagined would happen in America.
- My ben zekunim married.
- Many grandchildren married.
- The birth and bar/bas mitzvahs of grandchildren.
- The birth of great-grandchildren.
- A mishpachah of bnei Torah and future n'shei chayil, bli ayin hara.
- Many multi-generational siyumim that were made in the family during this period.
- Many simchos, much fun time.
- And so many accomplishments of harbatzas Torah in ArtScroll where Hashem allows me to contribute to daily with a special siyata d'Shmaya despite other health restrictions.

I could go on and on, but there is no need. Rav Yaakov Kamenetsky used to refer to his post-surgery years as "geshenkteh yahren," which we can translate as "matnas chinam" years: bonus years. That's why I work with the focus and intensity that I do, so Hashem's "geshenkteh yahren" should not be in vain, or wasted, chas v'shalom. (I apologize to each of you if I am not always available and attentive to you as I would want to be, and should be. But Hashem has kept me here for a reason; I can't let Him down.)

I give all of you a berachah that together we should continue to have good health, nachas, simchos, parnassah b'revach mitoch harchavah, along with arichus yamim v'shanim during which we can continue to enjoy one another, that we can be oveid Hashem b'simchah, and accomplish on behalf of Klal Yisrael and ourselves ad bi'as go'el tzedek. V'ad bichlal.

With my overflowing love to all of you,
   Dad

Reb Meir's attachment to his family defined him. His success in transmitting that love was never more evident than in his final weeks. When he — who had always insisted that children and children-in-law were equal to him — was hospitalized, he didn't have eight children vying to take shifts at his bedside, but sixteen. They seized the chance to be around him and serve him, devoted to him as he had been to them.

In 1976, when Reb Meir published his first *sefer, Megillas Esther,* he had kept a few copies for himself. He presented one to his wife, Rachel, with an inscription, a thank you for being the partner in this new venture.

Just a few weeks after Reb Meir's passing, a painter was working in the Zlotowitz home and as he worked, a *sefer* tumbled down from one of the shelves. Mrs. Zlotowitz bent down to retrieve it and saw that it was *that Megillas Esther,* one of the original copies with the letter to her.

It was fitting: a message from — and about — her husband. The slim volume had launched a revolution, but the one who had spawned it had never lost sight of that which was most important to him: his beloved family.

16

KI V'SIMCHAH SEITZEI'U

I N 2004, REB MEIR ZLOTOWITZ EMBARKED ON A NEW MIS
sion.

For centuries, Jews had immersed themselves in Talmud
Bavli, learning Mishnayos and then Gemara. They learned
Rambam and *Shulchan Aruch*, studied the commentators and
mastered practical halachah.

But the Yerushalmi was off-limits to all but elite *talmidei chachamim*.

As one of the erudite ArtScroll writers explained:

> It is one of the fundamental components of Torah
> Shebe'al Peh, the Oral Law, yet it has been one of the
> most difficult and neglected areas of Torah study. Dur-
> ing the years 200-350 C.E., roughly five generations of
> Amoraim (sages of Talmud) flourished in the Galilee, the
> northern part of the Land of Israel.
>
> Their task was never easy. They lived under brutal
> Roman occupation and there were periodic episodes of

persecution. But Torah is the lifeblood of the nation, and, with stubborn courage and unfathomable dedication, they persevered. Until finally, brutal anti-Semitism decimated the land's yeshivos and its voice of Torah was silenced. Their teachings lived on, however, in the Talmud Yerushalmi, the Jerusalem Talmud.

In Babylonia, Amoraim continued to teach and debate for another one hundred and fifty years. The Babylonian Talmud was redacted and edited. Its text was refined and its halachic rulings clarified.

For this reason, the Babylonian Talmud remained the Talmud that was studied intensively. The Jerusalem Talmud, on the other hand, remained a closed book to all but the most accomplished scholars. Should the Jewish people continue to be deprived of this rich repository of Torah?[1]

Reb Meir had already made history once: he was poised to do it again.

There weren't too many others who shared the vision. Talmud Bavli had a natural customer base, but Yerushalmi does not; there are few organized *shiurim* and no widely accepted *Daf Yomi* programs. It isn't learned in yeshivos or *kollelim*.

Instead of discouraging Reb Meir, this motivated him even more. These words of Talmud Yerushalmi were Torah, dating back to the glory era of *Torah Shebe'al Peh*, and to him, their inaccessibility was a tragedy. It was as if they were stored on a high shelf, and there was no ladder with which to reach them.

He would provide that ladder.

The mission that had fueled him thirty years earlier, when he had followed *Megillas Esther* with a commitment to keep printing, continued to drive him.

---

1. Rabbi Nesanel Kasnett, "An Insider's View," included in *The Creation of the Talmud Bavli*, a limited-edition commemorative volume honoring ArtScroll's scholars and patrons.

Aside from finding funding for a series that would encompass forty-four volumes, he would need to convince his own staff as well. It was daunting, even for a team of brilliant, experienced *talmidei chachamim*.

"A bright person can do a crossword puzzle, and a brighter person can do *The New York Times* crossword puzzle," says editor-in-chief, Rabbi Yechezkel Danziger. "A really brilliant person can complete the weekend puzzle, when it's most difficult; but even that person wouldn't know what to do if you told him that he would have to complete the crossword puzzle without the black-shaded boxes, which indicate where words start and end.

"That," he concludes, "is what we felt like when Reb Meir gave us this challenge: to learn, translate, clarify, and elucidate the Talmud Yerushalmi."

Reb Meir had spent his life defying the naysayers; once again, he found his way to those friends he knew would encourage him. Jay and Jeanie Schottenstein believed in this vision as well and undertook to sponsor the project.

Presenting Rav Chaim Kanievsky with a new volume of Schottenstein Yerushalmi

But the most meaningful ingredient in realizing the dream came on a 2005 visit to Eretz Yisrael, when Reb Meir and Reb Nosson, joined by their children, entered Rav Elyashiv's room and articulated their hope of publishing Talmud Yerushalmi, just as they had done with the Bavli.

"*Yerushalmi iz a shvereh limud*, it's a difficult text," remarked Rav Elyashiv's devoted *talmid*, Rav Yosef Efrati, who was present.

Rav Elyashiv smiled. "Yes, but they have *siyata d'Shmaya*."

Now, everything was in place.

The next twelve years would be a stream of accomplishments and milestones, personally and professionally. He would celebrate his seventieth birthday and that of his wife, rejoice in the marriage of grandchildren, and welcome grandchildren and great-grandchildren to the world.

The financial downturn of 2008 put the Yerushalmi and other ArtScroll projects at risk, as many of the donors were forced to reevaluate their commitments. Rav Elyashiv passed away, but both Rav Aharon Leib Shteinman and, *yibadel l'chaim tovim*,

With Rav Aharon Leib Shteinman and Shmuli Zlotowitz

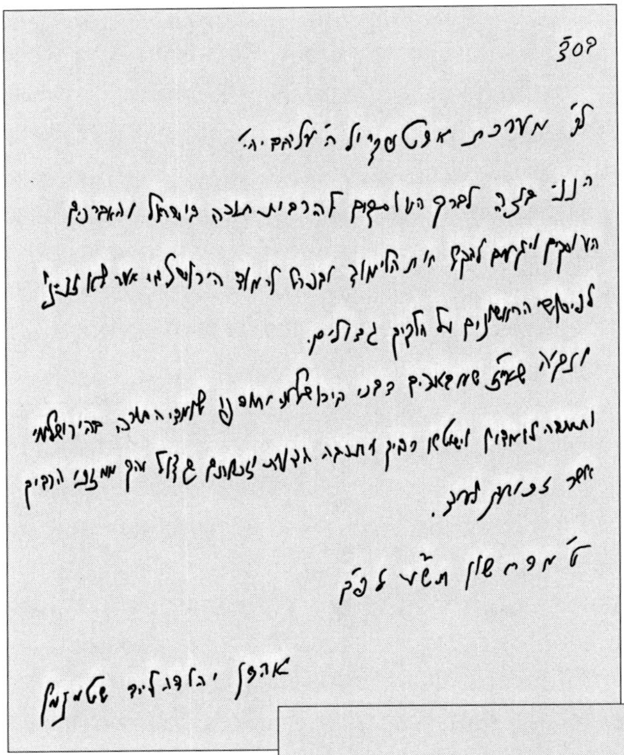

Letter from
Rav Aharon Leib
Shteinman to
the editors of the
Yerushalmi

בס"ד
לכ' מערכת ארטסקרול ה' עליהם יחי'

הנני בזה לברך העוסקים להרבות תורה בישראל,
והאברכים העוסקים ויגעים להקל את הלימוד,
ובפרט לימוד הירושלמי אשר לא זכינו לפירושי
הראשונים על חלקים גדולים.

ונקוה שעי"ז שמבארים דברי הירושלמי יתוספו
לומדי התורה בהירושלמי, ותרבה לומדיו וישוטטו
רבים ויתרבה הדעת וזכותם גדול והם ממזכי הרבים
אשר זכותם לעד.

ט' מרחשון תש"ע לפ"ק

אהרן יהודה לייב שטיינמן

Rav Aharon Leib learning from the Schottenstein Yerushalmi

Rav Chaim Kanievsky would welcome Reb Meir to their homes, filling the void left by Rav Elyashiv. Ultimately Rav Aharon Leib would use the Schottenstein edition of the Yerushalmi in the *shiur* he delivered at his home, a source of *nachas* to Reb Meir. Rav Aharon Leib would eventually write a letter, an unsolicited *michtav berachah,* to the editors of the Yerushalmi, acknowledging their extraordinary work.

There were high points and low points, all against the backdrop of the Yerushalmi, the project closest to Reb Meir's heart.

The Bavli was special, he would say, but he didn't feel that ArtScroll had given Gemara to the people. "They learned Gemara before ArtScroll too, and they would be learning it without our Gemara; but the Yerushalmi is waiting for us to do it."

In addition to being a sponsor, Asher David Milstein would also order volumes of Talmud Yerushalmi to be delivered to shuls, yeshivos, and outreach centers all over the world. When Reb Meir received confirmation that one of these shipments had reached their destination, he emailed his friend:

> *Dear Asher,*
>
> *I love the Yerushalmi undertaking. It's truly historic. I am sorry to repeat it so often but I get on a high whenever a new volume comes out. I can't help it. There is something awesome to have the zechus to plant seeds today that will sprout and provide peiros for future generations.*
>
> *Thank you for so substantially helping make it possible!*
>
> *B'ahavah,*
> *Meir*

Reb Meir would say that the day would come when the world would see the Yerushalmi as ArtScroll's defining work, and he took pride in each letter or email of thanks that arrived, testimony to one more Jew who was learning Yerushalmi.

Reb Meir — never a completely healthy person — was in near constant pain, and suffered several health scares. It became even more difficult to walk, and tasks as simple as putting on his socks or tying his shoes required assistance.

In a moment of reflection, Reb Meir looked at his close friend Rav Eliyahu Meir Klugman and said, "I'm not afraid. If the Ribbono Shel Olam sees fit to take me, then He will do so and I'm ready; until that time, I will keep doing the job that He gave me."

2016 was a difficult year for him. The Mesorah Heritage Foundation faced unprecedented financial pressures and Reb Meir worked feverishly to access new sources of funding. He traveled extensively and was only somewhat successful. For the first time in forty years, he had to officially cut employee hours and cancel projects. It caused him inordinate distress and added to his physical pain.

Only those closest to him knew how tough things were; the

smile remained the same, the warmth and generosity of spirit as abundant as ever.

With Reb Gedaliah at the *Siyum HaShas*

In March of 2017, Jay Schottenstein had a surprising proposal. Reb Meir had arranged for a meeting to discuss certain projects, and Jay suggested to Reb Meir that perhaps it was time that the next generation should get to know each other: Jay invited Reb Meir to bring his son, Reb Gedaliah, along, and he included his own son, Joey. The four men enjoyed a delightful conversation, none of them seeing it as anything more significant than just that.

After Pesach, Reb Meir traveled to Eretz Yisrael for a short visit. On Motza'ei Shabbos, he called his friend Reb Chaim Smutni and asked him to meet him in the Plaza Hotel. Reb Chaim arrived, and Reb Meir apologized that he hadn't gone to his friend's apartment. He really should have, he said, but he wasn't feeling up to it. "I'm sorry to have bothered you, but I just needed to see you, Reb Chaim."

He and Rachel had been planning to go to Eretz Yisrael for Shavuos. She left several days before he was slated to travel, because there was an all-important family *simchah* at which she would represent him. Reb Meir had work commitments and was planning to join her closer to Yom Tov.

But it wasn't meant to be.

In the middle of work one day, he told Reb Gedaliah that he was headed to the hospital unexpectedly.

Reb Meir had been experiencing pain in his hip and he had gone for x-rays; the doctor had just called with the results. He didn't say that Reb Meir needed emergency surgery, but he

Reb Meir with grandchildren, Chaya, Aliza, and Nosson Tzvi Zlotowitz, at their home on Motza'ei Shabbos shortly before he entered the hospital

did say that if they would do the procedure sooner, rather than later, the recuperation would be easier.

Reb Meir was a man of schedule and he had several meetings lined up for the next few days — but the idea of being self-sufficient, not to burden others, meant even more to him. Reb Meir was determined to have the surgery done before the situation worsened. Reb Gedaliah immediately left the office and accompanied his father to the hospital; Mrs. Rachel Zlotowitz made plans to come home from Eretz Yisrael.

The surgery was successful, and Reb Meir spent the next Shabbos at Joint Disease Hospital in the company of his sons, Yisroel and Baruch. He and Rachel spent Shavuos at the Haym Salomon Home for Nursing and Rehabilitation, where he appeared to be on the road to recovery.

During that week, he was in the middle of an ongoing back-and-forth debate with his friend and donor, Adam Sokol, who was sponsoring a new volume of the Mishnayos. Adam had chosen to dedicate the work anonymously, and Reb Meir was unhappy with the decision.

Adam explained that he was worried about *ayin hara*, having dedicated other volumes the previous year, and Reb Meir spoke with confidence and conviction. "There is no *ayin hara* when it comes to supporting Torah," he said, "because there is no greater source of protection and merit than Torah. Torah safeguards. You don't have to worry."

Adam still wasn't convinced and the issue was left unresolved.

On Sunday, Reb Meir was home, planning for his return to work the next day, when he felt weak: Hatzolah was called and he was rushed to Maimonides Hospital, where he underwent two emergency surgeries.

From the hospital, he sent an email to a friend of his in the administration of Haym Salomon, hoping he could spend the next Shabbos there. He was weak, but the style — the elegance and warmth and graciousness — was the same as always.

> *I want to thank you again for your superb, selfless care. After I was discharged from Haym Salomon last Friday I felt great. I had a beautiful Shabbos, and I had a wonderful Sunday. Then Sunday evening I threw up a massive amount of blood so Hatzolah rushed me to Maimonides where I had two stomach surgeries in two days. I am still in Maimonides waiting to be transferred to NYU where I will be under the care of a liver specialist.*
>
> *I really don't know what to do after NYU. I was doing so great in therapy. Now I had a serious setback. If it's nogei'a, may I call upon you at the end of the week to join you again? I've been telling everyone how exemplary the care was.*
>
> *You didn't receive the sefarim I told you I would send because I was never in my office since I left you. Sorry!*
>
> *Please let me know.*
>
> *Thank you!*
>
> *Meir*

While in NYU, he experienced another scare. On Tuesday, June 13th, the doctors detected internal bleeding, and as they tried to stabilize him, he went into cardiac arrest on the

operating table. The doctor urgently summoned all the Zlotowitz children to the hospital as the situation appeared grim. From
various directions, the family members descended on the hospital and joined in prayer for their beloved father.

The situation worsened and the doctors determined that there
was little choice other than to perform a risk-laden procedure.
They warned the family that there was a strong possibility that
Reb Meir wouldn't survive.

Throughout his life, Reb Meir had preferred giving to taking:
that day, he received as never before. The message to daven
swept through Klal Yisrael, with *Tehillim* groups forming and
people spontaneously going to holy sites to plead on behalf
of a Jew who meant so much to his nation. In the rooms of
the *gedolei hador* and the classrooms of small children alike,
words of supplication and hope were offered: the people he
had reached came together for him.

He woke up from surgery the next day, clearly aware that he
had been given a gift.

In that final week, he got a commitment for a significant
sponsorship[2] for a new Siddur.

Visitors came and left, and for each he had kind words and a
warm, if somewhat wan, smile — but those weeks were about
his family. His beloved children, children-in-law, and their children surrounded him in a final dance of devotion and love.
They created a round-the-clock rotation, each of them eager
to take a shift with Dad, to be at the side of a father who had
never left theirs.

He joked with visitors about discovering that he was expend-
able. "I didn't think I could leave the office for five minutes, and
now I've been gone for five weeks and they're managing just
fine," he remarked to Rabbi Paysach Krohn.

He was calm and tranquil, rooted in the faith that had sustained him his entire life.

---

2. The Siddur would be called *Zichron Meir*, given its name during the *shivah* by
the sponsors, Simcha and Shani Applegrad, close friends of the family.

In that last week, he was in touch with the editors of the French language *Edition Edmond J. Safra du Talmud Bavli* and *Houmach Edmond J. Safra* regarding the release of *Masechta Bava Basra*, Volume 2. In what would be his final message to them, he wrote, "Belief in Hashem is what keeps us together and helps override all challenges. I hope to be well soon and back at my desk in the coming weeks."

A close friend emailed him good wishes: *A stream of tefillos from all over the world for a holy man? It's a cinch.*

Reb Meir wrote back: *What we can be certain of is that all the tefillos are working, whether we see it or not. No tefillah ever goes unanswered.*

Toward the end of the week, he spoke on the telephone with Jay and Jeanie Schottenstein, who were visiting Europe. Jay, a Kohen, blessed his partner and friend. Reb Nosson came to visit; the conversation was routine, Reb Meir engaged in what was going on at the office, eager to get back to work.

And always, there were the children; married grandchildren came in with their own little children, turning zaidy's room into a happy commotion.

At one point, Reb Meir, discussing the *chasdei Hashem* that had accompanied him over the previous weeks, admitted that he worried that he was using up his *zechusim*. "Don't worry, Dad," one of his daughters quickly responded, "every second of the day, someone, somewhere, is using an ArtScroll Siddur, *Tehillim*, or *sefer.* They are able to understand what they're saying or learning because of you, so you're always getting more and more *zechusim*."

Too weak to argue, he smiled, but it was clear that he appreciated it.

From his hospital bed, Reb Meir kept giving.

One granddaughter searched for a gift to bring her grandfather: what does a person in the hospital need? She finally decided on a red lollipop, which he generally enjoyed. When she gave him the candy, he noticed that her own toddler seemed to want it. Reb Meir handed the treat to his great-grandchild, reveling in the opportunity to give.

One of his younger grandsons was sitting on the couch at home, saying *Tehillim* for his zaidy. He called his mother, who was visiting the hospital, and told her that he had said all fifteen of the *pirkei Tehillim* that begin with *Shir HaMa'alos;* she complimented him and told him to go help himself to ices from the freezer.

"But how can I eat ices if zaidy is sick?" the boy asked.

His mother shared the conversation with her father, who insisted that she take a picture. "Send him a picture of me, he'll see that I'm okay and he'll enjoy his ices."

Reb Meir's children, Chaim and Shira, brought a card written by their own young son, a *refuah sheleimah* letter to zaidy. Reb Meir asked for a pen, and wrote, *Dear Nosson Tzvi, thank you very much, I love you! Zaidy,* and asked them to give the card back to their son, perceiving that the worried little boy needed some sort of acknowledgment that his card had been read and appreciated.

Reb Meir in the hospital with his grandson Moshe Perlowitz on the day of his bar mitzvah

On Thursday, Reb Meir was released from the hospital and transferred to Boro Park Center, a rehabilitation facility across the street from Maimonides Medical Center. On Friday — Erev Rosh Chodesh Tammuz — a stream of children and grandchildren came by to say *Gut Shabbos* and wish him a *Gutten Chodesh.*

In his preface to the Rav

Moshe biography, Reb Meir had written of his rebbi: *When we were finished speaking and ready to leave, he always gave a berachah or encouragement. We never left him without a good word.* Those final days were Reb Meir's opportunity to part from his beloved family with *berachos*, encouragement, and good cheer. He wouldn't leave them without a good word.

The situation was calm on that Erev Shabbos: Reb Meir appeared on the road to recovery, and his children were optimistic. As Mrs. Rachel Zlotowitz prepared the room for the onset of Shabbos, Reb Meir remarked that he wanted to change, to get dressed in honor of Shabbos. "And it's Rosh Chodesh, so I'd like to wear a new shirt."

Jack Jaffa was with them in those final pre-Shabbos moments, and he removed a fresh shirt from the package and helped Reb Meir put it on.

Once Reb Meir felt ready, he joined in the *minyan* at the center. Reb Chaim Dovid Zwiebel, who happened to be davening there while visiting his own mother-in-law, davened next to Reb Meir in the small shul. "All his qualities were on display," Rabbi Zwiebel recalls. The two men danced together during *Lecha Dodi*, welcoming Shabbos, welcoming a new month.

Reb Meir and Rachel ate the *seudah* in peaceful solitude, a rare moment alone after years of perpetual motion, of accomplishment and activity, of shared *nachas* and fulfillment.

In the pre-dawn hours, Mrs. Zlotowitz noticed something amiss, and she summoned the nurses. Hatzolah was called.

Late that Shabbos morning, the 30th day of Sivan, the soul of Rav Meir Yaakov ben Harav Ahron returned to its Heavenly abode.

The light had been dimmed.

On Motza'ei Shabbos, the bitter news spread through communities across the world. Jews with little in common united in grief for the man who had opened up the world of prayer for them, of learning, of connection and growth.

The *levayah* was held Sunday morning. Since it was Rosh Chodesh, Rav Dovid Feinstein ruled that only children should deliver *hespedim*.

Those who knew Reb Meir well appreciated both aspects of the *psak*. They perceived the symbolism of his *levayah* prompting a halachic discussion and novel *psak*: Reb Meir had been an expert in *Hilchos Aveilus*. He had served as chief editor of ArtScroll's classic *Mourning in Halachah* and from then on, he would carefully review every manuscript that dealt with those halachos.[3]

And they appreciated the fact that ultimately, testimony to what he had accomplished with his years was expressed by his beloved children. They were his life's work, his connection with them his greatest source of pride, and the families they had built his true legacy. It was appropriate that they be the ones to bid him farewell.

The *aron* was taken to Eretz Yisrael, where a *levayah* was held in Beit Shemesh. The throng of mourners was a reflection of Reb Meir's essence. Graced with the presence of *gedolei Torah*, his most loyal patrons and his beloved family sat with Reb Meir's friends from the Kosel and so many of the ArtScroll users — people who had felt drawn to pay their respects. Reb Meir was laid to rest not far from his parents.

The *shivah* drew masses of comforters to the home on Avenue K in Flatbush, and spawned articles, tributes, and letters to the family, expressions of raw pain from Jews who lived in gratitude to him though they did not know him.

During that week, Adam Sokol, who had been deliberating with Reb Meir just a few weeks earlier whether to sponsor the new Mishnayos anonymously or not, reached a decision: He sponsored the very first ArtScroll *sefer l'iluy nishmas* Rav Meir Yaakov ben Harav Ahron — dedicating it with his own name

---

3. Interestingly, for Reb Meir's *sheloshim*, his friend Reb Zvi Ryzman released a new *sefer* in his memory. The *sefer*, *Ratz Katzvi*, deals with *Hilchos Aveilus*.

and message of tribute, as Reb Meir had wanted.

At the end of *shivah*, the family stood up, united as one. It was Erev Shabbos, *Parashas Chukas* — the day that meant so much to him, marked as a time of mourning the holy books that had been burnt in 13th-century Paris. Reb Meir Zlotowitz had worked to recapture those letters and pages, to restore the Torah that had been lost and give the Jewish nation back its very heart, the Torah itself.

One month later, the ArtScroll staff gathered in the *beis medrash* at ArtScroll headquarters, the room where *talmidei chachamim* would argue the nuances of a halachah, where Reb Meir had celebrated so many milestone events — late-night *siyumim* and impromptu celebrations after completing a volume.

Rav Yisroel Simcha Schorr, rosh yeshivah of Ohr Somayach in Monsey and a senior ArtScroll editor, spoke of two of the great figures in the modern-day dissemination of *Torah Shebe'al Peh*, two men who had given the most precious gift possible to an entire nation; he remarked that they had shared the same first name. Rav Meir Shapiro had illuminated the world with his concept of *Daf Yomi,* and Reb Meir Zlotowitz had revealed the light of Torah and *tefillah* to a new generation.

The Lubliner Rav, Rav Meir Shapiro, passed away at the age of 47. Reb Meir Zlotowitz was 73 when he left the world. Together, said Rav Schorr, they had lived for 120 years, considered a complete life — the years given to Moshe Rabbeinu, who manifested the ultimate act of lovingkindness in bringing Torah to Klal Yisrael.

Reb Meir Zlotowitz confided in a friend that he had once heard his rebbi, Rav Moshe, recite a few words of *tefillah* with special concentration, and from then on, he had also focused on those words: "*L'ma'an lo niga larik*, so that our work may not be in vain."[4] Man toils, Reb Meir said, but without Divine assistance, his work isn't guaranteed to endure.

---

4. From *U'va L'Tzion Goel,* in *tefillas* Shacharis. See *Mishnah Berurah.*

פ"נ

בעלי, אבינו וסבנו

הרב ר' **מאיר יעקב** זללה"ה

בן הגאון הרב אהרן זללה"ה

זלוטוביץ

מייסד ומנהל המפעל התורני הגדול

ארטסקרול - מסורה

פ"נ

הרב

מאיר לסולם על ידי המהדיר ביומדי התורה

אשר מתורה הפיץ למאות ולאלפים בכל תפוצה

אשר היה רבם ולמדין ולשמואל לא הטעם

ד"ע אתיו ונאמן היה בתחום רב שליחת

לזיו במעשיו וקצלותו גדולי הדור בתערוצה

עבר עבודת ח' במרץ וזנות ביתו עזרה

קירב רחוקים וחיזק קרובים בדרכי האמונה

בני משפחתו תלווהו

על מסירותו להם הנאמנה

בן הגאון הרב אהרן

וזוגתו פרומא זכרונם לברכה

זלוטוביץ

נלב"ע בארה"ב בשבת קודש

ל' סיון, א' דר"ח תמוז תשע"ז

ת נ צ ב"ה

On the 10th of Tammuz, 1943, the doctors had warned an anxious father that his child would probably not live.

They were wrong. The child defied their prediction, coming forth to live a life of accomplishment, generosity, and strength, igniting a flame that will burn for eternity.

Reb Meir lived.

HESPED
OF JAY SCHOTTENSTEIN
AT THE LEVAYAH
IN BEIT SHEMESH

I T IS WITH A HEAVY HEART THAT MY FAMILY IS HERE TODAY to say goodbye to our dear friend Meir. There is never a right time to say goodbye, so please indulge me one last time to speak directly to Meir.

On behalf of my wife Jeanie, our children, Joey and Lindsay, Jonathan and Nicole, and Jeffrey, allow me to tell you again how much we adore you.

Each one of us has a special connection and friendship with you that has withstood years of sharing and caring. For years we have considered each other as family.

Whenever a new book was released, whether it be a cookbook or any other volume, you always told Jeanie, when she asked for copies, "Feel free to pick from the garden we planted together." You and Lindsay had a very special relationship; you were notorious for texts back and forth for all the charitable causes Lindsay would present. Many times you brought to our attention how proud you were of her, her good works, and how the generations continued.

I remember the day my father *OBM* told me of his meeting with you and Nosson and the opportunity to dedicate the Talmud volume *Eruvin*.

The volume was first published when my father was taking chemotherapy. His participation made him so proud and happy at a very difficult time. He passed out copies of "his volume" to many of his friends with great optimism and joy. For that alone I will be forever grateful to you.

What you and Nosson did for me, and my family, I could never repay. You always refer to our partnership. I pray that you know how honored we are to have had the privilege of partnering with you and all that you stood for and accomplished. You made Torah accessible to millions of people in a most beautiful way. Your desire for a book to be not only halachically correct but also beautiful to the eye is well known. Attention to detail is within your character. I remember going to see the facility where the Talmud is printed and how proud you were of how each book is hand-finished with the sponge-painting on the edges of the pages.

An ArtScroll event was another time your attention to detail showed in many ways. You were involved in the planning of the agenda right down to the menu. Without a doubt, no one ever went hungry while attending an ArtScroll event.

Many know you as the co-editor of the Talmud, as a man who changed the landscape of the accessibility of learning Torah, as a pioneer in reaching all Jews with the written word. I have the honor to hold you as a beloved friend.

Meir, 25 years ago when my father passed — you were there for me. I will never forget your faith, confidence, and unwavering support in me through the difficult times that followed.

You have stood at my side at my father's grave on every one of his *yahrzeits*, in Columbus, Ohio, in some very nasty weather, for the last 25 years. Your presence was always comforting and never taken for granted.

We are not through, in fact far from finished...we have many projects we are still working on together.

Just like the faith you had in me, and the support and wisdom you gave to me, I hope to do the same for your son Gedaliah.

To your beloved family — Rachel and the children. It was Meir and Rachel at *every* *simchah* — bar mitzvahs, weddings, *brisses*. Spending holidays together in Israel it was always you and Rachel. Your love for her and your family was always so obvious; you worried for everyone in a quiet, loving way.

Meir, today when you go up, you will be welcomed and take your place with all the great Jewish leaders who went before you. When you see my father, please give him a big hug and kiss from us and thank him for introducing us.

I am forever grateful to Hashem for having you as a friend who changed my life and who also impacted so positively on hundreds of thousands of Jewish people.

I will never forget you.

Yehi zichro baruch, may your name always be remembered as a blessing.

Bs"d   The 10th of Tamuz 5777

Letter of Condolence

To my dear and honored friend, a man distinguished and esteemed who pursues charity and good deeds Rav Yehoshua Eliezer may the L-rd strengthen and preserve you.

We spoke by phone concerning the tremendous loss incurred by the passing of our friend the renowned Torah scholar who worked ceaselessly for the good of all our people and who spread the learning of Talmud through the Schottenstein edition of Shas, our Rabbi the Rav HaGaon Rabbi Meir Ya'akov of blessed memory.

We are all richer and elevated with him in his portion.

He merited and shared merit with the many.

Blessed is the L-rd who did not remove the Redeemer from Israel but allowed him sons whom like him go in his way.

His merit should guard his sons that they succeed to further his works in spreading Torah learning amongst the Jewish people in the continuance of his ways.

The family should receive condolence.

It is my part to bless you Mr. Schottenstein that you may merit to continue the Rabbi's great way and his vision to merit the People of Israel with more projects and good works to bring closer the Holy Redeemer speedily and in our days.

           Rabbi David Chai Abuchatzeira

Translation of the letter on facing page

Handwritten letter by Rabbi Dovid Abuchatzeira to Jay Schottenstein
upon hearing of Reb Meir's *petirah*

Bs"d   The 4th of Tamuz 5777

Letter of Condolence

To The Zlotowitz family may you all have long life.

We have been informed of the sad tidings of the passing of your father,

the Rav HaGaon Rav Meir Ya'akov of blessed memory.

Through his vision he increased the learning of Torah in general and in particular the learning of the Talmud as facilitated by the Schottenstein Shas.

And with this in mind we convey our condolences to you.

And we hope and pray that the Good L-rd bring you no more sorrow and may He console you amongst the other mourners of Zion and Jerusalem.

Rabbi Aharon Leib Shteinman

Rabbi Chaim Kanievsky

Translation of the letter on facing page

בס"ד

לכ' משפחת זלוטוביץ שיחי'

הגיע לנו הבשורה הלא טובה בפטירת אביכם
הרה"ג ר' מאיר יעקב ז"ל אשר בחזונו הרבה
גבולות לימוד התורה, ובפרט בלימוד הש"ס
ע"י מהדורת שוטנשטיין, והנני בזה לנחמכם.
ונקוה כי ה' הטוב לא יוסיף לדאבה עוד וינחם
אתכם בתוך שאר אבלי ציון וירושלים.
ד' תמוז תשע"ז

Nichum Aveilim letter sent to the Zlotowitz family
signed by Rabbi Aharon Leib Shteinman *zt"l*
and *ybl"ch* Rabbi Chaim Kanievsky *shlita*

This volume is part of
THE ARTSCROLL® SERIES
an ongoing project of
translations, commentaries and expositions on
Scripture, Mishnah, Talmud, Midrash, Halachah,
liturgy, history, the classic Rabbinic writings,
biographies and thought.

For a brochure of current publications
visit your local Hebrew bookseller
or contact the publisher:

Mesorah Publications, ltd

4401 Second Avenue
Brooklyn, New York 11232
(718) 921-9000
www.artscroll.com